The Age of Ideology

Also by John Schwarzmantel

STRUCTURES OF POWER: An Introduction to Politics
SOCIALISM AND THE IDEA OF THE NATION
THE STATE IN CONTEMPORARY SOCIETY

The Age of Ideology

**Political Ideologies from the American
Revolution to Postmodern Times**

John Schwarzmantel

First published 1998 by
MACMILLAN PRESS LTD
Houndmills, Basingstoke, Hampshire RG21 2XS
and London
Companies and representatives
throughout the world

ISBN 0–333–65044–1 hardcover
ISBN 0–333–65045–X paperback

A catalogue record for this book is available
from the British Library.

10   9   8   7   6   5   4   3   2   1
07   06   05   04   03   02   01   00   99   98

Copy-edited and typeset by Povey–Edmondson
Tavistock and Rochdale, England

Printed in Malaysia

For Ernst and Maria Wangermann
in gratitude and affection

Contents

Contents

Preface

The aim of this book is to analyse the contemporary relevance of some of the main ideologies that have been central to political struggle over the two centuries since the American and French Revolutions. While there are many texts on this topic, this book offers a distinctive approach on several grounds.

First, it seeks to present the main political ideologies not as separate and unrelated sets of ideas, but as sharing a common agenda, the agenda set by modernity. Modernity is seen here as both a distinctive type of society and a broad philosophy.

Second, this book addresses the contemporary crisis of ideology and analyses the challenges to the whole ideological tradition of modernity. The focus is thus on a double crisis: the crisis of the ideologies of modernity, the question of whether they are still valid as frameworks for political thought, discussion and action in the changed circumstances of the contemporary world; and the crisis of modernity itself, as identified by the critique of post-modernist theorists.

Third, the book contrasts the more traditional analysis of political ideologies – their main themes, historical development and contemporary relevance – with the discourse of postmodern theory in order to identify the main lines of theoretical challenge to ideological discourse in general, to the specific ideologies of the Left–Right spectrum and to the whole tradition of modernity. The book contends that this tradition is still relevant today, and that ideological discourse is still necessary to the process of democratic politics, despite the disastrous consequences of imposing totalitarian thinking on society, as illustrated by the communist and fascist regimes of the twentieth century.

Finally, it aims to relate the theoretical discussion and analysis of ideologies to the transformations occurring in the real world, to identify the problems faced by the ideologies of modernity in their adaptation to a fundamentally changed social reality. It thus attempts to provide some kind of answer to the question 'where do we go from here', in terms of the ideas and theories that are necessary to stimulate political thinking and citizen action in the postmodern world of globalisation.

The arguments developed in this book suggest that the ideological thought that developed in response to the coming of modernity has a place in contemporary politics but needs to take account of the diversity of those politics. Ideologies are still necessary, but the ideologies of modernity need to be 'reinvented' to respond to a world that is very different from the world of modernity.

I am extremely grateful for the help and encouragement I have received from a number of friends and colleagues. I am particularly obliged to Ricardo Blaug for some very stimulating and helpful exchanges; to Erika Harris, Marion Kozak, Duncan McCargo and Max Silverman for reading draft chapters and suggesting improvements; and to a number of other friends who provided intellectual support and general encouragement, especially Nina Biehal, Cathy Bryan, David Cesarani, Cindy Daugherty, Ellis Tinios, and Ernst and Maria Wangermann. I also acknowledge some stimulating exchanges with Faisal Khan on the topic of nationalism and modernity. I am grateful for the advice and perceptive comments of my editor, Steven Kennedy, and the comments of anonymous reviewers of both the initial proposal and of a later draft. I am very grateful to all these friends and colleagues for the trouble they have taken.

JOHN SCHWARZMANTEL

Introduction: Ideology and the Crisis of Modernity

The aim of this book is to determine whether the central ideologies of modernity are still relevant to contemporary politics, and meaningful as organising frameworks for political debate and action. Ever since the great revolutions of 1776 in America and 1789 in France, political struggle has been expressed as a conflict between Left and Right, a spectrum of ideologies that offered different views of 'the good society', of how society should be organised. As Bobbio notes in his recent book defending their continuing relevance today, ' "Left" and "Right" are two antithetical terms which for more than two centuries have been used habitually to signify the contrast between the ideologies and movements which divide the world of political thought and action' (Bobbio, 1996, p. 1). The familiar terms of socialism, liberalism, conservatism and nationalism, along with later additions such as communism and fascism, among others, were labels for these different ideologies and for the parties and movements that sought to realise them.

In the state of contemporary politics, there is a world-wide crisis of ideologies, provoked by a series of rapid social and political transformations that have created a new framework for political action. The collapse of communist regimes and the difficulties encountered by social-democratic and labour parties suggest deep problems for socialism. Liberalism, so long the basic principle of liberal-democratic societies, has been challenged by ethnic and national conflicts, religious fundamentalism and by those searching for forms of community that have been ignored or underestimated by liberalism, with its emphasis on separate individuals. Likewise conservatism, with its attachment to tradition, seems irrelevant to a world of rapid transition and modernisation in which continuity and the weight of the past have been swept away. Do these ideologies, then, which formed the basis of politics for the past two hundred years, have anything to say to us as citizens of contemporary societies, or should the whole framework of political ideologies and the Left–Right spectrum be

1

rejected as of purely historical interest, of no concern to the 'postmodern' world? If this is indeed the case, do we need new ideologies of politics that offer alternative and more relevant frameworks for political action and debate? These might take the form of feminism, or environmentalism, or ethnonationalism. Alternatively it might be suggested that the whole concept of 'ideology', with its connotation of a broad view of how society should be organised, is itself the problem. Any general theory that seeks to dictate how society should be structured is itself dangerous, and cannot deal with the large variety of viewpoints, equally valid, that flourish in the pluralistic society of today.

Political ideologies provide central organising frameworks for political debate and action. Each ideology contains three elements: critique, ideal and agency. Political ideologies offer a criticism of existing society, which is condemned as imperfect and contrasted with some vision of 'the good society' that is to be attained. Each ideology offers a view of agency or the means by which the movement from an imperfect to a better, if not wholly perfect, society is to be achieved. Furthermore a political ideology operates with a certain view of human nature, sketching out the potentialities and limitations of the human subject. The individual chapters on particular ideologies in this book assess the ways that each, from socialism on the Left to conservatism on the Right, criticise existing society, what view each holds of the 'good society', and how theorists within each ideology think that this good society can be attained.

The focus of this book is also on the contemporary crisis of the great ideological currents of the nineteenth and twentieth centuries, and their relevance to present-day politics. In order to tackle this, another type of discourse or level of analysis is needed. This involves confronting the ideologies of modernity with the analysis of postmodernity, and some central themes of postmodernist theories. Postmodernity here refers to a range of explanatory theories that collectively suggest the world of modernity has been fundamentally transformed in such a way as to make irrelevant those ideologies and movements that arose out of the Enlightenment and the American and French Revolutions. Those ideologies, whatever their different prescriptions, all took for granted certain assumptions about the real world. If that world has been changed in essential ways, then the empirical and also conceptual bases of those theories are shaken. If, for example, modernist assumptions about the primacy of industrial production and the centrality of class conflict no longer hold in the world of postmodernity, then this has important implications for the relevance of socialism in this changed world.

The ideologies of modernity are equally challenged by postmodern ism, meaning here the constellation of theories that in various ways celebrate difference and diversity, problematise the notion of the individual as a rational and autonomous subject of action, and question the notion of a collective agent as the bearer of emancipatory politics. Theorists of postmodernism also criticise ideology as oppressive and constricting, unable to appreciate (or 'valorise') the multiple sources of identity and political and social action. In short, postmodern critiques can be said to undermine each of the three central elements of the ideologies of modernity: critique, goal or vision, and agency. Such postmodernist perspectives suggest that the critique offered by each ideology is partial, stemming from a particular or limited perspective that cannot sustain the universalism it claims. By the same token, the goal or vision of 'the good society' held out by the different ideologies of modernity is held to be fraudulent and oppressive, because it rests on assumptions of rational consensus and agreement that cannot be sustained in a world of difference and diversity. Finally, postmodern theorists have questioned the whole notion of individual subject and collective agency, suggesting that these are often the constructs or inventions of the particular ideology, and hence have no privileged position or even any real identity, so any theory of social change based on such ideas is unsustainable. Such concepts as 'emancipation' and 'revolution', which are central to the politics of modernity, come under fire from these postmodern theorists and are criticised as arbitrary postulates internal to the particular ideology in question, with its unsustainable pretensions to universality.

Hence the 'crisis of ideologies' suggests a double crisis and a double critique. The crisis is of modernity itself, as a form of society, and also of the ideologies that emerged from it. The critique of modernity and its ideologies stems from a set of changes in the real world, and also from a range of theories that are deeply hostile to ideological thought and its central assumptions, notably universalism and unity as opposed to pluralism and diversity. Ideological discourse and the politics stemming from those ideologies are condemned because of their monolithic implications and claims of universal validity. The argument that will be maintained here is that the ideologies of modernity and the framework provided by the Left–Right spectrum can survive, though not in unaltered form, the crisis provoked by developments in postmodern society and the criticisms raised by postmodern theory.

The two centuries that followed the American Revolution are termed here 'the age of ideology', a historical period that was marked by the conflict between the different ideologies of modernity. These ideologies shared a common agenda and made similar assumptions about society, although their prescriptions and conclusions were quite different. The particular form of society, 'modernity', that emerged at the end of the eighteenth century gave rise to a common set of problems and questions, to which the different ideologies provided distinctive answers.

'Modernity' is also used to refer to a set of attitudes, a broad philosophy whose elements formed the material of the ideologies discussed in this book. This philosophy involved a belief that the power of reason could shape and remould the whole structure of politics and society:

> The most powerful Western conception of modernity, and the one which has had the most profound effects, asserted above all that rationalization required the destruction of so-called traditional social bonds, feelings, customs and beliefs, and that the agent of this modernisation was neither a particular category or social class, but reason itself and the historical necessity that was paving the way for its triumph (Touraine, 1995, p. 10).

Ideology and modernity went together in that both shared the perspective that society and the state were creations of human action, the result of conscious human purpose, rather than the legacy of the past, moulded by the weight of tradition and custom.

What linked the different ideologies of modernity was the debate on social improvement, reconstruction and emancipation, as all took the Enlightenment view that it was possible to transform human society. Liberalism and socialism shared the modernist insistence on progress and the belief that society could be changed for the better through the application of human reason. Conservatism took a more negative view of this matter, stressing the weakness of human reason and the limits to social transformation. Yet all the ideologies concurred with the modernist perspective on the possibility of political change and social improvement.

The social context in which the modern ideologies emerged had three features (cf. Mulgan, 1994, pp. 11–12). First, modernity meant a society in which industrial production was constantly growing and drawing in the larger part of the population, even though the progress of industry was uneven and varied in speed and extent from country to country. Nevertheless Marx's words in *Capital* that 'the country that is more developed industrially only shows, to the less developed, the image of its own future' (Marx, 1977, p. 19) suggest a perspective that went well beyond Marxism and socialism generally. The fact that industrial development did not progress evenly across the world, and that modernity developed at an uneven tempo, is of huge significance for such ideologies as nationalism, which is seen by many theorists as a response to this uneven development (Nairn, 1981; Greenfeld, 1996). Nationalism is a means by which the more backward areas could catch up with more developed or advanced ones, though this does not exhaust the significance or causes of nationalism.

Second, the epoch of modernity involved the formation and creation of large nation-states, and in turn the nation-state, originating in Western Europe, was the terrain of modernity. The modern nation-state combined three functions that offered its members an identity (cultural and political) within a clearly defined community: a single economic unit (the national market), political sovereignty (the state protecting its national citizens), and cultural unity and identity (citizens of the nation-state spoke the same language and shared a common education system).

Third, the modern epoch was the era of class politics, stemming from the industrial structure of society. Modernity was an age in which large and increasingly well-organised social classes engaged each other in conflict, although this was not necessarily or at all times a violent confrontation. Class identities and loyalties came to play a central part in political life, sustained by class-based parties and movements. While both bourgeois and socialist mass parties received support from outside their 'natural' or 'normal' clientele – respectively the property-owning classes and the working class – the epoch of modernity was one whose politics were dominated by sharp class divisions, and the class struggle was acted out in the institutions and processes of liberal-democratic politics (Miliband, 1989).

The dominant ideologies of the 'Age of Ideology' reflected all three themes (industrial society, the nation-state, and class conflict). Irrespective of their position on the Left–Right spectrum the 'classical' ideologies were all concerned with the following issues. First, how should the newly developed productive resources of society be organised; could industrial society develop the necessary cohesion, or was it doomed to divide, as socialist theorists insisted, into warring classes until society could be organised on collectivist lines?

Second, the nation-state and nationalism were central to the politics and ideologies of modernity, especially with the rise of nationalist movements. Such movements demanded national unification and independent nation-statehood for those nations that had not yet achieved it, for example Italy and Germany, and later the nations of Eastern and Central Europe. Both liberals and (to a lesser extent) socialists supported the struggle of oppressed nations against foreign rule in the Russian, Ottoman and Austro-Hungarian Empires. Adherents of both these ideologies thought that the nation-state was a stage on the way to a more international organisation of society, and that nationalism, a philosophy that accorded primacy to the national unit, would eventually become a thing of the past. Both put the nation-state at the centre of their philosophies, as the capture of government power at the level of the nation-state was seen as the central means by which their various ideologies could be realised.

Finally, the centrality of class identity was recognised and 'theorised', in positive or negative vein, by those who contributed to the formulation of the dominant ideologies of the modern period. Whether deeply opposed (by conservatives and liberals, who feared that democracy would empower the propertyless masses and lead to revolutionary consequences) or espoused (by socialists as the means by which the new society would be introduced), class conflicts and class identity were central to the politics of modernity and to the ideologies that reflected its core issues. Thus industry, nation and class were the three central pillars of modernity, both as features of that society and as objects of the theories or ideologies that reflected it.

However at the present time both modernity and the ideologies that emerged from it are in crisis, with significant implications for political theory and practice. These problems stem from the transformations that have simultaneously affected all three central features of modernity, leading to a more fragmented society with a plurality of identities that challenge the more structured and stable identities of the modern era.

While contemporary society is still predominantly industrial, the nature of industry and the productive system has been fundamentally changed with the growth of smaller productive units, the demand for new technological and other skills, and the more specialised industrial structure. Added to this are the concerns of environmentalism and 'risk society' (Beck, 1992): an awareness of the costs of industrial society in terms of its negative impact on the environment. This challenges two of the assumptions of the modernist ideologies, namely that humanity is able to control nature, and that industrial production will constantly develop and grow.

Industrial society has come into crisis because of the development of new skills and knowledge, leading to an undermining of the traditional social structure based on heavy industry and a cohesively organised proletariat confronting an antagonistic (to varying degrees, in varying places) class of owners of productive resources. This has considerable implications for the ideologies of modernity, especially for socialism with its emphasis on the organised working class as the agent of social transformation. However these developments impinge on all ideologies that place industrial society at the centre of their view of 'good society'. The restructuring of industrial society has thrown into uncertainty a central strand of these ideologies, namely the idea that society is controllable. Some social scientists suggest the development of a system that eludes control: 'a *global system*, which is systematically disorganised, that is, based in a global structuration of disorganisation' (Featherstone *et al.*, 1995, p. 23). This leads to consideration of a crisis of another pillar of modernity – the nation-state.

The classical idea of the nation-state, and the aspiration of post-French Revolution nationalism, was 'one nation, one state'. Each nation, however defined, should have its own state to rule its own affairs – economic, cultural and political. The state would preside over the affairs of the nation and would be the lever for ideological and social transformation. However, in the contemporary world both the idea and the reality of the sovereign nation-state have been radically challenged by a variety of events: by the phenomenon of globalisation, by the rise of supranational bodies such as the European Union, by cultural and religious movements emphasising their own separate identity and rejecting that of the supposedly homogeneous national culture. Each of these developments is problematic and carries with it contradictory implications. For example globalisation has been seen as 'an outcome of the universal logic of modernity', representing a situation in which 'global *flows* are coming to assume as much, or greater, centrality than *national institutions*' (ibid., p. 2). Yet while at one level such developments seem to represent 'the triumph of the universal' and introduce 'substantial measures of abstraction, of "disembedding" and the hollowing out of meaning in everyday life' (ibid.), this process of globalisation seems to be

giving rise, by way of reaction, to the 'universalisation of particularism' and the 'global valorization of particular identities'. The complex
relationships between global flows and national particularities give
rise to 'hybridization', to 'multiple identities and the decentring of the
social subject . . . grounded in the ability of individuals to avail
themselves of several organisational options at the same time' (Pieterse, ibid., p. 52).

All these developments cast doubt on the sovereignty of the nation-
state and on the pivotal role of national identity as a focus of loyalty.
The nation was one of the most powerful sources of identity in the
modern era, and the nation-state was the chief focus of power, seen as
providing the levers for social and political transformation. The
'contemporary crisis of the nation-state' (Dunn, 1994) has many
facets, and these have implications for modernity and all its ideologies. One issue in particular is that of plural identities and of national
minorities in supposedly culturally homogeneous nation-states. This
raises the question of whether the nation-state can command the
loyalty of all its citizens and act as the source of identity in the way it
was intended to in the period of modernity (Kymlicka, 1995).

Finally, the crisis of modernity and the ideologies of modernity find
expression in transformations in the class structure of advanced
societies. Instead of polarisation into 'two great hostile camps', as
announced by the *Communist Manifesto*, modern society seems to
have taken a more pluralistic form. Class divisions have become less
salient. Consumer sovereignty functions, in however misleading a
way, as a way of suggesting that all are sovereign in the marketplace,
not as producers but as individualistic consumers. Furthermore class
movements and political parties based on class seem less able to
capture the loyalty of their constituents than in the era of modernity.
Indeed in some cases social-democratic parties have abandoned class
politics and replaced it with much more broadly based 'catchall'
politics, with 'modernisers' moving away from the traditional ideology of socialist politics (Sassoon, 1996).

The implication of all these points is that the structure of modern
society that gave expression to the modern ideologies has changed,
causing severe problems for those ideologies. This leads to a consideration of post-modernist theories which deny the possibility of
any all-embracing theory of 'good society', in other words rejecting
not only the 'traditional' ideologies of the post-French Revolution
period but undermining the very notion of ideology as such (see Part
III of this book). Just as the ideologies of Left and Right arose on the

basis of modernity, postmodernist theories – with their rejection of totalistic ideological thinking – can be seen as reflecting a new social structure. Social fragmentation, the apparent erosion of the nation-state as a coherent framework, the problematic status of any collective agent and the absence of any organised movement that can claim to articulate the general grievances of society are all features of postmodern society. They point to the demise of those great over-arching theories of society (ideologies) that have provided prescription, critique and some idea of agency. Hence 'the postmodern political condition' is held to rule out 'redemptive politics of any kind' (Heller and Feher, 1988, p. 4) and to undermine the old agenda of politics shared by the ideologies of modernity. Such analysis calls for new ideas and theories of politics that are less grand and oppressive in their scope and less than universal in their claimed validity.

This criticism of ideologies invokes what Foucault called 'a sense of the increasing vulnerability to criticism of things, institutions, practices, discourses', and a critique of what he termed 'the inhibiting effect of global, *totalitarian theories*' (Foucault, 1980, p. 80). If these criticisms are correct, the age of ideology is indeed over, along with the structured and organised modern society that gave rise to it. The crisis of modernity and the crisis of ideology are intertwined, and the combined impact of this crisis is not just social fragmentation and increased complexity, but also that traditional ideological thinking is undermined and rendered irrelevant.

The postmodernist attack also involves, at least in some of its forms, a critique of the idea of progress and of the belief that social emancipation is possible. The rejection of ideological thinking is connected with radical scepticism about the possibility of social improvement and total transformation by a single agent of change. Postmodern theories emphasise the problematic nature of the collective agent of political and social action and they attach great weight to the plurality and complexity of contemporary society. They deny the validity of any of the 'grand narratives' provided by the dominant ideologies in the period of modernity (Lyotard, 1992). The ambivalence, conflicting identities and plurality of perspectives that characterise the postmodern period make the old ideological map (with its Left–Right guiding thread) too simplistic for a society that has been fundamentally stripped of its modernist structures and features.

This raises the question of the future of ideology. If ideology is indeed dead, what chance is there of any politics of emancipation –

must this aspiration too be consigned to the rubbish dump of history, to be replaced by politics emphasising particularistic identities and differences, 'the politics of identity and recognition' (Calhoun, 1995, ch. 7)? This form of politics finds its expression in debates about multiculturalism, demanding recognition for particular identities and cultures, and hostile to the broad, totalising sweep of global ideologies. Such demands for recognition come 'to the fore in a number of ways in today's politics, on behalf of minority or "subaltern" groups, in some forms of feminism and in what is today called the politics of "multiculturalism"' (Taylor *et al.*, 1994, p. 25).

All these issues are discussed in depth in this book, which is organised as follows. Part I investigates the nature of modernity, focusing on its core ideas on politics, society and philosophy, as well as providing a sketch of the social, economic and political transformations that underpinned those ideas and gave rise to modern society. What is crucial here is the 'discourse of modernity' (Habermas, 1987), seen above all in terms of a philosophical theory of universal progress and emancipation, a prescriptive view of the political system of a democratic republic, and a theory of civil society, with its market-dominated view of the organisation of the economy.

Historically and politically, this agenda of modernity found expression in the American Revolution in 1776 and, to an even greater extent, the French Revolution in 1789. These revolutions were the practical expression of the modernist outlook and opened the way to modern political thought and activity. As the ideologies of the modern period stem from these revolutions, one can understand nothing about modernity unless their impact is taken into account. Recent 'revisionist' accounts of the French Revolution give priority to the new democratic discourse of politics that emerged during the course of that revolution. As one account explains, 'a revolution can be defined as a transformation of the discursive practice of the community, a moment in which social relations are reconstituted and the discourse defining the political relations between individuals and groups is radically recast' (Baker, 1990, p. 18). This new discourse invoked ideas of citizenship in the context of the democratic nation as the new subject of politics (Baker, 1990; Furet, 1989; Sewell, 1994). These fundamental concepts constitute the language of the politics of modernity, and formed the agenda for the modern ideologies whose present relevance is being called into question by postmodern theorists. Hence Chapters 1 and 2 set the scene for the subsequent examination of the ideologies in question. The concept of modernity is explained in terms of the type of society prevailing at the time and the concepts (emancipation, democracy, nation and nation-state, citizenship, progress, revolution) that formed the language of politics and the various political ideologies that have dominated for the last two centuries.

In what ways did these ideologies respond to the new type of society and its accompanying political challenges? This is the subject of Part II, which divides the ideologies of politics into two broad camps: liberalism/socialism and conservatism/nationalism. Both liberalism and socialism saw themselves as 'modernist' but had a different vision of 'the good society'. They also shared some of the assumptions of the Enlightenment and modernity. Viewing these two ideologies as expressions of, and responding to, modernity, gives a coherence to each and helps explain the problems they face today.

Conservative theorists adopted a much more critical stance with regard to the promise of modernity, above all to the Enlightenment principle of the supremacy of reason. Nevertheless their reliance on tradition as a source of social cohesion, and the extreme emphasis on authority and hierarchy in some forms of conservatism, left conservative writers unable to offer any constructive alternative in the later world of constant transformation, where established certainties were being undermined. Similarly nationalism is instructive in its ambivalence about modernity, being at one and the same time a vehicle for the transition to modernity (Gellner, 1983) and defender of traditions that were threatened by the onward sweep of modernity. This Janus-faced (Nairn, 1981) feature of nationalism has helped it to emerge, it seems, as one of the winners of the age of ideology, as it is able to accommodate itself to the postmodern defence of fragmentation and particularity, and critique of universality. Hence the examination of nationalism serves as a bridge to Part III, which discusses whether the ideological traditions of modernity have a future.

The final chapters deal with the intellectual (postmodernist) challenges to modernity as well as the changes in state, civil society and economy which underpin these challenges. The question is whether the recent social and political transformations justify the jettisoning of the ideological traditions reviewed in Parts I and II. The challenge comes from a range of new and critical theories such as feminism, environmentalism and pluralism, which are symptoms of the crisis of Enlightenment optimism and constructivism. Postmodernism is critical of all ideologies, which are seen as dangerously rigid and incapable of coping with multicultural and pluralistic politics, and hence the question posed in the final chapter, does ideology have a future?

Chapter 9 defends both the modernist tradition and the need for ideology, which can still offer broad principles and goals for the structuring of society. Against the view that ideology is dead, and against the theory that suggests profound social and cultural transformations undermine the possibility of social emancipation, the conclusion seeks to measure the significance of ideology as a necessary condition for a truly democratic politics, rather than imposing a rigid blueprint on society. Modernity and the ideologies it spawned, with their tradition of universalism, are necessary to maintain a common identity and bonds of citizenship in the face of the potentially divisive particularism and multiple identities that proliferate in contemporary politics. But how this universalism can be maintained in times of rapid social change and the onward march of progress is a key problem for the politics of our time. Faced with forces of globalisation and economic development that undermine local traditions, there is a reaction in favour of the assertion of such particular identities. This reaction challenges the universalist aspirations and themes of the ideologies of modernity.

Ideology, it is argued, remains indispensible to contemporary politics, to democratic culture and to emancipation and progress. This does not mean that the traditional ideologies can ignore the criticisms and challenges levelled against them by the proponents of new ideologies and postmodernist critics of ideology in general. The changes in contemporary capitalism, the collapse of communism and the spread of free-market economics in the former communist world, the rise of ethnic and national particularism and forms of 'multiculturalism' have all modified the context in which modern political ideologies are developed. If these ideologies are to have a future they must take account of such transformations or run the risk of becoming irrelevant.

If democracy and emancipation are to be more than pious aspirations, the ideologies must once again be linked to social movements and political parties that are capable of putting them into practice. Without ideologies of emancipation, politics risks degenerating into an unprincipled struggle for power without any general aims or purposes, other than power for its own sake. On the other hand, unless they take a practical grip on the transformed reality and gain an understanding of the changes that have shot through society, the ideologies of modernity (notably socialism) risk becoming dinosaurs.

Ideologies offer a range of ideals whose total absence makes democratic politics an unlikely pursuit. Yet ideologies need to interact with and have a sense of reality, to avoid becoming abstractions or empty slogans. One of the aims of this book is to establish the continuing relevance of the ideologies of modernity in these times of division, complexity and unsettling social transformation.

Part I
Enlightenment and Emancipation

1

The Politics of Modernity

At the end of the eighteenth century, in the epoch opened up by the American and the French Revolutions, a new type of society emerged – *civil society*, a term that will be explained more fully below. The period of modernity was the era of civil society, a society free from the grip of the old regime, an individualistic and liberal society that promised its members progress, freedom and happiness in this world rather than the next.

The emergence of civil society gave rise to a whole new agenda of political and social theorising and a new range of ideas, including ideas that justified and celebrated this transformed society, seeing it as the achievement of emancipation and enlightenment. Yet the new agenda also included theories that were deeply critical of the changed society and of the ideas that justified it. These theories included different forms of socialism, which did not reject the premises of modernity as such, or its theoretical basis, but argued that in its present form civil society could not fulfil its defenders' promise of universal emancipation and happiness. Conservatives and nationalists warned of the costs of the new society, animated as it was by Enlightenment principles of material and moral progress and the achievement of happiness in the here-and-now. These critics sought to emphasise the limits and frailty of human reason, the conditioning of human activity by the weight of past history, and what Taine, a French conservative writing at the end of the nineteenth century, called '*la race et le milieu*' – forces that could not be penetrated or controlled by human reason. As Taine wrote, the real 'masters of man consist of physical temperament, bodily needs, animal instinct, hereditary prejudice, imagination, generally the dominant passion, and more particularly personal or family interest, also that of caste and party' (Taine, quoted in McLelland, 1970, p. 72).

Thus there were two lines of criticism of the politics of modernity, which could be called internal and external. The former – broadly the socialist Left – shared the assumption that there would be progress and emancipation, but argued that to achieve these goals radical, even revolutionary, changes would be necessary, and that this would transform the structure of society. The 'external' critics were much more sceptical of the whole Enlightenment project, and what Habermas called the philosophical discourse of modernity (Habermas, 1987). These critics thought the modernist programme was deeply flawed because it rested on false assumptions about the transformability of the world and the malleability if not perfectibility of human nature. They argued that Enlightenment or modernist philosophy neglected the conditioning effect of tradition and the weight of the 'real', of circumstances which were not transformable by human effort, except at disastrous cost. This, then, is what is meant by the politics of modernity: the attempt to bring about total social and political transformation, and the debate for and against this attempt in the sphere of political and social thought.

Habermas's *The Philosophical Discourse of Modernity* contains some useful pointers on what 'modernity' involves. Habermas saw Hegel as 'the first philosopher to develop a clear concept of modernity' (Habermas, 1987, p. 4). The crucial idea of modernity was that the new age was the modern age, dated (for Hegel) 'from the break that the Enlightenment and the French Revolution signified for the more thoughtful contemporaries at the close of the eighteenth and the start of the nineteenth century' (ibid., p. 7). Two features characterised this new age, both of which were highlighted by Hegel. The first was the idea of subjectivity, or individual freedom, that the basis of the new order was and had to be the freedom of the individual. Individuals were free to apply their critical faculties, to accept responsibility for their actions, to see the social and political order as the result of human action.

Secondly, the core feature of the modern age was the separation of two orders: state and economy. As Habermas put it 'the commodity exchange (organised under civil law) of the capitalist economy has detached itself from the order of political rule . . . Through the media of exchange value and power, two systems of action that are functionally complementary have been differentiated out' (Habermas, 1987, p. 37). Thus the main problem for society was that the modern order was fundamentally divided, and individual reason as an aspect of subjectivity could not unify society. The task therefore was to transcend subjectivity so that unity could be established. This would be particularly difficult, according to Hegel, given the divisive tendencies of civil society.

The Origins of Modernity

In order to understand the political ideologies of modernity, it is necessary to grasp why these ideas emerged when they did, and how they related to economic, social and political change. Faced with a situation in which the social, economic and political dimensions of life were being totally and rapidly transformed, the conceptual maps that had guided human endeavour for previous generations were evidently out-of-date and could provide no guidance in the urgent task of social reorganisation. Hegel's famous words in his Preface to *The Phenomenology of Mind* express very well this sense of transition to a new form of society and a different philosophy of human life:

> For the rest it is not difficult to see that our epoch is a birth-time, and a period of transition. The spirit of man has broken with the old order of things hitherto prevailing, and with the old ways of thinking (Hegel, 1966, p. 75).

Hegel greeted the French Revolution as 'the sunrise, which, in a flash and at a single stroke, brings to view the form and structure of the new world' (Hegel, 1966, p. 75). But what exactly were the transformations (economic, social and political) that gave rise to modernity, that its ideologies sought in their different ways to 'theorise', in the sense of providing a framework for the social and political organisation of this 'new world'?

In the different areas of economy, society and polity, radical changes had occurred that required new maps or frameworks for political action, and it was these frameworks that the various ideologies of modernity provided. In the economic sphere, modernity was marked by the emergence of a new mode of production, whereby commodities could be produced in far greater quantities for distribution in the world market. Globalisation, which is often claimed to be a feature of postmodern times, can actually be said to have begun with the discovery of America and the subsequent expansion in world trade. The lines in Marx and Engels' *Communist Manifesto* remain unsurpassed as a description of the world-wide sweep of this commercial and productive society:

> The need of a constantly expanding market for its products chases the bourgeoisie over the whole surface of the globe. It must nestle

everywhere, settle everywhere, establish connections everywhere (Marx, 1973a, p. 71).

As a characterisation of modernity this could hardly be bettered, for it describes a new form of society increasingly dependent on industrial production and world-wide distribution, a society in which science and technology were applied to conquer nature. Socialist thinkers best captured this economic aspect of modernity and emphasised its lack of organisation. The followers of Saint-Simon, Bazard and Enfantin, drew attention to the economic crises and danger of over-production to which the new society was constantly exposed: 'The necessary consequences of these uncoordinated efforts and of this overproduction in some areas is that the balance between production and consumption is continually threatened' (Iggers, 1972, p. 14).

Hence modernity refers to a society in which the expansion of the productive process and the application of science to production radically altered social relationships. This was recognised not just by socialists, but by all those who saw the need for new principles of social organisation. The ideologies of modernity emerged in response to the economic upheaval of the industrial revolution, the develop-ment of new methods of production and the expansion of market relations ('the cash nexus') to embrace all aspects of social life in a wider, increasingly international, context.

This economic transformation clearly had social and political consequences. The traditional, hierarchical society, where human contact for the most part was restricted to a geographically confined area, was undermined by the switch from agrarianism to industriali-sation. As noted by Gellner, this transition also necessitated new forms of communication and different institutions:

The modern industrial machine is like an elephant in a very small boat . . . [It] presupposes an enormous infrastructure, not merely of political order, but educationally, culturally, in terms of commu-nication and so forth (Gellner, 1979, p. 7).

Nationalism could be seen as a possible 'solution' to the problems of modernity, because a nation-state provides and maintains a common culture that is serviced by a shared education system and integrated by a common language, all of which are necessary to provide the sense of community needed for an industrially productive society. However in their different ways all the ideologies of modernity were preoccupied with harnessing the fruits of this new industrial society while at the same time preserving some degree of community and integration in a dangerously fragmented modern society:

> Words like *industrialist* and *industrialism* were coined to complement this concept of an 'industrial revolution' . . . predictions of the total transformation of society by means of this revolution began to be confidently made from a variety of ideological points of view (Hobsbawm, in Feher, 1990, p. 39).

The social changes consequent on the transition to modernity can be further specified as a movement away from traditional society marked by an unchanging hierarchy, in which everyone remained in his or her allotted place, to one of social mobility, the possibility of individual (and collective) advancement and the 'pursuit of happiness' on an individual or collective basis. Modernity involved a search for new identities to replace the traditional and religiously sanctioned ones of the previous epoch. Moreover it was made clear that these new identities were the creation of human action and agency, rather than God-given and unalterable. Modernity also endowed old words such as 'nation', 'citizen' and 'worker' with new meaning, opening them up as labels or categories that applied to a much wider constituency than hitherto. For example, 'nation' no longer referred to a group of people born in a particular area, it came to mean a sovereign people that possessed some unique quality that distinguished them from the people of other nations (Greenfeld, 1992, p. 9). Nationalism as an ideology sought in various ways to heighten people's identification with 'their' nation through a common education system and political mobilisation, even though this would take a long time to accomplish. Likewise 'worker' became endowed with new meanings that were often specific to particular ideologies, as in the Marxist idea of the 'proletariat', where the label was applied not just to those who formed a part of the 'collective labourer', but also to those who had, or would come to have, a particular consciousness and set of aspirations ('class consciousness'). In the same way, in its French Revolutionary usage the term 'patriot' came to mean a friend of the revolution, a person committed to the realisation of ideas of popular sovereignty and hostile to émigrés and counterrevolutionaries.

Thus new identities were created, to some extent consciously, identities comprising wider sections of the population, identities which were seen as attainable by will and conscious action.

The Rise of the Masses

If the new ideas of modernity were related to economic and social changes, they were also dependent on fundamental political changes. These political transformations can be called the rise of the masses, the challenge of democracy, or in general terms the demand that political participation be extended to the mass of people hitherto excluded from political society. Clearly these new demands for inclusion were related to the economic and social transformations outlined above, to the rise of new methods of production, and to ideas challenging God-given traditions and hierarchical structures, ideas that were based on the Enlightenment principle of rationality. What has been called the 'imperative of inclusion' (Rosanvallon, 1992, p. 43) sought to overturn any exclusion from political participation on the basis of property, education, gender, race, ethnicity and age.

All the ideologies of modernity had to reckon with the 'unfinished journey' of democracy (Dunn, 1992). This was exemplified by Marx saluting the Chartist demand for universal suffrage as 'a far more socialistic measure than anything which has been honoured with that name on the Continent' and having as its 'inevitable result . . . the political supremacy of the working class' (Marx, 1973b, p. 264). An alternative perspective came from the liberal thinker James Mill who suggested the age of forty 'as that at which the right of Suffrage should commence; scarcely any laws could be made for the benefit of all the men of forty which would not be laws for the benefit of all the rest of the community' (Mill, 1992, p. 28). What de Tocqueville called the demand for 'equality of conditions' was presented by him as inescapable in the tide of modern politics. Any attempt to fashion new principles or frameworks of political action had to take account of this democratic pressure, as the politics of modernity was a politics of democracy and participation. Indeed only legitimation based on popular sovereignty was acceptable in the modern age (Beetham, 1991), although this was distorted in various ways by ideologies such as fascism, which sought to justify absolute power by claiming that the leader could represent the masses better than any person who emerged from the divisive process of democratic politics.

Thus, 'modernity' refers to the series of profound transformations in economic, social and political relations that took place from the end of the eighteenth society and eventually created an entirely new form of society throughout the world. From this new society emerged the ideologies that were to provide the language of politics for the next two centuries, and create competing frameworks for political action and debate.

Enlightenment Philosophy

Modernity as a broad philosophical view started with the idea that the aim of political activity was not, as the dominant thought of the Middle Ages put it, to prepare people for their salvation in the next world. From the onset of the modern period the quite different assumption was made that happiness, progress and emancipation were possible in this world for all human beings. These beliefs were highly contested, and not just by diehard opponents of modernity. Even those who believed in the possibility of human happiness in this world, and in the construction of a political system appropriate to that end, had doubts about all human beings sharing in the benefits of a rationally organised society. Defenders of the Enlightenment project were deeply divided on the question of the role of the masses, of democracy, on the criteria determining who should be included in the new society and profit from it. Was the struggle for progress and rationality to be waged by and ultimately won for the benefit of a cultured elite, who alone were the worthy beneficiaries of an enlightened age? Some strands of the Enlightenment philosophy certainly suggested that such a restricted group of people should form the backbone of any republic, and that the vulgar masses (*la canaille*, the rabble) were not capable of playing a role in an enlightened social order. In part the tensions of the politics of modernity arose because of its link with democracy: if reason, or rationality, were part of the inherent apparatus of every human being, then the distinction between the cultivated few and the ignorant many, the enlightened minority facing the vulgar masses, could not be sustained for long.

The politics of modernity were marked by several tensions, of which the debate on democracy was one. The political project and the associated ideas that dominated world politics for two centuries stemmed from a core idea of the Enlightenment, namely that progress, rationality and unbounded human capacity were achievable aims in the real world. It was the French revolutionary Saint-Just who proclaimed that 'happiness is a new idea in Europe', meaning that before the French Revolution happiness was not considered to be achievable except in the afterlife. Goethe echoed this idea through the words of Faust, confronting the spectre of *Sorge*, anxiety or care: his response is an affirmation of this-worldly activity and the possibility of improvement: 'The world is well enough known to me now. Our view beyond it is blocked; only idiots turn their blinking eyes up yonder, and dream of beings in our own image above the clouds!' (Luke (ed.), 1964, p. 190).

The principles of modern thought cannot be grasped by studying some ahistorical sequence of 'great ideologies', of a number of 'isms' parading in succession. The politics of modernity and the ideas that made it up rested on certain core assumptions: progress, rationality, the achievement of happiness in the human – as opposed to the divine – world, and the construction of political and social institutions to realise those ends. However these assumptions and this philosophical discourse of modernity have been severely challenged in more recent times because of scepticism about human nature, arising in part from the experiences of totalitarian politics in the twentieth century. The prospect of progress and rationality has taken a severe blow in the light of 'the challenge posed by history itself, not least recent history, to the fundamental optimism about human capabilities which per- vades the socialist enterprise – a belief, inherited from the Enlight- enment, in the infinite perfectibility of human beings' (Miliband, R., 1994, p. 58).

The phenomena of twentieth-century politics include the barbarism of fascism and the mass terror of Stalinism, to which so many intellectuals (and others) were blind, as is demonstrated by François Furet in *Le passé d'une illusion* (1995). Indeed Furet and others like him seem to suggest that it was precisely because of the uncritical acceptance of certain elements of 'the Enlightenment project' that many people were reluctant to acknowledge the true face of the Stalinist system. They acquiesced in its atrocities and thought that the terror was an acceptable price to pay for the progress brought about by the Russian Revolution. The implication is that particular views of historical progress, in this case Marxism (itself taking over certain beliefs of the Enlightenment tradition), functioned to veil the huge sacrifices of human life and the disasters of Stalinism. Though a movement of quite different historical origins, fascism, with its brutality, cruelty and manipulation of myth and irrationality, rivalled Stalinism in its total denial of individual rights and the concentration of power in a swollen state apparatus.

These central episodes of twentieth-century politics illustrate the elusiveness of the Enlightenment principles, the core elements of the politics of modernity. To take a more contemporary example, the resurgence of nationalism and 'ethnic cleansing' in the Balkans suggests the irrelevance and naive optimism of the Enlightenment project and the ideas of modernist politics that stemmed from it. Miliband's answer to this problem is to argue that while 'it cannot be expected that the demons which have been at work throughout history will not continue to cast their evil spell for a long time to come', collective cruelty and individual acts of cruelty are not an incradicable part of human nature but 'are mainly produced by the insecurities, frustrations, anxieties and alienations that form an intrinsic part of class societies based on domination and exploitation' (Miliband, R., 1994, p. 61). In other words human nature is not fixed, but is influenced by the prevailing social conditions, the political and social institutions within which people associate, and which to some extent affect and mould human nature.

Arguments like this are certainly part of the tradition of Enlightenment theorising. The classic articulation of the position was that by Robert Owen, who is usually placed within the tradition of early or (to Marxists) 'Utopian' socialism. It was Owen in his 'Report to the County of Lanark' who suggested that human nature is moulded by the environment and the circumstances in which people grow up, and hence a change in the environment will create a different type of human nature. In Owen's view, it is the controlling elite, the educated classes, who have the power to change these circumstances, as Owen himself sought to do through better education and working facilities in his factories in New Lanark.

Here too there is a central problem with the Enlightenment tradition. Clearly such a perspective is capable of distortion, such as uncontrolled 'social engineering' to create a 'new man' or 'new woman' through indoctrination and compulsion, as exemplified by the fascist and communist regimes. In their different ways these regimes tried to force people into a particular mould, to inspire them with loyalty to the Führer, the party or the great leader Stalin. Of course this was not remotely what Robert Owen had in mind. His argument was that people's nature is shaped by the circumstances and environment within which they live, and in his view it was absurd to preach Christian morality and expect cooperation in a society that inculcated the opposite values of competition and selfishness. By creating a more humane and attractive working environment, fostering attitudes of cooperation and solidarity, manufacturers like him could contribute to the transformation of human nature and the making of a more cooperative society. Thus one of the principles of the Enlightenment tradition, and by extension one of the elements or core assumptions of the 'politics of modernity', is what could be called the malleability of human nature. In contrast to the religious argument of the time that individuals were irredeemably marked by original sin or unalterable wickedness, the Enlightenment tradition took a more optimistic view of human nature and suggested the possibility of cooperation and altruism. These more positive attributes of human nature could be fostered by political or social institutions designed to encourage the cooperative aspects of human nature and limit the antagonistic ones.

Modern ideologies thus have to be understood as products of the debate on modernity. At the heart of this project lies the Enlightenment idea that progress and transformation are possible. The politics of modernity has three core ideas, which can be discussed under the headings 'philosophy', 'politics' and 'society'.

The Philosophy of Emancipation

By 'philosophy' is meant certain core ideas, some of which have already been suggested above – ideas of progress, human rationality and enlightenment. As a starting point for characterising the ideas that form the basis of the politics of modernity, one can do no better than refer to Kant's famous essay of 1784, *What is Enlightenment?* (Kant, 1991, pp. 54–60). Two central points emerge from this essay. The first concerns Kant's bold statement that enlightenment involves thinking for oneself, daring to use one's reason. This is seen as the emergence of humanity from immaturity, an immaturity that is 'self-incurred' if people do not have the courage to think for themselves and require authoritative guidance to form their ideas:

> *Enlightenment is man's emergence from his self-incurred immaturity. Immaturity* is the inability to use one's own understanding without the guidance of another. This immaturity is *self-incurred* if its cause is not lack of understanding, but lack of resolution and courage to use it without the guidance of another. The motto of enlightenment is therefore: *Sapere aude!* Have courage to use your *own* understanding! (ibid., p. 54).

The other point is the central one of an informed and critical public. Kant argued that it is difficult for isolated and separate individuals to emancipate themselves from intellectual tutelage. This is easier to achieve through the force of public opinion: 'There is more chance of an entire public enlightening itself'. Hence all people must be free to address themselves to the public. It is interesting, however, to note two things. First, the progress of enlightenment, for Kant, was necessarily gradual and could not be achieved by means of violent revolution:

> Thus a public can only achieve enlightenment slowly. A revolution may well put an end to autocratic despotism and to rapacious or power-seeking oppression, but it will never produce a true reform in ways of thinking. Instead, new prejudices, like the ones they replaced, will serve as a leash to control the great unthinking mass (ibid., p. 55).

Hence Kant's political caution: the present age was, he thought, not an enlightened age, but an age of enlightenment, the process had started but was by no means accomplished. The other significant aspect is Kant's distinction between the public use of reason and its private use. The public use is, as he put it, 'that use which anyone may make of it *as a man of learning* addressing the entire *reading public*' (ibid.). This is contrasted with the private use of reason, which is bound up with the particular position a person occupies, as taxpayer or soldier, religious or academic functionary, in which the use of reason can be limited without, as Kant put it, hindering the cause of enlightenment. Thus the model of progress is of individuals addressing themselves to an educated public, and this intellectual discussion and criticism goes hand in hand with social order and avoidance of revolution. Indeed the essay contains praise for Frederick the Great ('our age is the age of enlightenment, the century of *Frederick*'), and suggests that 'a lesser degree of civil freedom gives intellectual freedom enough room to expand to its fullest extent' (ibid., p. 59). Kant's preferred model was one of enlightened despotism:

> A ruler who is himself enlightened and has no fear of phantoms, yet who likewise has at hand a well-disciplined and numerous army to guarantee public security, may say what no republic would dare to say: *Argue as much as you like and about whatever you like, but obey!* (ibid.)

In this way the peaceful spread of enlightened and rational ideas could continue to affect both the mentality of the people and of the rulers, who 'find that they can themselves profit by treating man, who is *more than a machine*, in a manner appropriate to his dignity' (ibid., p. 60).

Kant's essay is interesting indeed, not least for the tensions within his Enlightenment message, of daring to think boldly, emerging from immaturity and thinking for oneself, and yet accepting, if only temporarily, the existing political structure. Furthermore, his crucial theme is an informed and intellectual public opinion, a particular kind of public sphere. Humanity is faced with the task of emerging from 'self-incurred immaturity', but the way to enlightenment is through the development of an educated public, rationally discussing common concerns and contributing to the improvement of society.

The Ideal of the Republic

The second pillar of the politics of modernity is what is termed here 'politics', meaning a certain kind of political system that is appropriate to the realisation of the philosophical and social ideas of freedom and progress. In this category comes the idea of the republic, the tradition of republicanism. This term not only involves a set of political institutions, but also certain ideas of citizenship, participation and indeed democracy, as the republican regime both depends on and inculcates certain virtues in its citizens. The politics of modernity involves as one of its strands the idea of a republic, defined minimally as a public sphere, a set of political institutions inviting citizen participation, and creating and recreating an idea of virtue and republican zeal.

However the idea of the republic, while basic to the politics of modernity, has taken on different forms in this tradition. What is the nature of the republic in this tradition, what are its central institutions, how inclusive and exclusive are its boundaries, who are the citizens, and what are their duties and responsibilities? These have all been contested questions within the politics of modernity and the republican tradition, questions that were raised to a new degree of actuality by the American and French Revolutions. If 'the invention of the modern republic' (Fontana, 1994) is a central part of the politics of modernity, what is the nature and inclusiveness of this republic and its relationship to democracy? Kant's text on 'Perpetual Peace' draws a clear distinction between 'republic' and 'democracy'. The republic is a system in which there is no fusion of powers, and the republic is contrasted with despotic systems, of which 'democracy' is one example:

> *Democracy*, in the truest sense of the word, is necessarily a *despotism*, because it establishes an executive power through which all the citizens may make decisions about (and indeed against) the single individual without his consent, so that decisions are made by all the people and yet not by all the people; and this means that the general will is in contradiction with itself, and thus also with freedom (Kant, 1991, p. 101).

The tradition of the republic came from classical antiquity. Republicanism there meant a small-sized unit, composed of citizens who participated directly in the affairs of the *polis*. This arrangement was made possible by the existence of a class of slaves to carry out the productive work of society and thus free the citizens to attend to the deliberative affairs of the *polis*. The big problem for the early theorists of modernity was how, if at all, to preserve this tradition of classical republicanism, the face-to-face direct democracy of the ancient city state, in the quite different situation of modern society. In such conditions there were at least two huge differences from the context of antiquity: first, there was no slave caste, given the totally different type of society and economy that prevailed in modern society. Modern society was a society based on commerce, and later industry, where the task of production and of accumulating wealth could not be left to slaves. It was precisely the task of individuals in a commercial society to devote much of their time and energy to production, if necessary at the expense of 'politics', at least in the form of direct unmediated participation. One of the central dilemmas of modernity stemmed from this fact. If wealth was the chief preoccupation of its citizens, if their productive tasks kept them occupied for most of their time, how could their political tasks be fulfilled? Could the aspirations of classical republicanism be satisfied in modern conditions?

The second difference, which also gave rise to deep problems for the politics of modernity, was that the ancient city states were states of direct democracy, direct citizen participation. How could such a system be recreated in the modern world, given the increased size of the political unit, the demands of productive and professional activity, and the greater complexity of political life? This dilemma has been compounded in the conditions of twentieth-century politics, but it was present at the beginning of modernity in the epoch of the American and French Revolutions. Broadly speaking there were two responses to the problem, the first of which insisted that in the conditions ,of modernity the civic virtue, solidarity and sense of involvement that typified the ancient republic could not be achieved. This response was given by Rousseau, who in his *Social Contract* suggested that democracy as a form of government in which all participated in making the law, creating the general will, would be exceedingly hard and perhaps impossible to achieve in the modern world. Rousseau lamented the fact that the virtues of the city state could not be recreated or rediscovered in a modern, large-scale, commercial society.

The second response was exemplified by the liberal writer Benjamin Constant in his essay on the difference between the liberty of the ancients and the liberty of the moderns. Constant's answer was that there was a crucial difference between the two types of freedom (Holmes, 1984). The freedom available to a citizen of the ancient world was not relevant to the conditions of modernity. In Constant's view, under modern conditions the type of freedom the ancients enjoyed was not only impossible to achieve, but even if it could be recreated it would be undesirable. In the ancient republics citizens had indeed participated directly, but they had no freedom from the *polis*, their private beliefs and thoughts were held in common with all other citizens, there was no private sphere. The nature of the modern republic had to be different, it had to be representative, because ordinary citizens had no time to devote themselves continually to public affairs. Representative democracy made possible an economy of time. Nevertheless Constant, while welcoming the necessity in modern times for a private sphere, expressed concern that the politics of modernity might become too privatised an affair, in which citizens lost any interest in the sphere of politics and became totally absorbed in their personal money-making concerns. His fellow liberal Alexis de Tocqueville shared the same fear, which was so typical of the dilemmas of the politics of modernity – the pressures and demands

of a commercial society might well undermine the civic virtu
solidarity necessary for a healthy political system.

Civil Society

The third element of modernity refers to a particular type of society,
namely 'civil society'. Theorists of modernity included people such as
David Hume, Adam Ferguson and other theorists of the Scottish
Enlightenment, who welcomed the coming of a new type of society
civil society – and sought to delineate its chief features.

The idea of civil society has had a long history, and has been
resurrected in our own time (Cohen and Arato, 1992; Gellner, 1996;
Hall, 1995). In contemporary conditions it has come to signify
opposition to an all-powerful state, as typified by the communist
and fascist systems; although it is in the context of the former and
their collapse that civil society has become so popular. Contemporary usage stresses the idea of civil society in pluralistic terms: as a
society rich in groups and associations, in which individuals interact
and participate. The network of groups and associations is seen as a
bulwark against a totalitarian state seeking to atomise its citizens,
reducing them to cogs in a machine controlled by the unrestricted
power of the state. Civil society, in the recent understanding of the
term, is thus a necessary antidote to the state and a precondition for
democracy.

However the concept of civil society started its career by denoting
the particularly modern characteristics of the new age. Civil society
was described by the theorists of modernity in the following terms: it
was *individualist*, it was *commercial* and *productive*, and it was *pacifist*
compared with the belligerent societies that had preceded it, be these
feudal or, more distantly, societies such as Sparta, where war was the
only way of life, and as a result 'luxury' was not possible. Such
warlike societies were doomed to remain at a low level of production,
hence new and sophisticated needs could not be met. These societies
might have been powerful, at least in military terms, because human
energies were put to the service of the state and its army. As Hume
wrote in his essay 'On Commerce',

In short, no probable reason can be assigned for the great power of
the more ancient states above the modern, but their want of

commerce and luxury. Few artizans were maintained by the labour of the farmers, and therefore more soldiers might live upon it (Hume, 1994, p. 96).

However, what modern civil society lacked in military might, it made up for in terms of productive power and the satisfaction of new and more sophisticated needs, or 'luxuries' (Berry, 1994).

The antithesis between 'ancient' society and 'modern' society was commonplace in late-eighteenth-century thought. The new civil society was seen as a society in which individuals pursued their interests, and were free to do so, to the resultant benefit of society as a whole. The classical example of this is Adam Smith's idea of the 'invisible hand'. Modern civil societies were liberal or free societies, in which the private sphere was marked out and separated from the area of the state. Progress was made possible by the liberation of individuals from the thralls of the state, and the devotion of most, if not all, individuals to the cause of productive activity. A civil society was one of 'civilisation', of the growth of production and refinement in arts and sciences, as noted by Hume in his essay 'Of the rise and progress of the arts and sciences'. Relationships between individuals became more refined and softer, as opposed to the rude militaristic ruggedness of past society. Contract and commerce replaced combat as the chief interaction between human beings, with resultant gains in art and literature.

Civil society was a liberating force, which set individuals free from the stifling grip of the state and other associations such as the clan, which in 'ancient' or premodern societies had imposed their customs on individuals and made impossible any private sphere and individual initiative. The second part of Adam Ferguson's *Essay on the History of Civil Society* deals with what he calls 'the history of rude nations': such 'rude' nations were distinguished from the civilised ones of modern society. Initially, 'rude' nations had no idea of private property: they 'intrust their subsistence chiefly to hunting, fishing, or the natural produce of the soil. They have little attention to property, and scarcely any beginnings of subordination or government' (Ferguson, 1995, p. 81). Rude nations were militaristic, rapacious and governed by arbitrary power. In such a society 'the warlike and turbulent spirit of its inhabitants seems to require the bridle of despotism and military force' (ibid., p. 101). By contrast, in modern civil society people could choose their occupation, and diversity of profession and opinion held sway: 'the occupations of men, in every condition, bespeak their freedom of choice, their various opinions, and the multiplicity of wants by which they are urged' (ibid., p. 13).

However this new-found civil society was not without its problems. It was prone to corruption and decay, and above all to a dissociation between its members, a lack of social solidarity (Gautier, 1993). How could community be maintained in the new civil society, and could modernity, with all its advantages, be made compatible with a sense of social obligation and reciprocity? Excessive individualism and self-interest could be as harmful as the violent and rapacious societies of 'rude' nations:

> To the ancient Greek or the Roman, the individual was nothing, and the public everything. To the modern, in too many nations of Europe, the individual is everything, and the public nothing (Ferguson, 1995, p. 57).

The more polished age of civil society brought with it new problems, including the difficulty of reconciling 'the several arts of personal advancement' with some idea of civic virtue. The chief concern of the theorists of modernity and civil society was that in unleashing the generally beneficent force of individualism and opening up a free path to self-interest, the new society might not cohere. It might fall into decadence and corruption, because commerce could loom so large in people's lives that they would neglect the public and political spheres.

The thinkers of civil society did see ways of mitigating and controlling these dangers. One of the sources of cohesion, even in the new individualistic civil society, was what the thinkers of the Scottish Enlightenment called 'sympathy', an awareness of common human qualities that transcended what a later generation would call 'the cash nexus'. Part of the constitution of human beings was a fund of sympathy and compassion for their fellow creatures, and this limited the selfishness and individualism to which otherwise they might be prone. Ferguson pointed out the potential danger of a commercial society setting people against each other, which could lead them to neglect their fundamental social nature. The comparison between the ancient and the modern was this time rather in favour of the ancient. In civil society, '(man) has found an object which sets him in competition with his fellow-creatures, and he deals with them as he does with his cattle and his soil, for the sake of the profits they bring' (ibid., p. 24). Ferguson contrasted this picture of instrumentalism with the idea of human beings' essentially social disposition and feeling of union with the rest of their species (ibid., p. 23).

Public Opinion and the Public Sphere

The second antidote to fragmentation was the force of public opinion. The society that the thinkers of modernity welcomed was one in which the accumulative impulses of individuals were released. An essential part of this new civil society was the emergence of an informed and active public opinion, seen as part of the Enlightenment tradition. There existed a range of groups and associations, societies in which informed citizens could come together to exchange ideas and catch up on the progress of the sciences and knowledge, and in so doing create a source of pressure on the rulers of modern society. This is part of the meaning that civil society still preserves today, the idea of an informed and active public that does not have to accept what the government tells it, that can act as a source of opposition to the government of the day and articulate a range of perspectives and opinions. The force of 'the public opinion tribunal' was saluted by Jeremy Bentham as one of the ways in which the potentially danger-ous power of government could be negated and contained. Anyone, Bentham wrote, who sought to reduce the power and influence of this public opinion tribunal was an enemy of the public and of liberty, and should be exposed as such (Parekh, 1973, p. 215).

In similar vein are the words of one of the French Revolutionaries, Brissot. He was a defender of representative democracy and defined 'republic' (on 5 July 1791) as 'a government in which all powers are, firstly, delegated or representative; secondly, elective by and for the people; thirdly, temporary or removable' (Fontana, 1994, p. 96). For Brissot, public opinion, expressed by a free press, was an essential mediator between the public and the representatives. He wrote that public opinion, 'bursting forth from all sides, from all parties at once, is elaborated and purified by frank and open opposition, and by comparisons which settle the dross to leave nothing on the surface but a limpid liquor', that 'limpid liquor' being reason (ibid., p. 103).

From a sociological point of view, the question must be asked, who articulated this public opinion in the newly formed civil society? It was the 'notables', the pillars of society, who were the leading lights in this movement of informed middle-class opinion. Kant defined the citizens as those who had the right to vote on 'a public law which defines for everyone that which is permitted and prohibited by right'. But who were these citizens? To be a citizen required a degree of independence that only male property owners could claim:

The only qualification required by a citizen (apart, of course, from being an adult male) is that he must be his *own master (sui iuris)*, and must have some *property* (which can include any skill, trade, fine art or science) to support himself (Kant, 1991, p. 78).

In a footnote to this passage Kant explicitly stated that 'The domestic servant, the shop assistant, the labourer, or even the barber, are merely labourers (*operarii*), not artists (*artifices*, in the wider sense), and are thus unqualified to be citizens' (ibid.). There were tensions between the rationalism of the Enlightenment tradition and its proclamation of universal principles, and the narrower limits that were imposed on it by the nature of the society in which these principles were being realised. The aim in theory was for truth to be discovered, for society to be brought together on the basis of principles rationally discovered and proclaimed for all human beings. Yet the leaders in this process of public-opinion formation were enlightened notables, who sought to exclude from the process the vulgar, the propertyless masses, the rabble. The philosopher Condorcet wrote in 1776 that popular opinion 'remains the opinion of the most stupid and most miserable section of the people' (quoted in Ozouf, 1989, p. 33).

Nevertheless civil society had as one of its strands the idea of citizens coming together to form *sociétés de pensée*, or circles of conviviality, to articulate their interests and come to some common understanding of the rational principles of politics and society. In this way too the potentially divisive impact of civil society and the dangers of the politics of modernity could be mitigated, if not avoided altogether. Through the naturally sociable nature of humanity and the associations through which public opinion could be expressed, citizens would come together to articulate their interests and ideas, society would express its power against the state and progress would continue.

The contemporary social and political theorist Jürgen Habermas has analysed the sociological foundations of this new public opinion (Habermas, 1993; Calhoun, 1992). This involved the idea of publicity and openness (*Öffentlichkeit*), a politically reasoning public that challenged and widened the role of the representative assembly or parliament. This informed and active public opinion was certainly a 'bourgeois' one, composed of property owners (as the above quote from Kant makes clear), but in principle the position of property owner contributing to the rational discourse of public life was open to all. However, as the socialist critique was to reveal, the class conditions of bourgeois society were such as to negate the promise of a public sphere open to all property-owning citizens. Furthermore Habermas' analysis suggests that the idea of this critical public, rationally discussing issues of public interest, rested on certain foundations that were undermined by later social developments.

The modern form of this bourgeois public sphere involved a definite separation between public and private. The private sphere was one of bourgeois heads of household, patriarchally controlling their own family affairs. The idea of the public sphere, according to Habermas, was one of a common and general interest, in which political issues were discussed by a rationally informed public opinion. Sociologically, this public was a public of educated 'notables', extending their influence down to the popular masses. These bourgeois strata were the *Träger*, or bearers of a 'reading public' (*Lesepublikum*), able to react against and control the holders of political power, and subject politics to rational discussion. Such politically effective groupings of rational discourse took form in institutions such as the coffee house in England in the period from 1680 to 1730, the salons in post-revolutionary France and the reading circles, with their own premises in which to read periodicals and discuss their contents, in Germany at the end of the eighteenth-century.

Habermas' analysis of the subsequent development of this modern form of public opinion suggests its later decline. With the emergence of the more interventionist state there was a shift from public reasoning on cultural matters to a public opinion that was more easily manipulated, and a consuming rather than a critically appraising culture. The public sphere became one of advertising, where the holders of political power developed a greater ability to manipulate and control public opinion. The idea of public interest, rationally appraised by a critical public, was replaced by politics as a pure clash of interests between on the one hand powerful pressure groups and associations (*Verbände*) that tried to politicise particular or partial interests, and on the other hand political parties that sought to mould public opinion. The idea of private individuals reasoning politically (*politisch räsonnierenden Privatleute*) and creating a well-informed public opinion no longer applied, even though this public opinion was, as Habermas notes, initially formed by property owners, with propertyless people excluded from the sphere of opinion formers (Habermas, 1993, p. 188). One of the key elements in the politics of modernity is the emergence of public opinion as a force in its own right – a mediating force between power holders and society – and Habermas' discussion reveals some of the sociological foundations of this idea. The aim was for this public opinion to be politically effective and to articulate and enforce ideas of common interest:

> This should transform arbitrary will into reason, a reason which through the open competition of particular arguments establishes a consensus over what is practically necessary to realise the general interest (Habermas, 1993, p. 153).

Through the very development of modernity itself, this aspiration to turn 'will' into 'reason' came to grief, and public opinion became something to be manipulated and squeezed out between the politics of interest groups and the state.

Towards Revolution

The three pillars of the politics of modernity involved a philosophical conception of progress and rationality; a political concept of the republican regime; and a concept of civil society which could realise the progress and enlightenment that typified modern times. These joint ideas of progress, republic and civil society led to an overall conception of the 'good society', one that was appropriate to and realisable in the modern age.

However the politics of modernity contained severe tensions that broke out into the open with the revolutions in America and France, which laid down the agenda, theoretical and practical, of modern politics. The key words here are revolution and democracy. Progress, rationality, republican values and civil society were espoused by a number of philosophers and social thinkers who claimed to be witnessing the birth of a new age, in which the principles they held would be realised. In the perspective of people such as Adam Ferguson it was a question of moving from the rude societies of the past to the civil or more polished ones of the present, a move that was taking place through the spread of rationality, without the need for political revolution. Indeed Hume, who offered a view of this new type of civil society, was politically conservative and saw revolution and democracy as values to be rejected. So a view of progress, of the achievement of this new type of society, did not commit its advocates to any association of this view with the defence of democracy, or that progress would be furthered by political rights being extended to the mass of the population. The republic they envisaged was not one in which all citizens would participate; they recognised that reason was part of all human beings, but this recognition went hand in hand with a contempt for the vulgar masses in whom the light of reason shone very dimly. Hence the view of these philosophers of modernity was that the transformations they desired were already occurring, and that the development of civil society would continue.

At the end of the eighteenth century a world view was enunciated based on ideas of reason and common rationality: the idea of a free society that was politically liberal though not democratic. Before this idea was put into practice in the American and French Revolutions, it was confined to a relatively small class of enlightened persons, an elite who saw progress as the gradual diffusion of the ideas of the Enlightenment. In part they saw these ideas as continuing their spread, being diffused through the institutions of public opinion across the civilised world. However the crucial question was that of the strained relationship between these ideas of modernity and the ideas of democracy. Ideas of enlightenment and emancipation had been proclaimed by the philosophes, as exemplified by Condorcet in his splendid *Esquisse d'un tableau historique des progrès de l'esprit humain* (Condorcet, 1988). There he gave a prediction of the future progress of the human mind. Condorcet envisaged the ending of inequality between nations, the spread of equality within each society, and the final growth of humanity to perfection. The hope was that all the peoples of the world would catch up with the most advanced countries of contemporary Europe. Condorcet thought there was no limit to the progress that could be made by the human race, and he went on to present his well-known vision of the fully free and rational society, in which the sun would shine on human beings that recognised 'no other master apart from their own reason' (ibid., p. 271).

The philosophers of modernity considered that the prospect of a new society was already being realised in Europe at the end of the eighteenth century. True, there was an awareness that this new civil society was bringing new problems, in particular the question of how this society could be prevented from falling into decadence and corruption. The answer given was that this depended not on the masses, the unlettered rabble, but on continuing the slow and steady diffusion of Enlightenment principles and understanding. However it was only when these principles came to be put into practice in the great revolutions that some of the tensions really came into full view. These included the question of republicanism and democracy, and civil society and democracy, together with the question of emancipation: emancipation for whom?

The universalism that underlay the rationalism of the Enlightenment principles seemed to imply a democratic attitude and a welcoming of the extension of political rights to the mass of the population. Yet several of the leading figures of the new philosophy of the Enlightenment and civil society had a fear of the masses, seeing them as an unenlightened body of people that should be kept at arms length from political power and the exercise of political rights. There was thus a severe tension, which found expression in liberal philosophy, between the desire for universal rights and power being put in the hands of the non-enlightened majority. This then raised the question of how the transition to a new society was to be continued. If the power holders refused to tolerate the spread of Enlightenment principles, or if they did not rule society according to the demands of reason, then how was a rational society to be achieved? Would the power of a rational minority be enough, or would there have to be recourse to the mass of the population, that uneducated mass who were not yet instructed in the principles of rationalist philosophy? These dilemmas were to be brought out in the era of the American and French Revolutions.

2

The Revolutionary Challenge

At the end of the eighteenth century the American and the French Revolutions set the agenda for the politics of modernity. They constituted and defined the politics of modernity in two basic ways. First, they invoked the idea of the rational reconstruction of society, through the application of reason to social and political institutions. Second, they promoted democracy through the attempt to create new forms of politics and invoke 'the sovereign people' as the new legitimate 'subject' of politics. It was in the attempt to realise democracy that a crucial part of the 'modernity' of these revolutions resided. One of the elements of modernity was the Enlightenment view of the application of reason to human or social affairs. Condorcet's *Esquisse* is exemplary in this regard: he presented a picture of humanity steadily evolving and casting off the shackles of prejudice, imposing science and reason on the world that surrounded them. Similarly Kant argued that enlightenment was the emergence of human beings from immaturity, especially self-imposed immaturity. Human beings were learning how to think for themselves, rejecting the guidance imposed from above – though this process of gaining intellectual maturity was compatible with acceptance of the existing law – in the hope that political change would gradually come about.

While many strands of the Enlightenment philosophy were politically conservative, or even timid, as in the case of Kant, the American and French Revolutions put into practice the principles of the Enlightenment in this respect: these revolutions proclaimed their task as that of creating a new society, free from the irrationalism that characterised the old order. They invoked reason and sought to achieve the 'good society', indeed the perfect society, by the application of reason to the social and political world. In this sense, whatever the political views of particular 'Enlighteners' or contributors to the Enlightenment tradition, there is an intrinsic connection between Enlightenment and revolution. If the Enlightenment in its broadest sense sought to invoke reason as the standard for judging social and political (and other) matters, those who carried out the American and French Revolutions used the same criterion. The revolutionaries in both America and France saw themselves as contributing to the realisation of human happiness. Human well-being would be achieved by the critical use of reason, and by sweeping away all irrational and outmoded institutions inherited from the past and justified by tradition alone. A core idea of both revolutions was that a new age was beginning, in which freedom could be achieved by the unfettered use of reason and its application to society. Hence the enormous surge of optimism and energy that was unleashed by the two revolutions laid the foundations of modern politics.

The Discourse of Democracy

The American and French Revolutions introduced a new discourse of politics, a new subject of political action, and a new basis for the legitimacy of the political order. All this can be encapsulated in the key terms of 'democracy' and 'popular sovereignty'. The differences between the Enlightenment ideas sketched out in the previous chapter and the experiences of the American and French Revolutions involve the differences between, on the one hand, a set of general ideas, philosophical principles and broad concepts of progress and rationality, and on the other hand, political movements and the practice of popular politics. The revolutions sought in their different ways to realise elements of the Enlightenment philosophy. Equally importantly, these revolutions created a new language of politics, centred around the people as the true subject of politics and the basis of the state. Hence the core importance of the idea of popular sovereignty and the attempt to bring this idea to fruition in both America and France. These revolutions brought 'the people' to centre stage, and not just in theoretical terms since both revolutions, each in very different ways, created new structures of politics in their attempt to realise the goal of popular sovereignty. The French and American Revolutions inaugurated the politics of modernity by creating a new democratic culture, which henceforward was the language of modern politics. This 'language' saw the mass of the people as the source of sovereign power, as opposed to the king, or any power derived from a religious or supernatural body.

Recent studies of the French Revolution by François Furet and his school see the true originality of the revolution in terms of political culture: it is in the political and cultural spheres rather than in the emergence of new economic relations of production that the true significance of the French Revolution lies. It inaugurated a new theory of political legitimacy: henceforward power would only be legitimate if it stemmed from the people. The fundamental problem was how to realise the goals of popular sovereignty. The fear was that new groups would emerge speaking the language of democratic politics but exercising power on behalf of – if necessary against the will of – the people as a whole. Hence the importance Furet accorded to the work of Auguste Cochin, a late-nineteenth-century analyst of the French Revolution whose originality was to identify the new political culture of the revolution, and to see Jacobinism as the theoretical and practical articulation of this new 'discourse' of politics:

> For Cochin the problem was not the causes which made the Revolution possible, but the coming into being with the Revolution of a new cultural legitimacy, equality, along with the development of new rules of the political game, 'pure democracy' – which we could call direct democracy (Furet, 1989, p. 306).

Indeed Furet explicitly writes that the French Revolution provided a new language, a language referring to a newly invented subject, the people, or, especially (but not exclusively) in the French case, the people-nation, the nation as the body of citizens. This was the 'invention' of the French Revolution, and the American Revolution too (Beer, 1993). The French Revolution created a new subject of politics which, according to Furet, it was Cochin's original intuition to perceive:

> More than a set of acts, the Revolution is thus a language, and it is in relation to this language, and the consensus on it, that the machinery of politics selects people; ideology speaks through the Jacobin leaders more than they spoke through it (ibid., p. 279).

This analysis suggests that what the French Revolution contributed most to modern politics was a new discourse of citizenship, the idea of sovereignty as exercised by a new body, that of the citizens, collectively forming the nation. Power was legitimate insofar as it stemmed from this newly created body, the citizens or the people-nation.

It is not the case that the French Revolution 'invented' this concept out of the blue. It can be found in Rousseau's *Social Contract* (1762), where he described a new association or collective body that would replace the disaggregated individuals of the prepolitical society:

> At once, in place of the individual personality of each contracting party, this act of association creates a moral and collective body, composed of as many members as the assembly contains voters, and receiving from this act its unity, its common identity, its life, and its will . . . Those who are associated in it take collectively the name of *people*, and severally are called *citizens*, as sharing in the sovereign power, and *subjects*, as being under the laws of the State (Rousseau, 1968, p. 13).

This idea was common to both the American Revolution and the French Revolution, and was to prove an essential strand of modern politics. The citizens, associated together, would form the sovereign body, taking the form of the nation. While Rousseau enunciated this idea theoretically, the American and French Revolutions were concerned with fully realising the idea of popular sovereignty, the people as supreme, the executive power as a mere agent of the people, with laws formed through the collective participation of all citizens. This democratic idea is part of the politics of modernity.

Sovereignty and Representation

One core problem of this idea was the obvious one of how popular sovereignty could be realised: who would speak for the people, indeed who were the people? For Furet, Cochin's analysis of Jacobinism was highly relevant here. The Jacobins, as the holders of power during the years 1792–94, sought to mediate and express the popular will. Cochin's analysis implied that after the creation or invention of this new political subject, the people-nation, political means must be found to express its will and give it a voice. Democracy required politics, but politics of a new type, of which the Jacobins were the first practitioners: they claimed to be acting in the name of the people, to be expressing the popular will, to be articulating a democratic consensus or a common will (the 'General Will' of Rousseau). In Furet's words, the French Revolution gave rise to a new type of

representation, democratic representation, which required professional politicians, a party functioning as a machine of democratic
representation:

> Politics thus appears as complementary to democracy: its speciality
> is to create a consensus mythically free from its social context.
> Politics thus involves replacing the 'natural' conduct of business
> with organised bodies: politicians, parties, ideologies (Furet, 1989,
> p. 275).

Hence the importance of Cochin's analysis of the French Revolution:
the Jacobins not only sought to articulate but also to manipulate
the public will. Modern politics, the politics of modernity, was based
on public opinion (cf. the analysis of Habermas in Chapter 1), on the
public or general will. The locus of sovereignty moved from the
monarch to the new association formed by all citizens. But democracy
required political formations and leaders to express and to lead this
newly sovereign public will. This led to the danger that such democratic representation could become distorted through the activities of
highly organised groups who claimed to express the public will or
public opinion. The experiences of the French Revolution in its
Jacobin phase (1792–94), which ended with the fall of Robespierre
in Thermidor in July 1794, revealed for many observers the danger
that a highly organised group could substitute itself for the masses,
for the people as a whole, and create a new despotism speaking in the
name of the people. In Furet's presentation of Cochin's ideas:

> Jacobinism, using the fictitious name of 'the people', substituted
> itself for both society and the State. Through the general will, the
> people-King henceforth mythically coincides with power; this belief
> is the breeding ground of totalitarianism (ibid., p. 281).

The revolutionary challenge in both America and France was to
apply the demands of reason to society, to create a new society that
would bring happiness on earth. It was this creative rationalist
scheme, applying Enlightenment principles to society, which appalled
conservative and reactionary critics of the French Revolution such as
Burke and de Maistre, leading them to construct a counter revolutionary philosophy that was critical of the philosophy of modernity.
The new language of politics invoked a new source of legitimacy – the
people – who would take over the sovereignty that had been the

personal preserve of the monarch. A number of new problems
stemmed from this transformation of the subject of politics. 'Subject'
is used here in the sense of the creative agent or maker of politics,
because the revolutionary transformations in America and France
can be seen as transforming 'subjects' in the political sense – passive
'subjects' of (in France) an absolute monarch, or in the American case
subjects of a less-than-absolute monarch – into citizens, co-equally
determining the laws under which they lived. Problems arose in
translating this new idea of democratic legitimacy into practical
politics, and in determining the bounds of the citizen body.

Hence the politics of modernity stemmed from the revolutionary
experience at the end of the eighteenth century when America shook
off English domination and France its monarchy. However this
'revolutionary experience' was highly differentiated. In the first place
there were large differences of style and degree between the American
and French Revolutions: traditionally, the former has been seen as
more limited, less radical, more confined to the assertion of political
rights and the creation of a new political system than the revolution in
France, which went socially and politically further. This judgement
seems valid as the French Revolution in its different phases assumed a
degree of social and political radicalism that exceeded that of its
American predecessor. Perhaps this was because, as de Tocqueville
noted, the American Revolution took place in a 'new' society, where
there was no ancien régime to overthrow. America was fortunate in
that, properly speaking, revolution was not necessary to establish
democracy:

> In America the democratic revolution is long since over, or, rather,
> there never was such a revolution. The Americans never had class
> privileges to abolish or exclusive rights to overthrow (Lamberti,
> 1989, p. 195).

As de Tocqueville observed in *Democracy in America*,

> The Americans have this great advantage, that they attained
> democracy without the sufferings of a democratic revolution and
> that they were born equal instead of becoming so (Tocqueville,
> 1968, vol. II, p. 656).

The American revolution was nevertheless a central element in the
politics of modernity because it represented the first attempt in

modern times to 'invent a republic', to realise Enlightenment principles and consciously create a political system based on ideas of
individual rights and popular sovereignty, a model of a modern
political system for the whole world. The key problem was the way
in which the idea of the republic was realised, the conflicting tensions
in the project of realising the goal of popular sovereignty.

As stated above, the French Revolution went further than the
American Revolution in all possible respects: socially, politically and
in its proclamation of a universal model of human emancipation,
whose ideals would spread throughout Europe and the rest of the
world. In its creation of a new style of politics, invoking the language
of democracy and the mobilisation of the masses, the creation of
myths and the attempt to create a 'people-nation', the French
Revolution can be seen as the archetype of modern politics and
creator of its central dilemmas. In addition, the French Revolution,
unlike the American Revolution, was the sum of a number of
different revolutions, which together constituted the central strands
of the politics of modernity. According to a recent study of the
French Revolution:

> What the French Revolution has lost as a *model*, it has gained as a
> *problem*. The more distant it becomes as a source of inspiration, the
> larger it looms as a necessary source for the understanding of our
> political world (Gauchet, 1995, p. 7).

The basic ideas of the American and French revolutions are those of a
rational political order guaranteeing basic and universal *rights of the
individual*; the idea of a political system guaranteeing the basic aim of
popular sovereignty or the *power of the people*; and associated with
that the creation of a *democratic nation*, of a unit (the nation) of self-
governing citizens.

The attempt to achieve through revolution the modern political
system and inaugurate the politics of modernity created a series of
dilemmas that formed the stuff of modern politics. These dilemmas
can be labelled 'dilemmas of unity and power'. The attempt to create
a system based on popular sovereignty was, at least in the French
case, premised on the idea of the unity of people as a collective
subject. However this risked the annihilation of difference or plurality, the attempt to force the very plurality created by modernity in
the sphere of civil society into one mould: 'the sovereign people' as a
single sovereign body.

The related dilemma of 'power' was that the revolutionary attempt to create a new subject, the people ruling itself, risked the danger of a democratic state with no limits, no checks, a political power speaking in the name of the people. The different experiences of the American and French Revolutions can be seen as attempts both to create this new power and to tame or limit it, and to grapple with the problems stemming from the project. If the modern political system was a democracy, based on popular power, how could the state that realised this popular power be contained or checked? The problem was all the more dangerous in that this new state power could be taken over by a political group (for example the Jacobins) that claimed to speak in the name of the people and substituted itself for the popular will.

The attempt in France to realise democracy and popular sovereignty through revolution created the danger, as so many analysts at the time and subsequently have argued, of an all-pervasive power, seeking to mould and create *l'homme régénéré* (new man): 'With the idea of "new man" one touches on a central aspiration of the French Revolution' (Ozouf, 1989, p. 116). Ozouf suggests that this aspiration, with its implications of abolishing any distinction between public and private, led to 'a project of all-seeing intolerance of any ambiguity, which denies democracy: and that is why the Gulag can be seen as the consequence of the revolution which was the child of the Enlightenment' (ibid., 1989, p. 120).

Hence the politics of modernity unleashed powerful forces whose collective impact was highly problematic. Modernity and the idea of revolution were intrinsically related, leading critics to suggest that modernity would lead to politics without limit, to the creation of a new society and a new humanity to fit that society, and that this would lead not to liberation but to a new form of despotism.

America: The New Republic

The American Revolution centred on the idea of a republic, a political system that would guarantee basic individual rights, remove the tyranny of the executive power and realise popular sovereignty. The aims of the American Revolution were more political than social, concerned with both the liberal – or classical Whig – aim of preventing the abuse of power and the democratic aim of popular sovereignty. Liberal and democratic, political rather than social, an appeal to a sense of rights supposedly acknowledged in the English system of common law rather than to the French Revolution's set of abstract 'metaphysical' rights – these are commonly seen as the characteristics of the American Revolution, in contrast to the more extreme and 'ideological' nature of the French Revolution.

Recent studies of the American Revolution suggest that its ideological origins lay in an appeal to existing rights, which were seen as threatened by the corruption and at least potential tyranny of the monarchy in England under George III (Bailyn, 1992). Hence the appeal was to the model of an existing constitution, to an ideal of what the existing constitution of England ought to be when freed from the corruption and overweening power of the crown. The model proposed by the American revolutionaries, at least initially, was of a mixed constitution, a balanced government, which they claimed had already been undermined by the dangerous power of the English monarch. The claim was that traditional rights, the liberties of the free-born Englishman, had been eroded, and that the revolutionaries in America were asserting rights that were theoretically recognised, if practically denied, in the English constitution.

The American Revolution was thus a 'moderate revolution', in contrast with the French Revolution, which was more extreme because it started from an idea of abstract and metaphysical rights, that were not deduced from or embedded in a particular system, but proclaimed as inherent in the nature of 'man'. Discrimination between the two revolutions can be seen in Burke, that scourge of the French Revolution, who adopted a more benign, even positive, attitude towards the revolution in America. Burke defended the American Revolution because the revolutionaries' claims rested not on abstract rights but on claims recognised in the English system. As Burke put it,

> The people of the Colonies are descendants of Englishmen . . . They are therefore not only devoted to Liberty, but to Liberty according to English ideas, and on English principles. Abstract Liberty, like other mere abstractions, is not to be found (Burke, 1993, p. 222).

Burke was later to contrast this moderate revolution – which he saw as a protest against arbitrary power, a protest animated by English ideas of liberty – with the much more dangerous attempt by the French revolutionaries to, as he saw it, create a totally new political system based on abstract metaphysical rights. Such rights had already been criticised by him in his speeches on America before the spectre of the French Revolution occupied his thoughts:

> Man acts from adequate motives relative to his interest; and not on metaphysical speculations. Aristotle, the great master of reasoning, cautions us, and with great weight and propriety, against this species of delusive geometrical accuracy in moral arguments, as the most fallacious of all sophistry (ibid., p. 258).

However, this contrast between the two revolutions is inadequate. The crucial contribution of the American Revolution to the politics of modernity was its attempt to give practical form to the modern republic, as a representative political system expressing the will of the people and avoiding the dangers arising from the concentration of power. Modernity involved a particular idea of a political system, and the American experience was a crucial element in the formation of the modern people-nation system. The American Revolution may have started as an attempt to claim rights that were being threatened, or so the revolutionaries thought, by the corruption and tyranny of George III. But from these moderate beginnings the revolution developed its own radicalism (Wood, 1992). This consisted in attempts to realise the goals of popular sovereignty, but through the different approximations of this goal the revolution achieved a dynamic of its own.

The initial goal of the American Revolution was to bring about a mixed government, with the emphasis on preventing executive tyranny. But it subsequently moved away from this idea to that of a republic – a democracy in which the people would rule and all the branches of government would be expressions of the popular will. The politics of the American Revolution thus shifted from the traditional principles of the English constitution – mixed government – to 'unmixed' government, where power would be held by the people. In the course of the struggle the revolutionaries progressed from suspicion of the executive power (representatives of the English king) to suspicion even of the American legislative assemblies as potentially subverting the popular will: 'In the 1780s the Americans' inveterate suspicion and jealousy of political power, once concentrated almost exclusively on the Crown and its agents, was transferred to the various state legislatures' (Wood, 1993, p. 409). The solution found to allay this suspicion was to announce explicitly that all power emanated from the people, and that all branches of government, as agents of the popular will, were responsible to the people. In the words of one of the founders of the federal constitution, James Wilson, the supreme power *'resides* in the PEOPLE, as the fountain of government' (ibid., p. 530). However this solution created a new problem – namely the danger that if all branches of government were emanations of the popular will there would be no check on power, which could come to lie in a single source, as de Tocqueville was to note in his *Democracy in America*. This problem was anticipated in a letter by Madison to Jefferson:

> Wherever the real power in a Government lies there is the danger of oppression. In our Governments the real power lies in the majority of the Community, and the invasion of private rights is chiefly to be apprehended, not from acts of Government contrary to the sense of its constituents, but from acts in which the Government is the mere instrument of the major number of the Constituents (ibid., p. 410).

The modern age was the age of the masses, of democratic pressures that could not be withstood, as even thinkers such as de Tocqueville understood, although he was less than fully enthusiastic about this irresistible onward march of democracy. The modern republic, in America as in France, was a republic that involved the mass of the people. This 'people' was a male people, even in America, where property qualifications were swept aside at an early date but women continued to be excluded from political life. Nevertheless the modern republic was envisaged as one that would allow the participation of a greater number of people than had been the case in the republics of classical antiquity, hence raising the question: how could these masses be integrated into the republic and how could the danger of a new despotism, which de Tocqueville called 'democratic despotism', be averted?

In America the solution offered to this latter problem was twofold: the constitutional separation of powers, and Madison's famous solution – splitting up the popular will into a range of separate groups and factions to avert the danger of a united, possibly radical, political will of the majority. This involved the invention of a particular type of modern political system, a representative democracy, which Madison called a 'republic' as opposed to a 'pure democracy' (ibid., p. 598). Yet this republic, if not a pure or direct democracy, gave rise to key problems. The republic as the classical tradition envisaged it, a tradition taken over by Jefferson and the other founding fathers, had 'virtue' as the unifying factor that would produce social homogeneity and hold the system together. As John Adams saw it, a balanced constitution would reconcile the aristocracy and the people. Yet with the idea of factions and acceptance of the notion of politics as the sphere in which people pursued their particular interests, the classical view of a 'virtuous' citizenry pursuing the common interest became irrelevant. The new American republic was one in which a much less elevated view of interests prevailed, a political system that was no longer the preserve of a republican elite pursuing political virtue. It was more open to a diverse and heterogeneous public pursuing their own interests.

It is in this aspect that the 'radicalism of the American revolution' consisted (Wood, 1992). The political sphere of the republic was open to all, at least in theory; political activity was a means, among others, by which individual citizens pursued their own interests. Hence politics in this modern system was not the securing of a common interest in republican virtue, though this may have been the intention of the original founding fathers of the American republic. Republican politics was a much more down-to-earth concern, the sphere of individual or group interests, in which any attempt to develop unity or common interest was impossible, given the diversity of interests in modern commercial society.

This is one of the key problems of the politics of modernity, and also furnishes a striking contrast between the American and French Revolutions. In both revolutions the attempt was made to unite all citizens in the newly created (or 'invented') republic. In America the attempt was abandoned at an early stage; the revolutionaries' wish to establish 'virtue' as the cement for the republic gave way to the idea of the republic as a democratic system in which all interests could and should be represented. Hence, among other consequences, public officials had to be paid, rather than be expected to work with no reward just for the sake of republican virtue:

> By the beginning of the nineteenth century the classical republican conception of government officeholding was losing much of its meaning. If each person was supposed to pursue his own private interests, and the pursuit of private interests was the real source of the public good, then it was foolish to expect men to devote their time and energy to public responsibilities without compensation (ibid., p. 293).

Thus the model of the American republic was one of individualism, where all could, and indeed should, devote themselves to work, to commerce, to making a living. The regime thrived not on an abstract conception of virtue but was seen as a limited state that allowed individuals to participate in the political system. Politics was seen in instrumental terms, as a means of favouring the pursuit of individual interests that were common to all citizens. The republic and commercial society went together.

France: The People-Nation

This model can be contrasted with the republic that emerged in France between the years 1789 and 1799. During those ten years an enormous variety of political regimes succeeded one another in France, but the key problem for the republic, whether in France or in America, was that of unity, or political (and social) cohesion. How could the new republic, as an association of citizens, hold together? One aspect of the politics of modernity was the emergence of a new language of politics, a democratic political culture, which found expression in the idea of the 'people-nation', a united association of citizens. This was much more prominent in France than in America: 'In contrast to the American revolution, the French Revolution had to be a total recasting of the body politic and of society' (Ozouf, 1989, p. 124). The French experience, the invention of the republic in France, was much more radical and thoroughgoing because of the search for unity and the desire to create a homogeneous community of citizens. The new language of politics, and the new rituals of *la fête révolutionnaire*, sought to express this unity, to create bonds to unite all citizens. This contrasts with the American Revolution, as illustrated by de Tocqueville's observation that American democracy was created without a thoroughgoing revolution.

In the French case, the opposition to the ancien régime and the fact that the republican system came about because of antagonism to the power of the monarch, meant a greater degree of radicalism than in America. Those who spearheaded the revolution in France, whether Girondins, Jacobins or *sans-culottes*, sought to achieve a system of popular sovereignty. Yet as the current historiography of the French Revolution makes clear, there were two concerns. The first involved different interpretations of 'popular sovereignty' and how it was to be achieved. Was it to be achieved as Girondins such as Brissot and others such as Sieyès envisaged, through a form of representative democracy, or as the *sans-culottes*, the popular masses, demanded, through a much more direct form of democracy, in which the active and ever-present people would keep a vigilant eye on the *mandataires* or representatives, who would be mere executors of popular power?

Thus the first concern was the means by which popular power was to be achieved. Marcel Gauchet, in his study *La Révolution des Pouvoirs* (1995), suggests that the dominant wish was for a single centre of power to express the public will, or a unitary republic. Certainly this was desired by the Jacobins, who operated on the basis of a single public will, of which the Jacobins were the sole bearers. Hence political practice and the language of the French Revolution were 'monolithic' in that there was seen to be a single source of political virtue, and in contrast with the American experience a unitary idea of the republic emerged.

Secondly, given the bloody struggles of the revolution in France, how could the concept of citizen virtue be sustained, and how could the unity of society be expressed and preserved? The idea arose that divergence and difference were somehow suspect, that the republic had to be indivisible. The new forms of politics, the revolutionary rituals and *fêtes*, were attempts to build up a sense of unity and cohesion in the face of the factions and different political currents of the revolutionary years. The sort of democracy that emerged from the French Revolution was very different from that of America.

The French Revolution went through different phases, of which Jacobinism was the culminating one, ending in Thermidor in July 1794. The model of the modern republic offered by the French revolutionaries consisted in a single, homogeneous nation-people, bound together as a group of virtuous and active citizens, and expressing their civic zeal through ceremonies and fraternal association. Hence the revolution created the concept of citizenship, the idea of fraternity as the bond linking these citizens. The problem was that this common interest did not allow for the diverse interests of commercial society, unlike the concept of citizen unity in the American republic. Indeed during the French Revolution commerce was regarded with suspicion, as giving rise to different interests and factions that could undermine the common fabric of citizenship.

Thus the revolution in France sought to create a culture of citizenship, unity and cohesion. This idea was fostered by the rituals and mass symbols that were exemplified by the *Fête de la Fédération* of 1790. But this civic unity also required scapegoats, or at least a target, and this was one function of the Terror, to identify those who were the 'bad citizens' or enemies of the revolution. It was also one of the features of Jacobinism: distinguishing the good patriot from the bad citizen.

The main feature of the French republican model was the creation of a unitary centre of power, untrammeled by any checking force, a focus of power that could claim to express the popular will. Whether this centre of power was the representative assembly, the Convention, the Jacobin club or the 'sections' of the *sans-culottes*, the point was that whereas the American example favoured the separation of powers, the French model was suspicious of all attempts to split up power. Hence Marcel Gauchet's argument that the control of power was a distinct undercurrent in the democratic discourse of the French Revolution, and that their legacy from Rousseau predisposed the French revolutionaries to the idea of a single, concentrated source of power. Through the *levée en masse* (the citizens army, the mobilisation of the masses), the nation was constituted as a democratic assembly of citizens requiring the expression of unity. Factions and subsections were not tolerated. Hence the French Revolution created a new discourse of politics, mobilised the masses and created a new subject of political action, the people, whose unity was formed by armed defence of the nation as an association of citizens.

Nevertheless the assumption of unity, homogeneity and democratic involvement was challenged by some of the other successive ideologies of modern times. From the side of liberalism came a welcoming of modernity in terms of the rights of citizens, but a fear that this new citizen body would become despotic and all-powerful. From the side of socialist theorists and movements came the charge that the representation of the people as a unitary bloc of citizens was false in that it neglected the deep social divisions that divided property owners from the rest of the population, the propertyless masses, and that 'citizenship' was merely a façade that concealed the falsehood of the universality of citizenship rights proclaimed by the revolutions in France and America. The French Revolution both provided the model for the politics of modernity, and revealed central dilemmas and problems of the modernist project.

Nonetheless the French Revolution stands as the great landmark of the politics of modernity, because it furnished a model that was to influence the whole world. As de Tocqueville pointed out, and as critics such as Burke and de Maistre agreed, the French Revolution offered a universal model of emancipation and preached a message of liberation for all human beings everywhere. In his study of *The Ancien Regime and the Revolution*, de Tocqueville analysed the message of the revolution in religious terms. He wrote, 'the French Revolution aspired to be world-wide, and its effect was to erase all the old national frontiers from the map . . . it created a common intellectual fatherland whose citizenship was open to men of every nationality and in which racial distinctions were obliterated' (de Tocqueville, 1966, p. 11). In contrast with the American Revolution, which appealed to particular rights embedded in a determinate national tradition, the French Revolution's Declaration of the Rights of Man and Citizen of 1789 proclaimed certain core rights as 'the natural, inalienable and sacred rights of man'. As a recent account of these rights explains, the circumstances in which the declaration was drafted, as well as more theoretical or philosophical considerations, helped account for the more universalist and 'metaphysical' tone of the French declaration compared with the historical reference of the American Revolution. Because recent French history seemed, in the eyes of those who drafted the declaration, to be the story of despotism, it could not be drawn on as a basis for the proclamation of liberty and the rights of man:

> If French history bore witness neither to a lost constitutional freedom in need of restoration nor to the civil benefits of a strong monarchy, it was clearly good for nothing, at best a record, in the abbé Sieyès words, of the long 'night of [aristocratic] barbarity and ferocity' pierced only by a few rays of 'pure despotism' (Van Kley, 1994, p. 93).

Hence the new regime of freedom and enlightenment had to be proclaimed in ahistorical and general terms. Prerevolutionary French history was damned as either despotic (the power of the absolutist state, which had to be resisted) or aristocratic (the attempt of the aristocracy or the *parlements* to keep power to themselves). In the words of one of the members of the National Assembly (Rabaut de Saint-Etienne), 'History is not our code' (ibid.). According to the historian Mona Ozouf, the negativity of the revolutionaries concerning the history of France explains the 'early radicalisation of the French Revolution': for the revolutionaries there was nothing in

French history worth preserving, 'no point of anchorage, no help to be expected in the adventure on which they were embarking' (Ozouf, 1989, p. 124). If history could not provide the 'code', then a rationalist and universalist set of rights had to be the key to liberty. One of the principal aspects of modernity was the proclamation of a set of basic rights, valid at all times and in all circumstances, and the revolutionary challenge in France was to create a political system that would guarantee and enshrine those rights in a rational political system. The challenge of modernity, then, was to design a republic in which citizens would enjoy and share those rights.

The rights proclaimed in the 1789 declaration, included both rights against the state (article 2: 'liberty, property, security, and resistance to oppression') and the right to participate in the state, to contribute to the making of what Rousseau called the 'general will' (article 6: 'The law is the expression of the general will. All citizens have the right to participate personally, or through their representatives, in its formation. It must be the same for all, whether it protects or punishes') (Van Kley, 1994, pp. 1–2). The rights in question were thus both *liberal*, in the sense of seeking to create a limited state, and *democratic*, in the sense of inviting and guaranteeing citizen participation, direct and indirect. Two questions that were fundamental to the politics of modernity were raised in the French Revolution in a highly practical form: the question of *citizenship* and the question of *the state*, more specifically the *modern democratic nation-state*, as a new 'subject' created by the experience of the revolution.

The Idea of Citizenship

The new discourse of revolutionary politics invoked the concept of citizenship: citizens as bearers of rights against the state and as persons entitled to participate in the state by making the law. The revolution in France transformed people from subjects of the king to citizens associated in a republic, making the law. In the words of William H. Sewell:

> Indeed one could characterise the aim of the revolutionaries, from Sieyès and Mirabeau to Robespierre and Saint-Just, as the transformation of 'sujets' into 'citoyens'. Rather than passive subjects of an absolute monarch, the French were to become active participants in the public life of the nation (Lucas, 1988, p. 106).

However the French revolutionaries, at least in the early stages of the revolution, made a famous distinction between active citizens and passive citizens, those who were entitled to make the law, and those who merely acquiesced in it. Those in the latter category were entitled to protection of their person and property, but not to any active involvement in creating the law. There was thus a tension in the French Revolution, and this tension was inherent in the nature of modernity itself, between the universality of the claims made by the revolution and their more limited extension in practice. Did the French revolution live up to the claims it made about the spread of rights to the mass of the citizens? Who were the active citizens and who the passive?

Among those who grappled with this question was the abbé Sieyès. The excellent analysis by William H. Sewell shows the ambiguity and hesitation this key figure of the French Revolution displayed when struggling to provide an answer. Sieyès moved from his bold words that 'The Third Estate is everything' which open his pamphlet *Qu'est-ce que le Tiers Etat?* to his admission that an active citizen had to be 'disponible', to have the leisure necessary to participate in the making of the law. Sieyès recognised that in any 'great nation' there was a necessary distinction between 'two peoples', those with leisure and property, and those, as he put it, who were 'the human instruments of production':

> A great nation inevitably contains *two peoples*, the producers and the human instruments of production, those who are intelligent and the workers who are only passive, educated citizens and the subordinates who are granted neither the time nor the means to receive education (Lucas, 1988, p. 109; Sewell, 1994).

For Sieyès, the category 'active citizen' could not include people of non-French nationality, women, people under 25, those employed as domestic servants, those not in gainful employment, and those who made no financial contribution to the state through the payment of taxes. Active citizens had to have taken a civic oath and fulfilled certain residency requirements, and be neither bankrupt nor facing accusation in the courts.

To sum up the discussion so far, citizenship was a key concept of the democratic discourse inaugurated by the French Revolution. Citizens would form the nation, in terms of the 'people-nation', and thus the concept of citizenship, bound up with fraternity, was one of inclusion, of a new form of bonding, of community. This was certainly the new idea that both the American and the French Revolution unleashed on the world. Yet at the same time the idea of citizenship was hedged about with qualifications, with criteria of exclusion that prevented some individuals from involvement in law making and thus from becoming citizens in the fullest sense. Hence from the very beginning the universalist claims of the French Revolution were shown to be less than they appeared.

This was a central dilemma of modernity because one crucial strand of modern politics was the debate about which groups would form the citizen body, of the limits of emancipation and liberty. The socialist critique was that the emerging divisions in civil society were preventing the mass of the people from sharing the benefits – social and political – of bourgeois society, from forming part of the community. Modernity was highly disruptive in its economic and social aspects, sweeping away the traditional community of the *ancien régime* in France, and more generally the stable preindustrial society. In its place the politics of modernity offered, or 'invented', a political community, an association of citizens, the republic, or the 'people-nation', the nation-state as the framework for democratic rule.

But the question remained of its limits, the criteria of admission to this new political community. The dilemmas of modernity were signalled from the beginning: who would form part of this new community, who would identify with it? The rhetoric of the French Revolution proclaimed universal rights that were not realised in practice. As one of the revolutionaries, Jean-Paul Marat, announced,

> Where is the fatherland of those who own no property, who cannot lay claim to any employment, who draw no advantage from the social contract? Everywhere they are condemned to servitude, whether under the yoke of an employer or of their fellow citizens. Whatever revolution occurs, their eternal lot is slavery, poverty, oppression. What can they then owe to the State which has done nothing but make their misery permanent and forge their chains? (Leroy, 1946, p. 282).

The popular bloc of the third estate was already dividing, new social divisions were emerging and the new collective subject, the people, was already being denounced, if not in so many words, as a 'mystification', and this veiled the forthcoming revolution of the fourth estate, the propertyless masses. A new democratic discourse had emerged, but it was already being criticised by those who saw new class divisions emerging. This interplay of universalist rhetoric and social differences will be probed further below.

Finally, there is the question of the democratic nation-state. This was announced as the new subject of politics, invented by the democratic discourse of the revolutions. Yet the dilemma was not just the problem of who could enter or constitute this new body as fully fledged citizens. There was also the question of the extent and limits of the newly constituted, democratic nation-state. This problem related to the distinction between liberalism and democracy, between the two strands of the French Revolution. Here the experience of Jacobinism was crucial. What kind of democracy was to be created by the French Revolution? Leaving aside the question of who constituted the people, how was this sovereign power to be exercised? The Jacobins saw themselves as carrying out the will of the people, but purifying it from above, exercising the collective will. In carrying out this popular will they came up against the democracy espoused by the *sans-culottes*, who wanted a much more direct and unmediated form of popular power. The fear expressed by liberals was that the newly created sovereign power, speaking in the name of the people, would be much more powerful, enjoy more legitimacy and be less restricted in scope than the prerevolutionary state. This gave rise to a concern that the new state, while purporting to express the will of the democratic community, would be used to mould people to its will. Both liberals and conservatives expressed the fear that an artificial machine of politics had been created: this machine was contrasted, by German philosophers such as Herder, with the natural community of the nation. Liberal thinkers, such as de Tocqueville, and some of the thinkers of the American Revolution, for example the authors of the Federalist Papers, were aware of the need to install checks and balances against the possibility of state despotism, or restrict its power through increasing the number of factions in society (Madison *et al.*, 1987, p. 122).

The spectre of Jacobinism hung like a threat over the post-revolutionary world. Jacobinism, for the defenders of the established order, seemed to exemplify the rationalist project taken to excess. It seemed to show the danger of seeking to establish a new society but ending up with centralised power, of creating a new community that was highly repressive towards individuals and much more unitary and monolithic than the American republic.

What then was the legacy of the French Revolution to the politics of modernity? The attempt to achieve the radical reconstruction of society seemed to result in a highly centralised state and the imposition of 'virtue' on its citizens. Modernity also involved a contradiction between the community of citizens in the political sphere and the divisions that commerce was opening up in the newly established civil society. Hence the following chapters seek to explore the legacy of the two revolutions, to analyse the politics of modernity and some of its central dilemmas, and to see in the third and final part of the book what can be made of them for our own time. Are the ideas of the Enlightenment and the American and French Revolutions, as expounded in these two chapters, of any relevance to contemporary times? Are we living in 'Enlightenment's wake' (Gray, 1995)? Has the whole Enlightenment project, taken a wrong turning, followed a false trail that was already evident at the time of the revolutions? These are the questions that the following chapters of this book seek to answer.

Part II
Ideologies of Modernity

3

Liberalism and Modernity

The preceding chapters explained the nature of modernity, and the way in which the two revolutions at the end of the eighteenth century sought to bring about a totally new way of ordering the social and political spheres. In the same way it is necessary to see that the very concept of ideology, and the particular ideologies that developed in the nineteenth and twentieth centuries, were all products of the revolution of modernity. In the course and aftermath of the American and French Revolutions there developed ideologies that sought to offer projects of total social and political reconstruction, or in the case of conservatism, to oppose this modernist project.

The concept of ideology – which had built in to it the idea of the transformation of society as a whole, and which functioned as a framework for political debate and action – was only possible as part of a modernist perspective that envisaged wholesale change as feasible, made possible by the power of human reason and its transformative potential. In this sense ideology was a profoundly modern concept, with its three elements of critique, goal and agency, since the ideologies of modernity held not only that human beings could effect purposeful and constructive social change, but that this could be achieved by rational methods of political organisation, using the state as a mechanism for improving the quality of human life on Earth, and seeking to capture state power through political organisations such as parties to articulate programmes of social change.

If social change and rational political action were not possible, if there were no coherent agency and means to implement political action, then the very concept of ideology would not have made sense, since the ideologies of modern politics functioned to provide the goals and framework for political action designed to produce 'the good society'. Ideology as a concept thus took as its basis the notion that it was possible to transform society and change human nature to make people into suitable members of this new society.

The Modernist Agenda

The ideologies that dominated modern politics from the time of the
American and French Revolutions have shared this modernist agenda, even when, as in the case of conservatism, they issued dire
warnings against its exaggerated implementation. The ideologies that
are treated in this and the following three chapters are liberalism,
socialism, conservatism and nationalism. They are seen as distinctively modern in the following way: they all envisaged the creation of
a new subject of politics, a new way of organising social life on the
basis of the transformations that were typical of modernity. This new
subject differed from ideology to ideology, ranging from the rational
individual and the limited state of liberalism; through the classless
society and the organised, class-conscious working class celebrated by
socialist and Marxist theory; to the nation as the subject of nationalism, 'the nation' being identified or conceptualised in many different
ways; and finally to the cohesive and in some ways backward-looking
or traditional society invoked by conservatism.

   These of course were not the only ideologies of modern politics, but
they remained central to political life for two centuries in Western
Europe, North America and beyond. They all shared a common
agenda, namely that in the face of the colossal transformations of
modernity (the transformation of state, society and economy, as
sketched out in Chapter 1) they each offered a perspective of how
society should be organised, they each held that total or holistic social
transformation (of whatever kind) was an eminently practical and
feasible task, and that it could be achieved within the parameters of
modernity that were outlined earlier: namely on the basis of developed industry and the conquest of nature, within the literal and
metaphorical terrain of the nation-state, and taking account of
democracy and the 'rise of the masses', features that all these
ideologies saw as defining characteristics of modernity.

   Even conservatism, which in some of its manifestations sought
to deny modernity and return to a premodern society, was forced to
accept the reality of modernity, and develop its stance as a criticism of
modernity and its features, rather than seeking to reverse it and return
to premodern forms of social life. The paradox is that conservatism,
despite its opposition to modernity and its defence of tradition, was a
child of modernity, since it sought to theorise and defend the virtues
of tradition, a reflexive and theoretical task that would not have been

necessary in a truly traditional society where tradition and the weight of the past were accepted unquestioningly as guides to action.

Hence the argument here is that, for all their differences, the ideologies of modernity shared certain themes, namely the possibility and (conservatism apart) desirability of large-scale social and political transformation, the conviction that the tools or institutions necessary for this purpose had been or were being created through the transformations of modernity, the three parameters of modernity noted above. Just what could be achieved on the basis of modernity was envisaged in different and contrasting ways by the ideologies considered here, so their solutions were different. However they shared certain presuppositions, namely that solutions were possible, that as Marx put it 'mankind only sets itself such tasks as it can solve', and that it was the developments of modernity that rendered such solutions possible. On all these points, and consideration of this is the purpose of Part III of this book, developments in contemporary society, both practical and theoretical, have come to challenge all the ideologies of modernity, their relevance to contemporary society, and the very notion and coherence of ideology itself, with its built-in concepts of total social transformation and rational political action.

The ideologies in question thus shared this deep structure of modernity, and arose from the foundations of modernity. A distinction can be drawn between those ideologies that reacted enthusiastically to the promise of modernity, and those with a more sceptical or ambivalent attitude towards it. In the first camp can be placed liberalism and socialism as modernist ideologies *par excellence*, which saw the coming of modernity as enabling a new form of society that would promote human freedom, as well as bring into being the agents and institutions necessary for the achievement of this desired society. Conservatism arose as an ideology that shared with its rivals a holistic view of 'good society', and it is argued here that conservatism as an ideology also arose from modernity, however critical it was of many features of modernity and sceptical of the possibility of total social transformation and human emancipation. Finally, nationalism is treated extensively here not just because of its undeniable impact and appeal throughout the age of ideology, but because it seems to have chameleon-like qualities that have enabled it to survive, perhaps better than its rivals, the transition to a postmodern age that challenges many of the assumptions and bases of modernity.

Nationalism had an ambiguous relationship with modernity. It too was a creation of the age of ideology, involving the creation of a new subject of social and political action, namely the nation-state, complete with the myths, ceremonies and rituals that made it a focus for human loyalty. However nationalism, at least in some of its forms, also invoked traditions, real or imaginary, of the nation in question. More importantly, nationalism as an ideology challenged the universalism that was an essential part of the tradition of modernity, and which has also come under critical attack in the politics of our time.

Modernity, and these ideologies that arose from it, envisaged a universalist end, a common destiny for all mankind, liberated from local traditions and particularist loyalties. However nationalism, and to some extent conservatism, challenged this universalism by elevating the nation, with its special and particular characteristics, to be the focus of human loyalty, thus giving supreme importance not to what was shared with all of humanity but to what divided humanity, namely specific national features, however mythical they might have been. Hence, to anticipate one of the themes developed later, when faced with the dual crisis of modernity – the crisis of the three pillars of modernity mentioned above, and the crisis of the ideas or ideologies that arose with modernity – nationalism seems to have a better chance of surviving this crisis and adapting to the relativism that is highlighted by postmodern critics of modernist universalism.

Hence the ideologies investigated here are studied both because of their historical importance and because in various ways they are now being accused of having lost their relevance, of being out of step with the contemporary age of postmodernism, which has rendered irrelevant all ideologies, with their universalistic and totalising views of social change. All these ideologies, in varying degrees, are jointly implicated in the current crisis: the debate about the relevance of these ideologies, which is really a debate about the crisis of modernity and the feasibility of emancipation, total social transformation, the existence of agencies of change and reform, and the future – if there is one – of the tradition unleashed by the American and French Revolutions at the end of the eighteenth century.

Studying these ideologies and their historical development and present relevance is thus a good way to approach the debate about the future of politics itself, in terms of schemes for social change and political action. The question is whether these ideologies can continue to function as frameworks for political debate and discussion and as guidelines of democratic action in a postmodern age where, it is argued, the three pillars of modernity (industry, nation and class) are fragmented and crisis-ridden, along with the general notions of emancipation and social progress.

It is well known that the categories of 'Left' and 'Right' arose as orienting terms for political debate in the course of the French Revolution: those who wanted more radical change were seated to the left of the President's chair in the National Assembly, while those who opposed change were seated to the right (Gauchet, 1992). This binary opposition does however suggest that both sides were party to a common debate on the pace and extent of change in the age of modernity, and that the various ideologies belonged to a single spectrum running from communism at the extreme left to fascism at the extreme right. The ideologies' position on the spectrum depended on their attitude towards two central features of modernity. how favourable they were to 'the rise of the masses', to the role of the people in political and social life; and how positively they evaluated the schema of rational and radical reconstruction of society. Ideologies that gave a positive value to popular power, to extending the bounds of participation in political (and later on economic) life, and to giving affirmative answers to the project of rational social reconstruction, can be assigned to the left of the spectrum.

The historical issue to be probed here is the development of, and relationship between, the different ideologies; the more contemporary issue is the relevance of the Left–Right spectrum in the postmodern age, which questions the universality and other assumptions of the main strands of the age of ideology. The latter will be discussed in Part III, but first it is necessary to review these four ideologies – liberalism (this chapter), socialism (Chapter 4), conservatism (Chapter 5), nationalism (Chapter 6) – which in their different ways arose as views of total social change and offered a framework for political discourse in a situation marked by colossal transformation in the realms of state, economy and civil society.

Liberty and Progress

The aim here is to probe some of the central dilemmas of liberalism by seeing how it reacted to the promise and problems of modernity. In the first place, liberalism can be seen as distinctively 'modernist' in its outlook. Liberal thinkers welcomed the new society that the American and French Revolutions had brought into being, in part under the impact of liberal ideas of the supreme value of the individual and the need for a political system that was suitable for an emancipated and rational population. It is not difficult to find examples of the highly positive outlook that liberal thinkers had of this new world of modernity, and their acceptance of the core ideas of the Enlightenment modernist project. The opening lines of Bentham's *Fragment on Government*, written in 1776, provide an excellent example of belief in progress and the need to extend the scope of scientific discoveries from the natural to the social and political world:

> The age we live in is a busy age; in which knowledge is rapidly advancing towards perfection. In the natural world, in particular, every thing teems with discovery and with improvement . . . . Correspondent to *discovery* and *improvement* in the natural world, is *reformation* in the moral; if that which seems a common notion be, indeed, a true one, that in the moral world there no longer remains any matter for *discovery* (Bentham, 1988, p. 3).

Bentham even suggested that there might still be discoveries, rather than just reformation, in the moral world, as a consequence of what he announced as 'this fundamental axiom, *it is the greatest happiness of the greatest number that is the measure of right and wrong*' (ibid.).

These quotations reveal an air of optimism, belief in progress and what could be called 'constructivism', namely the idea that the construction of 'the good society' was a task of which human beings were capable, animated by reason. Part of this task was to reform the political order, which was Bentham's project. Given that early liberals generally welcomed the new political and social order and saluted the coming of modernity, what exactly was the shape of the modern social and political order which they endorsed, and what were its central problems?

Some central guidance in answering these questions can be found in the writings of Benjamin Constant, notably in his famous distinction between the liberty of the ancients and the liberty of the moderns. Liberalism, in its broadest sense, was a philosophy or set of ideas that gave primacy to the idea of individual freedom, the freedom of the individual as the supreme social unit, untrammelled by interference from the state, other individuals or society as a whole, freedom from the 'tyranny of the majority', which weighed so heavily on nineteenth-century liberals. The new society of the post-revolutionary era opened up the era, at least potentially, of individual liberty. Yet at the same time modernity created new and highly powerful forces that threatened to undermine the emancipation and liberation promised and made possible by the modernist revolution. In this sense liberals were if not exactly schizophrenic, then at least profoundly ambivalent – not on the value of modernity as such, but on the characteristics of the society that emerged from the revolutionary era. These ambiguities have characterised the liberal attitude to the present day.

If individual liberty was and has remained the central value for liberals, what emerges clearly from Constant's writing, and the ideas of the other liberals to be considered here, is that in the modern world liberty had to be conceived in a particular way. The kind of freedom that was appropriate for individuals in a modern society was totally different from that which was possible in and suitable for the ancient republic of the classical world.

Modern society, as Constant saw it, was a commercial and pacific society, distinct from the bellicosity of the ancient world. A commercial society was one in which self-interest was the driving force, and hence the unity and cohesion that characterised precommercial, 'ancient' society could not be recreated, except through a necessarily futile and self-defeating despotic state. As Constant put it, 'we have finally reached the age of commerce, an age which must necessarily replace that of war, as the age of war was bound to precede it' (Constant, 1988, p. 53). The age of commerce did not necessitate a transformation in human nature, since 'War and commerce are only two different means to achieve the same end, that of possessing what is desired' (ibid.). However, bellicose and commercial societies represented different means of attaining this end, and through experience 'a man who was always the stronger' would realise that commerce was 'a milder and surer means of getting the interests of others to agree with his own'.

Constant was educated at Edinburgh University, and hence would have been familiar with the idea of civil society and the contrast between the 'rude' and 'polished' societies that existed there. He deduced that the modern, commercial, non-bellicose society had a number of implications for the shape liberty must take in the modern world – he (and other liberals such as de Tocqueville) were well aware of some of the negative implications and the kind of liberty that was appropriate to this modern society. Constant expressed well a theory about the kind of liberty that the 'moderns' sought and needed, and the danger of seeking in modern times the type of freedom enjoyed by the 'ancients'. To revert to that ancient freedom would be a form of regression for modern society as it would have to be enforced through a strong or despotic state, which would annihilate the liberty of the moderns in a vain attempt to impose a uniformity that had gone for ever. Such a doomed attempt, Constant thought, had been made by the French revolutionaries, acting under the misleading guidance of Rousseau's ideas. Finally, Constant is a useful source of another core idea of liberalism, the fear of some of the consequences of modernity and the unintended side-effects of the liberty of the moderns.

Constant distinguished between ancient and modern liberty, a contrast enunciated in 'The Spirit of Conquest' and further developed in his famous lecture of 1819. The liberty of the ancients was that of participating directly in the affairs of the *polis*, in making the laws. Liberty was the freedom to intervene in political life without any representation, to address one's fellow citizens. This was participation in an extremely real sense, however there were costs to this liberty, and these costs would be considerably higher in modern society. The liberty of the ancients, Constant wrote,

> consisted in active participation in collective power rather than in the peaceful enjoyment of individual independence. And to ensure that participation, it was even necessary for the citizens to sacrifice a large part of this enjoyment, but this sacrifice is absurd to ask, and impossible to enact, at the stage the people have reached (ibid., p. 102).

By 'the stage people have reached' Constant meant precisely the coming of modern society, in which 'almost all the pleasures of the moderns lie in their private life' (ibid., p. 104). The ancients directly participated in law making and in that sense were 'political beings', or *zoon politikon* as Aristotle put it. But there was a price to be paid in that they had no civil liberty, in terms of the existence of a private sphere, free from the incursions of politics or society as a whole: 'Thus what we now call civil liberty was unknown to the majority of the ancient peoples' (ibid., p. 103). In a way this was no great deprivation, because the immense and direct political influence each citizen had in the small sphere of the *polis* afforded a large compensation; and also because the relatively undeveloped or unsophisticated needs of individuals in such societies meant that there was no great sacrifice in doing without a private sphere in the pursuit of happiness. However in modern society a multitude of needs had developed. As Constant put it, 'the progress of civilisation, the commercial tendency of the age, the communication among the peoples, have infinitely multiplied and varied the means of individual happiness' (ibid., p. 104). Hence modern men and women found satisfaction in the private sphere of consumption, and the wealth of a commercial society multiplied their needs and wants.

What made the liberty of the moderns even more different from that of the ancients was the fact that the large-scale political unit required by modern society made it impossible for the majority of people to feel that their individual contribution made a significant difference. The direct, unmediated participation of the ancients was not an option for people in a large commercial society. Their participation was more abstract, and could never offer the gratification that direct involvement in the affairs of the *polis* gave the ancients. In modern states, 'Because their territory is much larger than that of the ancient republics, the mass of their inhabitants, whatever form of government they adopt, have no active part in it. They are called at most to exercise sovereignty through representation, that is to say in a fictitious manner' (ibid.). In the same manner as Sieyès, Constant accepted the necessarily representative and hence somewhat distant ('fictitious') nature of political participation in the modern commercial world, a participation that was bound to seem less attractive than the satisfaction of private needs. In commercial society people were more attached to liberty, in its modern sense, because they saw in it a guarantee for the private sphere, for the pursuit of pleasure, which was their primary concern.

Thus two themes are crucial to an understanding of liberalism and its relation to modernity. The first was the separation of the public sphere, or the sphere of the state, from the private sphere, which was one of difference and diversity, and the area in which human beings found their true identity and nature. Whereas the ancients found fulfilment in direct participation in politics and had little to lose by sacrificing the private sphere of existence, the moderns saw politics in instrumental terms. Political participation was representative and intermittent, liberty was freedom from politics, and commercial society was pacific rather than bellicose, since war and conquest were anachronisms in the modern age.

The second theme is equally important, because it suggests the ambiguous attitude of liberals to the French Revolution, which marked the start of the modern era. Constant argued that the French Revolution was an attempt to recreate the liberty of the ancients in modern times, to impose uniformity and direct participation, but that this could only be done, and then only temporarily, at the cost of annihilating diversity and halting the course of human progress. Thus those whom he called 'the modern imitators of the republics of antiquity' ended up by creating a new tyranny or despotism, which had been revealed in the French Revolution and which had been developed by Bonaparte, continuing precisely the spirit of conquest and usurpation. Constant believed that the revolution in France had resulted in

> the most absolute despotism under the name of republic . . . Our reformers wanted to exercise public power as their guides had told them it had been exercised in the free states of antiquity. They believed that everything should give way before collective authority, and that all restrictions of individual rights would be compensated by participation in the social power (ibid., p. 108).

However this attempt was doomed to fail, since the inhabitants of modern society were not resigned to despotism, they were too attached to their liberty, in the modern sense, to accept collective regimentation, which would bring only war and disrupt the peaceful life of happiness the moderns wanted.

Danger of Revolution

Modernity meant the achievement of a commercial, hence pacifist and non-belligerent society, one in which the pursuit by citizens of *private* happiness loomed much larger than the somewhat illusory concern with politics and public involvement, which could be nothing other than a spasmodic choice of representative. Hence a number of fundamental problems confronted liberals with respect to their attitude towards the French Revolution and the dangers of modernity and commercial society. The French Revolution was seen as an heroic series of events that unleashed modern society and made possible the progress of modernity, the creation of a sphere of private happiness to which individuals could devote themselves and in which they could find satisfaction. Yet at the same time the French Revolution had been animated by quite different, and for Constant misguided, ideas, which sought to impose on modern citizens the direct democracy and participation of the ancient world. Hence the Terror, the extreme manifestations of Jacobinism, which were the inevitable result of attempts to recreate old-style freedom. The names that crop up in Constant's account are those of Rousseau and the Abbé Mably:

> During the French revolution, when the tide of events brought to the head of the state men who had adopted philosophy as a prejudice, and democracy as fanaticism, these men were seized by a boundless admiration for Rousseau, Mably, and all the writers of that school (ibid., p. 108).

For liberals writing in the nineteenth century there was a deep ambiguity towards the French Revolution. This ambiguity was to some extent a matter of contrasting the glorious opening stage of the revolution with the excesses of the Terror, but it pointed to a fear of the masses, fear of the people. Why had the revolution taken such a wrong turning? The reason for Constant and de Tocqueville was that the wrong ideas had been invoked – for Constant it was the misconceived attempt to restore ancient liberty in circumstances where that was no longer possible. This raises the question of what kind of political system would prevent what Furet called *dérapage* (skidding off course), the movement typified by the transition from liberalism to Jacobinism between 1789 and 1793. What kind of democracy, what powers and limits of popular sovereignty were appropriate for a modern, balanced republic?

The answer that Constant gave was contained in his *Principles of Politics*, written in 1815. The idea he developed was of the necessary limiting of sovereignty in order to prevent the abuse of power. Like his fellow liberal de Tocqueville, Constant argued that in modern times the people should indeed exercise sovereignty, since the only legitimate power in the modern world was the power of the general will. So democracy had to be accepted:

> Our present constitution formally recognises the principle of the sovereignty of the people, that is the supremacy of the general will over any particular will. Indeed this principle cannot be contested (ibid., p. 175).

However for Constant the danger was that this popular sovereignty would be understood as unlimited power, exercised by a group of people who claimed to be representatives of the general will or of the sovereignty of the people:

> When sovereignty is unlimited, there is no means of sheltering individuals from governments. It is in vain that you pretend to submit governments to the general will. It is always they who dictate the content of this will, and all your precautions become illusory (ibid., p. 179).

Hence the only way of guaranteeing the liberty of the individual was to restrict sovereignty, because unlimited popular sovereignty would lead to the creation of 'a degree of power which is too large in itself, and which is bound to constitute an evil, in whatever hands it is placed' (ibid., p. 176).

Liberalism was a theory that welcomed the freedom that was typical of and made possible by modernity. In particular, it was the pursuit of individual happiness and the virtue of diversity, of individualism, that has characterised liberalism from the beginning of the nineteenth century to the present day. It was the liberal project to accept, perhaps even welcome, democracy, but to purge it of its associations with revolution. Certainly this was the key idea of de Tocqueville, whose attitude towards the revolution is well described by Lamberti: 'What he admired above all was the spirit of '89 and the Constituent Assembly, in which he found liberalism in harmony with democracy . . . At first (the Revolution) sought equality and liberty together, but the pursuit of equality quickly became its principal goal' (Lamberti, 1989, p. 187).

This sheds light on the liberals' ambiguous attitude towards modernity, ambivalent in the sense that for liberals modernity was the source of individual liberty, and the necessary precondition for the diversity and intellectual freedom they held dear. However it was also the source of two dangers: the danger of democratic excess, of a mass society that would annihilate individual liberty; and the danger of an excessively atomised and private society, in which a new despotism could be created, of a paternalist state rising up on the backs of an excessively privatised society.

Liberals enthusiastically endorsed the promises held out by modernity, at least initially. Those promises were individual emancipation, accumulation of wealth and the conquest of nature, a society in which the happiness of all individuals could be achieved. Constant's ideas are interesting in that he had a clear and decided view of the nature of modern liberty, and how the differentiating features of a commercial and individualist society made possible a new kind of freedom that was quite different from the homogeneity of the classical ancient republic. Hence the new republic, the democratic society of the modern world, would have to be a representative democracy. Similar ideas were expressed by Sieyès, who applied ideas of the division of labour to the political sphere:

> In the civil state, everything is representation. Representation occurs in the private sphere as well as in the public sphere; it gives birth to productive industry and to commerce, as well as being the source of liberal political progress. Moreover, I maintain that representation merges with the very essence of social life (Pasquino, 1987, p. 221).

As Pasquino points out, in a way Sieyès was anticipating the Italian elitist theorist Mosca, with his idea of a 'political class', a separate class of people running political affairs, even though the people as a whole possessed what Sieyès called '*le pouvoir commettant*', sovereign power. However in modern society this sovereign power could only be exercised by the representatives who made up the constituted powers (*pouvoirs constitués*) and exercised the constitution-forming power (*pouvoir constituant*) when necessary. As Sieyès said, it was only by choosing representatives that the people could exercise their sovereignty. This seems to signify the idea of exercising power by not exercising it, or at least not directly, so in this respect Sieyès and Constant were 'anti-Rousseau' and critical of the ideas of the author of *The Social Contract*, who insisted that representation meant the loss, not the exercise, of sovereignty. In Sieyès' words,

> The people must confine itself to be the principal power only, that is to say it must limit itself to choosing and delegating those persons who will put into practice the real rights of the people, starting with the (exceptional) right of establishing the constitution (the constituent power) (ibid., p. 226).

The interesting point about these theories is that Sieyès links representation and the '*concours médiat*' (mediated power) with the division of labour and specialisation that are typical of a modern commercial society. Indeed it appears that the Abbé, for all his ecclesiastical training, was well versed in modern political economy, the ideas of Adam Smith and the Scottish Enlightenment. Hence liberals had a distinctive idea of modernity, both in the sphere of the economy (commercial civil society) as well as in the

sphere of the polity, a representative republic where, in Sieyès' words
again, 'It is best to separate the profession of government and allow it
to be carried out by a class of men who are concerned solely with
politics' (ibid., p. 223). Hence the parallels with Mosca's idea of the
ruling class.

Individualism and Equality

The problems of modernity highlighted by liberals are the problems
of democracy and mass society, the question of democracy and
revolution, and the question of social cohesion, of modernity and
diversity. For liberals the modern age was the age of commercial
society and economic progress, making possible an expansion of
needs and their satisfaction, which marked a new epoch in the history
of humanity. In this respect liberalism and Marxist socialism had
something in common: they both welcomed the expansion of productive powers that was unleashed by the new social order (commercial society for liberals, capitalism for Marxists).

However for liberals, if the modern age was the age of productive
commercial expansion, bringing peace and prosperity throughout the
world, it was also the age of democratic pressure, towards which
liberals had a decidedly ambivalent attitude, linked to their stance
towards the French Revolution. Democracy meant the rule of the
masses, the coming of mass society, and demands and pressures for
social as well as political equality. Liberals had to grapple with the
central dilemmas thrown up by the arrival and development of
modernity. The liberal thinker Alexis de Tocqueville is important
for his analysis of these matters, and a convenient starting point is his
reflections on the subject of revolution in a democratic society: 'Why
great revolutions will become rare'. Democracy, de Tocqueville
suggested, created a mass of people with more or less equal fortunes
– it annihilated the extremes of wealth and poverty found in aristocratic societies. Hence in a democratic society everyone had something to lose. The polarisation of classes that Marx saw as
characterising capitalist society was not the future de Tocqueville
saw for societies emerging from the democratic revolution.

This contrast between Marx and de Tocqueville has been highlighted by Raymond Aron, who suggests that in some respects de
Tocqueville's picture is the more accurate one, or the better forecast
of the evolution of democratic society (Aron, 1976, Ch. 1). According

to de Tocqueville, 'Any revolution is more or less a threat to property. Most inhabitants of a democracy have property. And not only have they got property, but they live in the conditions in which men attach most value to property' (de Tocqueville, 1968, vol. II, p. 825). He saw democratic society as dominated by a host of small property owners, each jealous of the other, and eager to increase their individual fortunes: 'it is just the number of the eager and restless small property-owners which equality of conditions constantly increases . . . Therefore the more widely personal property is distributed and increased and the greater the number of those enjoying it, the less is a nation inclined to revolution' (ibid., pp. 825–6). The picture presented is of a society in which people were preoccupied with their private affairs and personal wealth, so that the heroic sacrifices and upheavals of a revolution were not for them, rather they were frightened of any prospect of radical change. In some respects both de Tocqueville and Marx shared the view that 'bourgeois' society was fundamentally unheroic, despite having been brought into being by revolution and violence, by human beings working themselves up to heroic actions by their imitations of the ancient world and invoking the stern classical virtues. As Marx wrote at the opening of *The 18th Brumaire of Louis Bonaparte*:

> But unheroic as bourgeois society is, it still required heroism, self-sacrifice, terror, civil war, and battles in which whole nations were engaged, to bring it into the world. And its gladiators found in the stern classical traditions of the Roman republic the ideas, art forms and self-deceptions they needed in order to hide from themselves the limited bourgeois content of their struggles and to maintain their enthusiasm at the high level appropriate to great historical tragedy (Marx, 1973b, p. 148).

While Marx and de Tocqueville agreed on the unheroic and privatised concerns of modern society, Marx and his followers thought that heroism and revolution would be the role of the nascent working class or proletariat of the new society, a claim whose fate is analysed below.

Modern society was democratic, and this democratic revolution was something de Tocqueville saw as a current or trend that could not be resisted, whatever his own personal regrets about the virtues of a hierarchical and aristocratic order. However, de Tocqueville was an especially interesting observer of the new society because he was aware of the ambiguities and dilemmas of this democratic current.

Democracy for him meant, in his oft-repeated words, 'equality of conditions', a move from political equality to social (and economic) equality. He argued that the predominance of small property owners, all of whom were attached to their property and fearful of revolution for that reason, was a factor of social stability. Radicalism and revolutionary politics were unlikely in such a society. His analysis has been born out by the non-revolutionary, non-socialist tradition of the American democracy, where despite the flux of modernity, the constant and dynamic search for innovation and personal accumulation of wealth, this modern democratic society has enjoyed a certain inbuilt stability. For de Tocqueville this had positive features, but negative ones also. He saw the danger, as did Constant, of excessive privatisation, of a concern for personal well-being that would undermine public concerns, including those necessary to preserve public liberty. Social stagnation could result:

> If the citizens continue to shut themselves up more and more narrowly in the little circle of petty domestic interests and keep themselves constantly busy therein, there is a danger that they may in the end become practically out of reach of those great and powerful public emotions which do indeed perturb peoples but which also make them grow and refresh them (de Tocqueville, 1968, vol. II, p. 836).

Democratic society had moved far away from the heroic rituals and celebrations that had brought it into being. The primacy of private acquisition in a civil society might give rise to a new form of despotism. People would become so preoccupied with their particular concerns that they would not be aware of the danger of increased state power.

Similarly de Tocqueville painted a picture of the danger of excessive individualism. Individualism was the central feature of democratic society, the celebration of the individual as the focus of life, the elevation above all of the private sphere and what Constant called the sphere of private pleasure. Any concern with civic republicanism or heroic republican values was out of place in such a society. The problem with this individualism was that it could undermine any concern with common citizenship and public values. de Tocqueville was pointing to the reverse of Sieyès and Constant's picture of a representative democracy, where there was a division of labour between representatives and represented, between the political class and the mass of the people bound up with their private concerns. This might produce, as Sieyès suggested, a rational republican system, but the danger was that it might create a mass of privatised citizens who had no interest in new ideas and could fall prey to despotism. de Tocqueville concluded his chapter on 'why great revolutions will become rare' with an astonishingly bleak statement, not exactly a forecast, but rather a warning of the possible stagnation of such a modern society:

> I fear that the mind may keep folding itself up in a narrower compass for ever without reproducing new ideas, that men will wear themselves out in trivial, lonely, futile activity, and that for all its constant agitation humanity will make no advance (ibid., p. 836).

This was not a statement of what would inevitably happen, but a warning of one of the possible consequences of an over-privatised modern society, in which politics would be left to professionals and any new ideas would be viewed with suspicion, and the fear of revolution would lead to the suppression of criticism or innovation, to the ultimate detriment of humanity itself. Modernity for de Tocqueville was the source of individual freedom, but it could give rise to a type of democratic society that would menace and stifle the freedom of the individual that liberals held so dear.

The liberal analysis of modern society thus portrayed modernity as possibly leading to a state of intellectual stagnation. However, and only apparently paradoxically, the picture presented by some liberals of the classical school was of social revolution and the annihilation of individual liberty through a strong state, and through socialism. In the liberal perspective modernity meant democracy, and democracy meant equality. Liberals feared that the outcome of this process could be the standardisation of humanity and the annihilation of diversity and progress. Two basic dilemmas or fears about modernity emerged from liberal thinking. The first was that modernity would lead to a dreadful society of the masses, dominated by a strong state, marked by low cultural standards and the politics of the lowest common denominator. The second, though not necessarily the preserve of liberalism alone, was that there would be too much disassociation and lack of community in modern society, that individualism would allow an all-powerful state to creep in and dominate the individual.

For both de Tocqueville and J. S. Mill, democracy was a product of modernity and not something that could be halted. Unlike conservatives, liberals accepted that the progress of modern society required the admission of the masses into the political sphere. While the classical liberals accepted that there was no halting the rise of democracy, the question remained of what kind of democracy, and the role of the masses in that democracy. Liberals accepted the need for an informed and active public opinion, but the danger was that the masses, the newly enfranchised people, would lower the tone of political discourse. They could also fall prey to demagogues and the new leaders, or manipulators, of public opinion.

Again, liberals were ambivalent about the promise, or the threat, of modernity. The politics of modernity, as liberals understood it, opened up the prospect of a rational politics, accessible to the mass of the population, a highly desirable state of affairs in the sense that, as J. S. Mill put it, 'There ought to be no pariahs in a full- grown and civilised nation . . . No arrangement of the suffrage, therefore, can be permanently satisfactory, in which the electoral privilege is not open to all persons of full age who desire to obtain it' (Mill, 1975, p. 277). Nevertheless, despite welcoming the participation of the masses as a necessary part of a rational political system, the fear was that an uneducated public would practice irrational politics. Hence the invocation by James Mill, in his *Essay on Government*, that it was the wise and sober middle class who should influence the opinion of the 'lower orders' below them. James Mill proclaimed a proposition that, he thought could be stated

> with a perfect confidence of the concurrence of all those men who have attentively considered the formation of opinions in the great body of society, or, indeed, the principles of human nature in general. It is, that the opinions of that class of the people, who are below the middle rank, are formed, and their minds are directed by that intelligent and virtuous rank, who come the most immediately in contact with them, to whom they fly for advice and assistance in all their numerous difficulties, upon whom they feel an immediate and daily dependence, in health and in sickness, in infancy and in old age; to whom their children look up as models for their imitation, whose opinions they hear daily repeated, and account it their honour to adopt (Mill, 1992, p. 41).

It is evident from this quotation that James Mill saw the question as being one of how to prevent those 'below the middle rank' from developing opinions that were critical of or hostile to the intelligent and virtuous rank of people in society, whom he saw as setting the standard for social conduct. For liberals modern society was one that promised emancipation and personal liberty, securing the basic rights outlined in the French Revolution's Declaration of the Rights of Man and Citizen. Yet for liberals of the mid nineteenth century this was jeopardised by the rise of mass society, threatening first political equality and then social equality.

J. S. Mill wrote in *Representative Government* of the dangers of 'class legislation'. Although he started by affirming his commitment to voting rights being extended 'to all persons of full age who desire to obtain it' (Mill, 1975, p. 277), he followed this with list of exclusions or exceptions. For Mill, admission to the suffrage involved a literacy test: it was 'inadmissible that any person should participate in the suffrage, without being able to read, write, and . . . perform the common operations of arithmetic' (ibid., p. 278). This he held to be a temporary exclusion, in the sense that the educational progress of society would result in all people (except those who could not be bothered to learn) being able to fulfil this qualification. Secondly, suffrage should not be given to those who paid no taxes, although Mill argued that because a direct tax would be imposed on every citizen, few people would be permanently excluded from suffrage on this ground. Nevertheless his conclusion remained that 'the receipt of parish relief should be a peremptory disqualification for the franchise' (ibid., p. 280), and that those who could not support themselves by their own labour should not have the vote. The reason for this was that such persons might use their vote to be lavish with public money: 'Those who pay no taxes, disposing by their votes of other people's money, have every motive to be lavish, and none to economise' (ibid., p. 279). The core of Mill's argument was that all these exclusions were temporary, and no-one, even those in receipt of parish relief, would on that ground be *permanently* excluded from the suffrage.

As many accounts of liberalism emphasise, at the core of liberal values was the idea of individualism. The principle of modernity for liberals was the emancipation of individuals from their traditional shackles, from the pressures of the arbitrary state of the *ancien régime* and the stifling conformity of public opinion. Hence it was the virtue of the solitary individual, self-reliant and autonomous, that was celebrated by liberalism, and made the central figure of modernity. It was in this sense that liberalism sought to set the individual free from tradition and arbitrary state power, and from the grip of any collective body. Constant's criticism of Rousseau was that Rousseau created an 'immense social power' that supposedly expressed the general will, a collective body to which each individual was subordinate. Constant thought that 'Rousseau himself was appalled by these consequences', that he had created a Frankenstein-like monster. The only protection Rousseau could envisage against this monstrous social power was, in Constant's view, to make this sovereignty unworkable by suggesting that 'sovereignty could not be alienated, delegated or represented. This was equivalent to declaring, in other words, that it could not be exercised' (Constant, 1988, p. 178).

The thrust of liberalism was to reject the concentration of power in one social body and to argue for the limitation of sovereignty. Hence the liberal critique of the French Revolution, a critique echoed in our own day by people such as Furet, that the French Revolution created a new power, a new collective subject, supposedly acting in the name of the people. However in reality this collective power was exercised by a minority, by people who claimed to speak in the name of the collective subject but were actually a dangerous group of power holders. In Constant's words, 'Because the action performed in the name of all is necessarily, whether we like it or not, at the disposal of a single individual or of a few, it happens that, in giving oneself to all, one does not give oneself to nobody, on the contrary, one submits oneself to those who act in the name of all' (ibid.).

Hence the collective subject – 'we the people' in the American version – turned into, or became the justification for, the domination of individuals by a particular group. Political power thus became a dangerous weapon used to dominate individuals, to intrude into the private sphere, 'a part of human existence which by necessity remains individual and independent, and which is, by right, outside any social competence' (ibid., p. 177). In the liberal perspective, this could only be prevented through the division of power, above all by insistence on a sphere of individual rights that political power could not transgress.

Dilemmas of Liberalism

As stated earlier, liberals welcomed the coming of modernity, which they saw as the coming of civil society and the rational representative republic, the modern political system outlined by Sieyès and Benjamin Constant. Philosophically, this liberalism was justified by the writings of Immanuel Kant, who developed the idea of the autonomous and self-determining individual, the subject of rights. There is a good illustration of Kant's liberalism in his essay *On the Common Saying: 'This May be True in Theory, but it does not Apply in Practice'*, where he defined the idea of the civil state according to three principles that he claimed were *a priori*: '1. The *freedom* of every member of society as a *human being*. 2. The *equality* of each with all the others as a *subject*. 3. The *independence* of each member of a commonwealth as a *citizen*' (Kant, 1991, p. 74). The liberal philosophy of modernity is summed up by the headings 'freedom', 'equality' and 'independence as a citizen', and in the liberal perspective a modern society was one in which these goals were met. Freedom, for Kant, meant the right of all people to choose their own individual plan of life:

> No-one can compel me to be happy in accordance with his conception of the welfare of others, for each may seek his happiness in whatever way he seeks fit, so long as he does not infringe upon the freedom of others to pursue a similar end which can be reconciled with the freedom of everyone else within a workable general law – i.e. he must accord to others the same right as he enjoys himself (ibid.)

Modernity was the setting free of individuals from any preimposed plan of life. Kant rejected the idea of a paternal government, which he called 'the greatest conceivable *despotism*' (ibid.), a situation in which governments would tell people how to be happy, and in which people would have no rights at all. All people, as human beings, had this right of freedom, the freedom to choose one's own way of happiness.

Equality involved equality between all 'subjects'. By this Kant meant that all were equal subjects and not exempt from the laws of the commonwealth: 'All who are subject to laws are the subjects of a state and are thus subject to the right of coercion along with all other members of the commonwealth'. However, he insisted that this equality before the law was in no way the same as equality of possessions: 'This uniform equality of human beings as subjects of a state is, however, perfectly consistent with the utmost inequality of the mass in the degree of its possessions . . . . Nevertheless, they are all equal as subjects *before the law*'. This equality before the law was compatible with an idea of equality of opportunity, or inequality of outcome: 'every member of the commonwealth must be entitled to reach any degree of rank which a subject can earn through his talent, his industry, and his good fortune' (ibid., p. 75).

Finally, Kant's idea of citizenship was restricted to those who could support themselves. A citizen was defined by him as 'anyone who has the right to vote' on 'a public law which defines for everyone that which is permitted and prohibited by right', which Kant said was an 'act of a public will, from which all right proceeds and which must not therefore itself be able to do an injustice to any one'. He insisted that 'The only qualification required by a citizen (apart, of course, from being an adult male) is that he must be his *own master* (*sui iuris*), and must have some *property* (which can include any skill, trade, fine art or science) to support himself' (ibid., p. 78). Hence the qualification of citizenship, in the liberal view, as with J. S. Mill, was bound up with the idea of property, and self-sufficiency, both economic and social, was seen as the necessary criterion for a citizen.

The dilemma of modernity for the philosophy of liberalism was that the political community was seen as an association of rational citizens, deliberating together and each forming their plan of life within the framework of the neutral state. Hence in this sense liberalism can be seen as the modernist philosophy *par excellence*, elevating the individual subject to the highest role, with all individuals determining for themselves their own plan of life. However, challenges arose to this liberal philosophy, challenges that were part of the very problems of modernity.

The basic problem stemmed from the idea of freedom, the debate over positive and negative freedom. The world of modernity, as posited by classical liberalism, was a world of property owners, in which all people were rationally pursuing their own self-interests, and in which the state acted as a neutral entity. However the structure of modern society was one in which a new class of people developed, the masses, or the working class, a group of people who had no property and therefore did not enter into the category of citizen. This was the problem of modernity for liberals. Modernity meant a society of individual emancipation, yet modern society was characterised by the emergence of the masses, whom liberals feared would threaten the rationality of that society.

Hence the propertyless masses had to be integrated into the new society, had to be given the chance of citizenship, given that democracy and the rise of the masses were features of modernity that could not be reversed. The central dilemma for liberalism was that modern society created the conditions for individual emancipation, yet it also created a threat to that emancipation, the threat presented by the proletariat, as the Marxist philosophy conceived it, or the propertyless masses. The question was how to achieve this integration without damaging, through revolution, the structure of liberal society.

One way in which liberalism sought to integrate the masses was by giving all people civil and political rights, as well as, no less importantly, rights of access to the market as consumers. Progressive liberalism, the new liberalism of the end of the nineteenth century, sought to increase the role of the state, to make it more interventionist, both to mitigate the inequalities of the market and to give the working masses a sense of integration, to make them citizens with a stake in the existing society. Hence liberal philosophy, especially in Britain, saw the state in a more positive light than the minimal state of classical liberalism; it saw the state as an institution for maintaining the sense of common citizenship that was being threatened by the mechanisms of modernity

As Charles Taylor notes in *The Ethics of Authenticity* (1991), the modern world was underpinned by a particular philosophy, or view of human nature, that was highly individualistic, 'a world where people have a right to choose for themselves their own pattern of life, to decide in conscience what convictions to espouse, to determine the shape of their lives in a whole host of ways that their ancestors couldn't control' (Taylor, 1991, p. 2). Yet this essential and supreme individualism of modern culture also gave rise to the malaises of modernity, which Taylor suggests were three.

First, as he puts it, there was the 'dark side of individualism', which de Tocqueville had already noted: de Tocqueville was afraid that modern people would neglect any common concerns and become wrapped up in petty self-interest. Second, what Taylor calls 'the primacy of instrumental reason' suggests that the characteristics of the modern age were ones of instrumentalism, that goals were seen in terms of narrow calculation, and that in Marxist language the world was one where everything was a commodity, where market relations prevailed in all spheres of life. Third, Taylor notes the fear that freedom would be lost, subject to what de Tocqueville called soft despotism, similar to Kant's paternal government, which would decide what its subjects wanted and provide them with it. This third malaise of modernity was that citizenship would cease to be of concern to people, and that any concept of defending rights, or common citizenship, would be subordinate to a very narrow concept of democracy. Political rights would only be seen as significant to a few individuals, and, as Taylor puts it, people might 'prefer to stay at home and enjoy the satisfactions of private life, as long as the government of the day produces the means to these satisfactions and distributes them widely' (ibid., p. 9).

In a sense these were the dilemmas of classical liberalism, and remain those of liberalism as a philosophy today. The fear is that liberal democracy is doomed to remain what Barber calls 'thin democracy', as opposed to 'strong democracy' (Barber, 1984), and that the liberal philosophy of individualism, seen as the highest point of the politics of modernity, is not enough to sustain a strong democracy of active and informed citizens, hence we live in a world where liberalism and the rights of the individual are increasingly threadbare notions. They cannot sustain any idea of community, democratic solidarity and citizenship.

In a sense the charges made against the liberal philosophy reflect the charges made against the French Revolution, that a revolution carried out in the name of liberty, equality and fraternity instead culminated in oppressive dictatorship. The argument against liberalism would be that it exalted and exaggerated the promise of modernity. Liberals defended the economic development, individual emancipation and citizenship rights that initially were the preserve of property owners but were later extended to all. They claimed that these features of modernity would provide a rational system, rational in the sense of safeguarding people's basic rights and affording them the opportunity to follow their own life plans. Yet according to the socialist critique, this liberal system was one of profound inequalities which prevented large sections of the population from acting rationally in this sense, precisely because without the provision of certain basic needs it was difficult to pursue one's life plans in a rational way. Hence the working out of liberalism and its attitude to modernity left unresolved certain basic dilemmas of modernity, with the result that liberalism has little to offer a postmodern society.

4

Socialism and Emancipation

This chapter develops the theme of modernity by considering the development and fate of socialist ideas and movements in the nineteenth and twentieth centuries. Socialism was a key philosophy or doctrine of modernity, perhaps even the epitome of modernity. Yet socialist ideas have had a problematic time in the period since the French and American Revolutions, leading to the question of whether the socialist project has failed.

The British sociologist Anthony Giddens claims that since the dissolution of the ancien régime socialism has been 'the standard-bearer of "progressivism"', which he defines as 'the notion that there is a direction to history and that appropriate sorts of political intervention can help us locate it as well as speed up the journey'. However, his argument is that socialism has become at best defensive, at worst irrelevant to an entirely changed world after the collapse of communism. 'Long accustomed to thinking of itself as the avant-garde, socialism has suddenly become archaic, consigned to the past it once despised' (Giddens, 1994, p. 51). Giddens argues that socialists are ill-prepared 'to cope with issues of life politics', life politics being 'a politics, not of life chances, but of life style', concerning 'disputes and struggles about how (as individuals and as collective humanity) we should live in a world where what used to be fixed either by nature or tradition is now subject to human decisions' (ibid., p. 14). This critique of socialism thus seems to suggest that it is an idea that was bound up with modernity, but whose time has now passed, a set of ideas no longer appropriate for the contemporary world.

The Organisation of Production

At the core of the socialist tradition was acceptance of the premises of Enlightenment thought, that society could be rationally controlled and organised through conscious human action. Giddens relates socialism to a 'cybernetic' model of society, in which 'a system (in the case of socialism, the economy) can best be organised by being subordinated to a directive intelligence (the state, understood in one form or another)' (ibid., p. 8). However many variations of socialism rejected the idea of the state as the 'directive intelligence' that organises the economy, and substituted for the state forms of worker self-management, the control of society by itself, the associated rule of the producers as Marx wrote in volume 3 of *Capital*: 'socialised man, the associated producers, rationally regulating their interchange with Nature, bringing it under their common control, instead of being ruled by it as by the blind forces of Nature' (Marx, 1974, p. 820).

The idea of socialism in all its forms is of organised society, of human beings mastering the forces of nature and production to achieve the common happiness of mankind. From its inception socialism was the child of the industrial revolution and the French Revolution. Socialist theoreticians, starting with those whom Engels called 'Utopian socialists' (Saint-Simon, Owen, Fourier), realised that a new world had come about with the development of industrial production, the application of science to production, the development of new needs and the productive capacity to meet those needs. In this respect the utopian socialists as well as those in the Marxist tradition would have agreed with the words of Jeremy Bentham quoted at the beginning of the previous chapter, to the effect that the present age was 'a new age teeming with discovery and innovation'. Likewise the originators of the socialist tradition hailed the discoveries of the industrial revolution as making possible an emancipated society. The writings of Saint-Simon, for example, are a clear case of 'a new view of society' (to use the title of one of Robert Owen's books) that placed the emphasis on the productive apparatus of society, as opposed to what Saint-Simon saw as the parasitic weight of the non-productive groups in society, *les oisifs*, the idlers. The often-quoted allegory in which Saint-Simon contrasts the loss that would be suffered by France if the skilled workers and productive people were disposed of, with the unimportant consequences if the nobles and court dignitaries were blown up, is a clear indication of the shift in emphasis to the productive apparatus of society as determining the nature of society, and indeed the possibility of human happiness (Ionescu, 1976, pp. 138–9).

Socialist theorists proclaimed that the key to realising the modernist promise of emancipation was the rational organisation of the economy, which alone could create the harmony and cohesion necessary for human satisfaction. Thus the socialist perspective shifted away from the individualist model of 'civil society' that was common to liberal thinkers and defined their view of the kind of society that was appropriate to the modern age. The liberal perspective was of a representative and constitutional republic, situated within a competitive civil society, a society of individuals who rejected any state despotism (as Kant put it) in the running of their lives. Socialists agreed with the premise that a new age had started in which a rational society was possible, in which human happiness could be achieved and social harmony was feasible. However liberals and socialists differed over how this modernist promise was to be fulfilled, how the fruits of modernity were to be achieved. Liberalism saw the progress of humanity in the achievement of 'civil society', the construction of a society in which individuals would be free to pursue their own interests, unfettered by the demands of society as a whole (the tyranny of the majority) or by a restrictive state. This was Hegel's *'bürgerliche Gesellschaft'*, a society in which each individual saw the other individuals in instrumental terms, as necessary to his or her own welfare, yet each individual was only a means to realise the goals of the other. However socialists saw civil society as a class structure in which a particular group of people, a ruling class, held economic power and dominated those who were excluded from the ownership and control of the means of production.

Hence the socialist critique of bourgeois society, or civil society, was twofold. The first part of the critique of civil society *'bürgerliche Gesellschaft'* was that it was fundamentally a sphere of inequality, that the profound divisions between human beings, dependent on their status as property owners or non-property owners, meant that the equality and citizenship rights proclaimed in the course of the American and French Revolutions would be unattainable as long as the class-dominated social structure continued to exist. The dominant relationship was one of exploitation, and thus the promise of a system of equality could not be fulfilled in the type of civil society that modernity had created. Modernity had created the preconditions for human emancipation, and the new age of industrial production and civil society was laying the groundwork for human freedom. However this could not be achieved within the existing structure of civil society, in which exploitation was preventing the true development of human freedom.

The other aspect of the socialist critique was that civil society was fundamentally irrational and badly organised, and that class relations and the ownership of productive resources by a particular group were preventing the use of those resources for the good of the whole society. A classic example of this argument was given by followers of Saint-Simon – Bazard and Enfantin – in their *Exposition of the Doctrine of Saint-Simon*. They argued that crises and disorganisation were endemic to the existing order of society. Hence the newly liberated productive forces were not being harnessed to secure the goal of general happiness and improve the lot of those whom Saint-Simon himself called 'the most numerous and the poorest class'. The followers of Saint-Simon called upon the bankers to be the true organisers and rational 'heads' of society, to move society on from a disorganised and chaotic arrangement to a rationally arranged structure in which credit would be channelled to the right sources, in which the crises and misallocation of resources would be a thing of the past. This was the promise of modernity that socialism held out: building on the new society that the industrial revolution had brought about, the idea was to create a modern society that would be different from the civil society that liberals exalted, organised by a conscious rational will. Saint-Simon and his followers envisaged a centrally planned and organised society.

Socialist theoreticians and politicians of all schools accepted the idea of modernity and saw themselves as fulfilling its promises. Indeed the socialists claimed that they alone could realise the goals of modernity. Liberalism was condemned by socialists as a philosophy that could not reap the fruits of modern society for the good of humanity as a whole.

For socialism as a distinctively modern view of the world, a new era had been opened up by the eighteenth-century revolutions. The revolution of modernity had brought into being a new society, industrial society, which had enormously increased the ability of human beings to produce, to dominate nature and also to expand their needs and provide the means of satisfying those needs. Hence for socialists the society of modernity was a productive society which for the first time could realistically envisage the overcoming of scarcity and the realisation of human happiness. Hence the key factor was the structure of the productive apparatus, the way in which production was organised. It was Saint-Simon who proclaimed that 'Politics was the science of production' (Ionescu, 1976, p. 108). The goals of the French Revolution, seen in purely political terms, were inadequate. A political revolution could not resolve the crucial problem of the epoch, namely the rational organisation of society's productive apparatus for the benefit of humanity. For Saint-Simon the Jacobins were the exemplification of power-hungry politicians who stirred up the masses for that end. Saint-Simon made a distinction between 'jurists' and 'industrialists'. Rather like Burke denouncing the leaders of the French Revolution for being intellectuals concerned only with abstract ideals, Saint-Simon complained of the power of the 'jurists' during the French Revolution: 'It is a fact that during the stormiest and most distressful years of the Revolution, France was governed by *jurists*' (ibid., p. 126). By 'jurists' he meant those who wanted political power and domination and pursued this aim by means of ever more centralisation and state domination:

> The Revolution gave the jurists an opportunity to reveal the spirit which motivates them: this is an unquenchable thirst for *power*, to the point where to possess it, even in a subordinate role, if they cannot be absolute masters, becomes the object of their desires and their efforts (ibid., p. 127).

Yet this Jacobin project was doomed to fail, because for Saint-Simon it did not tackle the real issue: the organisation of the economy, the system of production which alone held the key to social peace and harmony and the satisfaction of human needs. For him the error of the French Revolution and the subsequent epoch was the failure of society to place power in the hands of the productive classes, the industrialists (*industriels*), defined as all those contributing to production, whose importance should be recognised. Only in that way could the parasitic force of the state apparatus be curtailed and the productive forces of society rationally organised.

Socialism was thus a distinctively modernist philosophy, yet at the same time it offered a critique of the way in which modern society was organised. As Marshall Berman said of Marx, 'he hopes to heal the wounds of modernity through a fuller and deeper modernity' (Berman, 1983, p. 98). In general, socialists welcomed modernity but claimed that only social reorganisation – a social change that would go beyond purely political change – would allow modernity to fulfil its promise to satisfy people's needs and secure human happiness.

Harmony and Association

The core words of socialism thus included 'harmony' and 'association', and the vision of the Saint-Simonian school of socialism was one of a planned and organised economy. Saint-Simon himself has been seen as a sort of industrial corporatist, with his plans for representative bodies composed of industrialists, a House of Commons which 'should be made up of the leaders of the different kinds of industrial work', and other institutions such as 'Chambers of Invention', where engineers, artists and scientists would cooperate to put forward schemes of useful work. The implication for private property was that the status of property would have to be subordinate to the needs of production, 'property will be redefined and founded on bases which will make it more advantageous to production' (Ionescu, 1976, p. 151).

One of the clearest examples of the somewhat ambiguous socialist attitude towards modernity is the *Exposition de la Doctrine de Saint Simon*, a set of lectures given in 1828 by Enfantin and Bazard, two of Saint-Simon's followers. These lectures presented a picture of contemporary society as riven by egoism and disorganisation: 'Let us look at the society which surrounds us. Numerous crises and deplorable catastrophes afflict industry . . . the result of the application of the principle of unlimited competition' (Iggers, 1972, p. 102). The present social order was one of exploitation, hence of antagonism – the new society of the post-French Revolution era had not put an end to inequality and exploitation:

> At last the exploitation of man by man, which we have shown in its most direct and uncouth form in the past, namely slavery, continues to a very large extent in the relations between owners and workers, masters and wage earners (ibid., p. 82).

The worker, according to Bazard and Enfantin, was not directly owned by his master as slaves were, but the contractual relationship between worker and property owner was not a free and equal one: 'The worker is not like the slave, the direct property of his master. His condition, never permanent, is fixed by a transaction with a master. But is this transaction free on the part of the worker?' (ibid., p. 82).

What then was the solution these disciples of Saint-Simon proposed? How could the society of exploitation and disharmony be replaced by an associative society, in which the productive forces would be able to satisfy the needs of '*la classe la plus pauvre et la plus nombreuse*'? Certainly not through the principle of civil society and *laissez-faire*, which rested on the false assumption that individual interest was always in harmony with the general social interest: 'Let us add now that the basic principle *laissez faire, laissez passer* supposes that personal interest is always in harmony with general interest, a supposition contradicted by innumerable facts' (ibid., p. 14).

The solution proposed by Bazard and Enfantin was a planned economy, in which bankers would channel funds to productive enterprises that most needed them, and the future system of social organisation would be, in a striking phrase, an army of peaceful workers, '*travailleurs pacifiques*'. The organisation of property would be different, in that the only legitimate title to property would be the capacity for peaceful labour, the ability to put productive resources to rational use for the benefit of society as a whole. In short the solution proposed was not one of violent upheaval and political transformation, on the lines of the French Revolution, but rather of an evolution that all would accept in the interests of social progress and harmony: 'We want to repeat that the doctrine of Saint-Simon does not want to bring about an upheaval or a revolution. It comes to predict and to achieve a transformation, an evolution' (ibid., p. 111).

The 'Exposition' of 1828 clearly revealed some of the central themes of the socialist attitudes towards modernity: the possibility of satisfying of human wants and needs, improvement of the lot of 'the most numerous and poorest class', and the idea of a rationally organised productive society, in which armies of peaceful workers would cooperate and a central bank would channel credit to those enterprises that needed it. Only in that way could industrial society fulfil its promise.

One criticism of this perspective has important implications for the relevance of these ideas for the contemporary epoch. The theme of socialist thought from its inception was to emphasise the *social* as opposed to the *political*. The idea was that social organisation of the productive forces of society was necessary and that without such reorganisation and rational planning any political change would be futile. It would be, as Saint-Simon wrote of the jurists in the French Revolution, merely a case of the unscrupulous power seekers manipulating the ignorant masses in order to gain power, and such movements and upheavals could never lead to stability and harmony. It was organisation of the economy that was the key.

The charge against Saint-Simon's vision, and by extension against socialism more generally, was that it omitted any concern with democracy, and went too far in its underestimation of the significance of political rights. In short the charge was that there was a latent authoritarianism in this vision of a planned and organised society, which had no room for those who might not want to be part of the army of workers. In other words the argument, which has been taken up by more recent critics of socialism, was that Saint-Simonianism failed to show any concern with democratic rights and that the early socialists subordinated everything to the dictates of ordered production and a meritocratic or technocratic hierarchy. Certainly Saint-Simon's world was not egalitarian, and distribution would be unequal as people would be rewarded according to their contribution to the social product: 'In the organisation of the future each one will be classified according to his ability and remunerated according to his work' (Iggers, ibid., p. 89). The criticism is that for this brand of socialism the only possibility of reaping the fruits of modernity was through the rational organisation of the economy, but this neglected any possibility of organisation from below. Any assertion of democratic rights and indeed individual rights would be swamped in the need for centralised social organisation.

In an extreme presentation of this view, Stalinist centralisation and five-year plans were the inevitable outcome of the Saint-Simonian perspective. Furthermore, to take up Giddens' (1994) point of the cybernetic model of social organisation, this perspective seemed to rest on the assumption that the central planning and control of social life was possible, that a single unit could control the entire economy. The Saint-Simonian perspective neglected questions of democratic and political rights in general. They 'threw out the baby with the bathwater' in that they moved from belief that political rights and political transformations on their own were not sufficient, to belief that political, and especially democratic, rights were of no account. However socialists were highly enthusiastic about the modern industrial order that had emerged, and saw socialism as a means of realising the true potential of this modern order to satisfy human happiness.

Marxism and Modernity

As Marshall Berman points out in his study *All That is Solid Melts into Air* (1983), Marx was concerned with both the creative and the destructive aspects of modernity. The bourgeoisie, the class of people that owned and controlled the means of production, were the agents *par excellence* of modernity, sweeping away all prejudices, traditional modes of thought and barriers to economic development, dissolving everything in the cold reality of commodity relations and free trade. Some of these ideas are expressed most clearly in *The Communist Manifesto*: 'The *Manifesto* expresses some of modernist culture's deepest insights and, at the same time, dramatizes some of its deepest inner contradictions' (Berman, 1983, p. 89). Those contradictions are the opposition between the creative aspects of modernity and its destructive impact.

Modernity, for Marx, took the form of capitalism, in the sense that capitalism, the production of commodities for exchange value and the accumulation of further capital, was the agent of modernity. Berman is right to say that in some pages of the *Manifesto* Marx 'seems to have come not to bury the bourgeoisie, but to praise it. He writes an impassioned, enthusiastic, often lyrical celebration of bourgeois works, ideas and achievements. Indeed, in these pages he manages to praise the bourgeoisie more powerfully and profoundly than its members have ever known how to praise themselves' (ibid., p. 92). This praise involved celebrating the heroic role of the bourgeoisie in showing what human energy could do, in conquering nature, in expanding production, in creating a world market for its commodities. Only on that basis could a new social order (socialism) arise.

In the *Communist Manifesto* Marx and Engels criticised the crude egalitarianism of Babeuf, who has sometimes been called the 'first communist' and whose conspiracy of 1796 has been seen as marking the most radical point of the French Revolution. Babeuf and fellow conspirators such as Sylvain Maréchal organised the 'Conspiracy of the Equals', and Babeuf developed a scheme for '*un communisme parcellaire*', a kind of agrarian communism in which the products of people's labour would be put in communal warehouses and distributed on the basis of strict equality (Babeuf, 1976). However what divided this backward-looking communism from the communism of Marx and Engels was precisely the experience of modernity, or rather the sense in Marxist-type socialism or communism that the modern age was the era of the creation of new needs, not a period of ascetic egalitarianism and crude minimalism in the satisfaction of those needs. Modernity for Marx consisted in the expansion of needs, and the ability of the modern means of production to satisfy them. Thus the existence of capitalism was necessary to lay the basis for the new socialist order, in which people would be able to satisfy their needs, develop them, and yet exert a conscious control over society and its productive apparatus. Hence Marx's socialism was modernist socialism, whereas the egalitarian precursors of socialism in the French Revolution had no inkling of the possibility of a vast expansion of the production process.

However Marxism was also critical of modernity, of its destructive uprooting and dehumanising force. Again this can be explained with reference to the idea of civil society or *bürgerliche Gesellschaft*. This civil society was one of individual freedom, in which individuals could come together as self-sufficient individuals to realise their own ambitions and goals. Yet the division of labour and specialisation that was a necessary condition for the productivity of human beings in this type of society was a profoundly alienating force that would result in the stunting of human powers, and divide people from their fellow human beings and their true 'species being'. Hence modernity in its capitalist form was dehumanising, limiting and crippling, as well as being a system that in the Marxist view provided the necessary conditions for humanity to move forward to the realm of freedom.

The paradox highlighted by Marxism and by socialism more generally was that the capitalist system was the agent of modernity, it was in its capitalist form that modernity emerged and developed. Its main feature was the huge expansion of productive forces, which would make possible a society in which scarcity would be overcome and classes would disappear. Yet modernity was also profoundly disruptive, and stultifying in its effects, because it involved a division of labour that confined people to particular operations and modes of work, it swept away established forms of life, which in one sense was liberating, but capitalism as a system could establish no links between people apart from those of the 'cash nexus'. Only socialism could gather the fruits of modernity in a way that would heal its divisions and scars.

The passages in the *Grundrisse* where Marx discussed automation show this idea of modernity, and the ambiguous benefits it would provide in its capitalist form. It should be made clear that Marx did not use the concept of modernity, but of capitalism. For Marx, capitalism was a system not of the market as such, one could have markets without capitalism. Rather capitalism was a system in which the production of commodities became the chief end of life, and the production of commodities was the means to accumulate more and more capital. In its primitive form, it was through the direct labour of the producers that commodities were produced. However, with the growing sophistication of the means of production, the actual labour power expended would count for less and less:

> But to the degree that large industry develops, the creation of real wealth comes to depend less on labour time and on the amount of labour employed than on the power of the agencies set in motion during labour time, whose 'powerful effectiveness' is itself in turn out of all proportion to the direct labour time spent on their production, but depends rather on the general state of science and on the progress of technology, or the application of this science to production (Marx, 1973c, pp. 704–5).

The core problem of Marxism was that this programme of completing modernity came to be applied in practice in societies such as Russia that had barely begun the development and progress of modernity. Hence the socialist project as a whole generally became associated with forced development from above, which accentuated some of the problems noted above in the Saint-Simonian perspective, where democratic rights and political rights were generally neglected in favour of the planned approach.

Marxism, as the dominant form of socialism throughout the nineteenth and twentieth centuries, was an uncompromisingly modernist philosophy. This is clearly evident in Marx's writings on Germany. In the minutes of the Central Committee meeting of the Communist League on 15 September 1850 Marx was quoted as criticising 'a national German approach', which meant that 'The *will*, rather than the actual conditions, was stressed as the chief factor in the revolution' (Marx, 1973a, p. 341). Marx, in contrast, insisted that 'We tell the workers: If you want to change conditions and make yourselves capable of government, you will have to undergo fifteen, twenty or fifty years of civil war' (ibid.). Similarly, in his polemic against the anarchist Bakunin, Marx insisted that Bakunin's conception of social revolution was entirely misguided, again substituting 'will' for the real social preconditions under which revolution would be possible. As he put it, 'A radical social revolution depends on certain definite historical conditions of economic development as its pre-condition' (Marx, 1974, p. 334). Marx considered that Bakunin

> understands nothing about the social revolution, only its political phrases. Its economic conditions do not exist for him. As all

hitherto existing economic forms, developed or undeveloped, involve the enslavement of the worker (whether in the form of wage-labourer, peasant, etc.), he believes that a *radical revolution* is possible in all such forms alike. Still more! He wants the European social revolution, premised on the economic basis of capitalist production, to take place at the level of the Russian or Slavic agricultural and pastoral peoples, not to surpass this level . . . . The *will*, and not the economic conditions, is the foundation of his social revolution (ibid.).

The implication of this for modernity is clear: the promise of modernity could only be realised through radical revolution, which in turn would only be possible on the basis of capitalist modernity itself, brought to its highest and most developed point. Any other perspective would be futile, the idea of a non-modernist socialist revolution would be almost a contradiction in terms. Hence a revolution was necessary, but a revolution that would carry modernity forward and finish the task that the bourgeoisie were unable to accomplish.

Marxism and modernity go together in that the theoretical expectation was that the historical forces unleashed by modernity would themselves form the basis, the preconditions, for socialist revolution. For example, in the classical Marxist perspective the bourgeoisie in countries such as Germany had failed to live up to their mission, which was to modernise, to be ruthless in carrying out the task of modernity, as sketched out in *The Communist Manifesto*. In the *Manifesto*, as Berman says in the passage quoted above, Marx and Engels almost came to praise the bourgeoisie, not to bury them: they were credited with the heroic task of expanding the productive forces, of being the agents of modernity, of spreading the capitalist mode of production throughout the globe, of being the first agents of what now might be called 'globalisation'. Yet in other Marxist writings the bourgeoisie in particular countries and locations were depicted as shrinking from their allotted role as the ruthless agents of modernisation and modernity. For example, in Germany in the 1848 revolutions the Marxist charge was that the bourgeoisie did not live up to their heroic mission, but were prepared to compromise with the Junkers and the monarch rather than push for a democratic representative republic, which was the model of political modernity.

By the same token, the classic Marxist text *The 18th Brumaire of Louis Bonaparte* can be seen as an analysis of the unwillingness of the bourgeoisie to be agents of modernity. The political representatives of the property-owning classes were seen as handing power to Louis Napoleon because he was thought to provide the best protection against working-class revolution. The bourgeoisie, or at least their political representatives, were prepared to sacrifice their political power and abandon the democratic republic in order to preserve their economic power. Hence Emperor Napoleon III, as he became, was the agent by proxy of modernisation from above, accomplished through the imperial regime, since the bourgeoisie were frightened of realising modernity through a democratic republic. As Marx wrote of the Bonapartist regime, 'Industry and trade, i.e. the business affairs of the middle class, are to flourish under the strong government as in a hothouse. Hence the grant of innumerable railway concessions' (Marx, 1973b, p. 246).

Economic modernisation went hand in hand with political authoritarianism because the bourgeoisie were unwilling to assume the political responsibility required in a parliamentary democratic republic. The reason for this, in the classical Marxist tradition, was the fear of socialist revolution that gripped the property-owning classes, the bourgeoisie, in Germany in 1848, France in 1851 and Russia in the early twentieth century. 'The bourgeoisie' – those heroic agents of modernity, of economic and social progress, of throwing off tradition and creating the world market – were so haunted by the 'spectre of communism', the fear of social revolution, that even they grew half-hearted about the agenda of modernity. They came to realise that modernity could mean 'digging their own grave', in the sense that the further development of modernity would mean the rise of the proletariat and their political and social representatives, who in the Marxist perspective were better equipped to carry out the task of bringing modernity to fulfilment for the benefit of humanity as a whole. In Germany the bourgeoisie compromised with the Junkers, in France they accepted the authoritarian regime of Louis Napoleon, and in Russia they made only a feeble attempt to push for liberalisation and democratisation measures against the Tsarist system.

The socialist perspective was that the working-class movement would carry on where the bourgeoisie left off. The proletariat, the organised working class, would be the agent of modernity, and would bring humanity to a higher plane than the bourgeoisie ever could. The working class would become the ruling class, prior to the abolition of all classes and class rule generally. The expectation was that the working-class movement would represent a new community, a new society, built up on its capitalist predecessor, carrying on the work of modernity.

Problems of Marxism

What went wrong with this programme? Why has the socialist project not been fulfilled? Does it have any viability in the current epoch, however that epoch might be characterised? The core problem here is that the agents of modernity, the 'subject', were to be the members of the working class as they formed the majority of the population. Yet two further problems arose here, which have assumed a more acute form in today's world. The first was the question of the homogeneity of the 'subject', and the problem of representation and political power. The second was the problem of forces counteracting the modernising potential of this new subject.

In the Marxist perspective, the working-class movement would be the agent of modernity, a broader and deeper modernity in which the fetters or restrictions of capitalist production would be overcome. It would be the agent that socialised the productive forces for the benefit of all humanity. In an advanced, modern economy the working-class movement would not only be able to overcome its subordinate position in society, it would also be able to run that society, socialise the productive forces for the benefit of humanity, and overcome the crippling division of labour that blighted modernity's promise. However there remained deep divisions in this 'subject', the working class, and the need for political organisation created a separate grouping, the political party, which in Lenin's theory of the vanguard party played a very large role indeed. The Marxist project of revolution was one in which a cohesive subject, the working class or proletariat, would take power and bring the prehistory of humanity to a close with the realisation of modernity. This was premised on the collective subject developing its own awareness and identity, or in the language of Marxism, its own coherent class-consciousness. This would enable it to overcome the individualism and divisiveness of civil society, and for humanity to realise its own 'species-being'.

However there were a number of problems with this perspective. On the question of identity, the expectation was that human beings would shed other sources of identity such as religious and national affiliation, and in their place class loyalty would triumph, as part of a universal affiliation, in which particularistic identities would be lost.

Socialism and Emancipation 101

In this sense Marxism was the heir of the Enlightenment tradition, which insisted that human beings shared a common identity, and that social emancipation was a task in which rational beings everywhere could participate. The Marxist project was the same, at least in the sense that the rationalisation or modernisation of the capitalist system was seen as sweeping the globe, and hence people would become more alike and particular cultures and national identities would become lost. This comes out very clearly in the pages of *The Communist Manifesto* that deal with the process of globalisation, which is depicted as the heroic task of the bourgeoisie:

> In place of the old local and national seclusion and self-sufficiency, we have intercourse in every direction, universal interdependence of nations. And as in material, so also in intellectual production. The intellectual creations of individual nations become common property. National one-sidedness and narrow-mindedness become more and more impossible, and from the numerous national and local literatures, there arises a world literature (Marx, 1973a, p. 71).

This underestimated the degree of resistance there would be to the disruptive forces of modernity, which could and did take the form of religious, national or ethnic identity, which fragmented the idea of the unified 'subject', the agent of change. Hence just as the bourgeoisie had found it difficult to live up to their role as agents of modernity, so too did the body proposed by Marxism, because it was and remained divided by a variety of identities that also acted as barriers to modernity. Modernity meant disposing of the rubbish of past ages, getting rid of all 'the old muck' as Marx and Engels wrote in *The German Ideology*, and if the agent of this 'cleansing' remained affected by the 'muck' it could not be an effective agent of modernity. This stems from the basic problem that while modernity was progressive, laying down the preconditions for the new order, it was at the same time deeply disruptive and people needed identities to cling to as cushions against the disruptions of modernity. The politics of identity and nationalism was thus a key factor here.

The socialist project also involved a more profound aspiration, bound up with the sphere of production rather than the sphere of distribution, as is made clear in a recent study by Moishe Postone (1993). Postone distinguishes between what he calls 'traditional Marxism' and 'critical Marxism'. The gist of his argument is that traditional Marxism focused on the question of distribution. Capitalist society was seen as unjust because of its exploitative nature. Hence the working class did not receive the fruits of its labour.

However for Postone the Marxist critique went beyond this. The true concern of Marxism, the true nature of its critique of modernity, was that capitalism dominated all classes. It was not merely a question of the masses, the working classes, not receiving the distribution of the fruits of their labour, what was at stake was a particular structure of production in which labour, along with everything else, would become a commodity, a division of labour developed that would stultify human beings and their creative capacities. In Postone's words, 'the centre of his (Marx's) concern becomes the forms of wealth, labour and production of capitalism, rather than the form of distribution alone' (Postone, 1993, p. 57). As Postone further describes it, 'the capitalist-determined industrial mode of producing greatly increased humanity's productive power, but in an alienated form; hence this increased power also dominates the labouring individuals and is destructive of nature' (ibid., 1993, p. 68).

The solution that Marxist, and other, forms of socialism prescribed, and saw as 'immanent' in capitalism, was that the problems of modernity could only be dealt with through the development of modernity itself, and that capitalism was the unwitting agent of the unfolding of modernity. The capitalist mode of production not only massively developed the means of production, made possible the conquest of nature and the development of new needs, it also spread the new productive powers throughout the globe. In this sense Marxism appears not at all out-of-date but enormously prophetic, emphasising the globalisation of capitalist production and the fact that the production of commodities and the search for new markets brings all areas of the world into its reach.

However the Marxist perspective was not only an analysis of capitalism as developing modernity, it was also an analysis of the agent that would both carry on the work of modernity and at the same time gather the results of modernity for the benefit of humanity as a whole, in ways that the capitalist model could not. Through the agency of the working-class movement, modernity would be carried to its conclusion and yet in a sense transcended. The division of labour, which stultified and crippled human powers, would be overcome, but at the same time – and this is one of the problems of Marxism – the benefits of modernity would be maintained. Modernity was to be developed to its highest point, yet organised in a rational way that was not possible in 'civil society'. The civil society model was to be rejected: in other words the idea of an individualistic, competitive society was not one that could satisfy the social and creative nature of human beings, realise their 'species being'. An alternative model of modernity could only be realised after the transcendence of capitalism. It would in a sense realise the best of both worlds, the technological sophistication and modernity that capitalism had developed, but without the antagonisms that crippled civil society and the individuals who comprised it.

Socialism in Crisis?

The present crisis of socialism stems from the very modernity that Marxism itself so thoroughly analysed. The strength of Marxist analysis was precisely in its revelation of the 'commodification' of all aspects of human life, the remorseless encroachment of the market in its capitalist form on all areas of life, geographical as well as metaphorical. Yet Marshall Berman asked a pertinent question when he wrote:

> Even if the workers do build a successful communist *movement*, and even if that movement generates a successful revolution, how, amid the flood tides of modern life, will they ever manage to build a solid communist *society*? What is to prevent the social forces that melt capitalism from melting communism as well? (Berman, 1983, p. 104)

The Marxist analysis of modernity was that its capitalist form provided the basis for socialism to preserve the gains of modernity and overcome its disintegrative features, such as the division of labour, the commodification of all aspects of life and the creation of the 'cash nexus' as the only bond between human beings. Yet from the perspective of the late twentieth century it could be said that two things have happened: the process of modernity in its capitalist form has not led to the supersession of capitalism, but to its being given a renewed and extended lease of life; and in those societies where a single brand of Marxism (Soviet communism or Bolshevism) triumphed, the attempt was made to realise the modernist programme, to build modernity by design, by means of revolution from above.

Because of the generally low material base from which this attempt was launched, and because of the dictatorial political means that were employed, communism/Bolshevism was a very poor agent of modernity in comparison with its capitalist version. The Bolshevik revolution, or rather its aftermath, did represent the fullest attempt to remould society: the creation or forced development of an industrial base was seen as the necessary condition for the politics of modernity. Nevertheless while Stalinism did manage, at devastating cost in human terms, to build up an infrastructure of heavy industry, the total lack of democracy during the Stalinist period persisted after his death, although there was no further recourse to his unrestrained and all-encompassing terror tactics.

Largely because of the domination of the one-party system, Soviet society became rigid, incapable of allowing an autonomous 'civil society' to develop and therefore unable to allow the growth, except in a constrained and stifled way, of a modern, pluralistic and economically progressive society. Hence the revolution from above unleashed by Stalin was a distortion of Marxism, and created an authoritarian system that prevented the full emergence of a modern and diverse civil society.

Just such a society was the aim of Gorbachev's *perestroika*. Yet this could not be brought about within the straitjacket of even a reformed one-party system, and hence the continued modernisation of Soviet society (and other such systems) was incompatible with the communist version, or distortion, of socialism. Communist society collapsed under the weight of widespread protests and diverse political and social movements, some of which were no friends of modernity. Hence the argument is that socialism in the twentieth century, in its Bolshevik/communist version, did not live up to its Marxist promise of being the agent of modernity. This was because of a number of factors that were specific to that distorted form of socialism. Chief among these were the severe economic circumstances that led to the Bolshevik revolution, and the undemocratic nature of the instrument of revolution: Lenin's 'vanguard party' which after the revolution provided the framework for the organisation of all social and political life. This rigid structure functioned as the agent of forced modernisation, in a process imitating or perhaps parodying capitalist modernisation. The Soviet economist Preobrazhensky had warned that a process of 'primitive socialist accumulation' would need to be undertaken by the Bolshevik regime, and he told his fellow Bolsheviks that 'we do not live yet in a socialist society with its production for the consumer – we live under the iron heel of the law of primitive socialist accumulation' (Deutscher, 1970, p. 108).

This form of socialist accumulation did indeed succeed in developing an industrial infrastructure, but by means of a society atomised and dominated by the one-party system, once Stalin's dictatorship of terror was ended by his death in 1953. The absence of any autonomous civil society or forms of pluralist democracy, and the centralisation of economic decisions in a rigid planning apparatus remained as huge obstacles to the modernisation and democratisation of the Soviet system in the post-Stalin period.

Thus the Bolshevik or communist version of socialism collapsed, having failed to live up to the revolutionary promise that socialism would harness the fruits of modernity far better than the bourgeoisie could ever do. Nor has what one recent survey called 'the great crisis of socialism' (Sassoon, 1996, p. 645) spared communism's twentieth-century rival, namely social democracy, represented by organised parties operating within the framework of liberal-democratic politics, parties that in the conditions of late-twentieth century politics 'are the only Left that is left' (ibid., p. 777). Here too the discussion needs to focus on the theme of socialism and modernity. The social-democratic aim can be defined as humanising and reforming capitalism, and the history of 'one hundred years of socialism' is well summed up by Donald Sassoon in terms of a transformation of socialism and its goals: 'At its origins the socialist movement had the ambition of leading the workers towards self-emancipation; one hundred years later, the goals were more modest and not centred on workers' (ibid., p. 690).

The classical Marxist view was, as discussed above, that the bourgeoisie would be unable to bring the process of modernity to its conclusion, and that this task would fall to the working-class movement as the new and increasingly unified and self-conscious subject of history. In the Bolshevik model of Marxism this transformation would be achieved through a tightly organised party, bringing class consciousness to the workers. In the classical social-democratic perspective, on the other hand, it would be realised through a mass party supported by the majority of the electorate, the workers as the majority of the population. In this sense socialism would emerge through reforms that humanised capitalism and developed modernity in that way. Social democracy, and the socialist parties that were its agents, coexisted with capitalism, seeking the terms of such coexistence in three areas – politics, society and economy – through extending political democracy by the introduction of universal suffrage and civil rights; through the creation and extension of the welfare state by implementing social rights; and through economic reforms to regulate the labour market and take key industries into public ownership (ibid., p. 765). In this way socialism would create a regulated and humanised form of capitalism whose benefits would be extended to all the population, who would become full citizens and economic beneficiaries of a capitalist system where the anarchy of the market had been tamed by an interventionist state.

This social-democratic perspective can claim full validity within the Marxist tradition. Engels' 1895 preface to the reissue of Marx's text of 1848, *The Class Struggles in France*, spoke of the irrelevance of streetfighting and barricades, and saluted the use of the ballot as the means of working-class emancipation: 'We, the "revolutionists", the "overthrowers" – we are thriving far better on legal methods than on illegal methods and overthrow' (Marx and Engels, 1973, vol. I, p. 202). The Austro-Marxist Otto Bauer spoke of the working class as coming to share in the national culture from which they had been hitherto excluded because of its monopolisation by the ruling class (Bottomore and Goode, 1978). In his 1899 text Edouard Bernstein wrote that social democracy 'ceaselessly labours to raise the worker from the social position of a proletarian to that of a citizen (*Bürger*) and thus to make citizenship universal' (Bernstein, 1993, p. 146). Socialism for Bernstein was 'organised liberalism', a movement that was carrying to fruition the great emancipation started by liberalism. He argued that while liberalism had initially benefited the bourgeoisie, this was only a result of historical circumstances: 'The circumstance that, at first, it [liberalism] strictly maintained the form of bourgeois liberalism did not prevent it from expressing, in actual fact, a much more far-reaching general principle of society, the fulfilment of which will be socialism' (ibid., p. 150).

All these different contributions of Engels, Bernstein and Bauer express a similar idea: that through majority-backed and peaceful transition, socialist movements, unless provoked by ruling-class violence into insurrection, would complete the task of modernity begun by liberalism, but which the bourgeoisie were unable to bring to fruition because of their class-bound interests. Hence social democracy as a movement democratically expressing the interests of the majority would complete the process begun in 1789 by the bourgeoisie. The socialist movement would achieve citizenship rights for the majority of society, the non-property-owning classes. Democratic political rights would extend to the economy, society (welfare rights) and not least culture, as emphasised by Bauer, so that the working class would share in the national culture and become members of the nation in a cultural sense. The socialist movement thus claimed admission to the nation: 'the socialisation of the nation has as its corollary the nationalisation of socialism' (Carr, 1945, p. 19). Socialism as an ideology and social democracy as a movement were jointly premised on the three pillars of modernity defined earlier: the centrality of industrial production (hence of the proletariat as the majority class in a capitalist society); that the nation-state and the political institutions of liberal democracy would furnish the structures through which the majority working-class movement would come to power; and the removal of class division in society, even if Bernstein acknowledged that the Marxist prediction of 'two great hostile camps' was not being actually realised. Bernstein suggested that instead of society being polarised the evolutionary trend was an increase in the number of those making up the intermediate strata of society.

Hence the implication was that social democracy as a movement would complete the transition to modernity, and was itself the product of the social developments that characterised modernity. Modernity involved a social structure and form of production in which the industrial proletariat formed the majority class, and where the organisation and control of the productive resources of society depended on socialist transformation, achieved democratically and without violent revolution. Socialism produced modernity, modernity helped to produce socialism, and social democracy and its mass organised parties were both the vehicles and the beneficiaries of this process.

However, the relationship between socialism in its social-democratic form and full development of modernity was more problematic than expected, leading to 'the great crisis of socialism' as part of the wider crisis of modernity and the ideologies that sprang from modernity. To quote once more from Sassoon's wide-ranging survey of the West European Left in the twentieth century,

The crisis of the socialist and social-democratic tradition in Western Europe is not the crisis of an ideology defeated by the superior political and organisational strength of its opponents – as communism has been. It is an integral component of a fin-de-siècle turmoil reshaping the planet at momentous speed (Sassoon, 1996, p. 773).

This turmoil altered what Bernstein called 'the preconditions of socialism', so that the relationship between socialism and modernity became problematic in a society in which modernity was itself transformed.

This chapter thus ends with a brief statement on the crisis of socialism, whose implications will be explored further below. Modernity created the agent of socialism (the majority working class), the economic preconditions for socialism (a predominantly industrial society) and the framework (the democratic nation-state) through which the peaceful assumption of power could be achieved. The democratic nation-state provided the state power required to socialise and regulate the economy. However the development of modernity in some ways undermined those preconditions for socialism, and this led to its present 'great crisis', which is also a crisis for other ideologies of modernity. Modernity has led to postmodernity, a society in which the working class has become fragmented, disunited and just one of a range of different agencies. It now shares its transformative role with a wide variety of social, ethnic, national and religious movements, which in some situations may have a much more powerful appeal than class. In the words of a contemporary sociologist, 'Societies are confusing battlegrounds on which multiple power networks fight over our souls. In modern societies, class is just one of the more important forms of self-identity' (Mann, 1993, p. 28). Hence the development of postmodernity has undermined the cohesion and identity of that agent of change (the organised working class) in which classical Marxism and early-twentieth-century social democracy invested their hopes for revolution and reform.

By the same token, contemporary developments have given greater weight to people's identity as individual consumers, who find their freedom and identity in separate and disaggregated acts of purchasing and consuming commodities. The reform of capitalism, of which social democracy was such a powerful agent, has rebounded against the further development of socialism or social democracy, because greater purchasing power and the ingenuity of capitalism in furthering the process of modernity by producing ever more goods and commodities of ever increasing sophistication, has made people's individual acts of consumption more salient than their propensity for collective struggle and group (class) identity. 'In Western Europe', according to Sassoon, 'the main achievement of socialism in the last hundred years has been the civilising of capitalism' (Sassoon, 1996, p. 767). However the problem may be that this 'civilising of capitalism' has undermined or at least reduced the popular appeal of these institutions and organisations that formed the socialist counter society, and were meant to prefigure an alternative collective society.

In this sense socialism in its twentieth-century form could para-doxically be said to be the saviour rather than the grave digger of capitalism. Socialist theorists and movements did indeed develop the theme of modernity and call for its continued progress, but this served to give capitalism a new lease of life and defer indefinitely, perhaps for all time, the idea of socialism as an alternative society, collectively organised and a better representative of modernity than its capitalist rival.

By the same token, the continued development of modernity has helped to undermine the 'regulatory framework' of capitalism (ibid.), namely the nation-state, and this has hindered the social-democratic agenda of regulating and humanising capitalism, let alone transcend-ing it for an alternative society. The collapse of the Soviet model may have removed from the scene an undemocratic model that could be used by opponents of socialism to tar all socialists with the Soviet brush, but it also dealt a blow to ideas of collective provision and centralised regulation of the economy, spawning a search for alter-native models of 'market socialism' that can reconcile market dis-tribution with the idea of social ownership of productive resources (Pierson, 1995).

In short, the socialist perspective from the beginning was that modernity would lead to, and could only be realised by, a socialist society. Socialist movements harnessed the masses for this end, organising them into well-structured social-democratic parties for the capture of power. Yet the dilemma of socialism, its crisis in both theory and practice as the age of ideology draws to a possible close, is that capitalism, rather than socialism, could be the main beneficiary of 'the civilising of capitalism' that socialist movements have striven for throughout the course of twentieth-century politics. In that sense, no less than liberalism, socialism as an ideology is facing a crisis arising from the deep changes in modernity itself. This crisis is analysed further in Part III of this book.

5

Conservative Critiques

In the preceding chapters the aim has been to explain the core features of the politics of modernity, and the impact of the two revolutions that created the agenda for the politics of modernity and its core assumptions. Liberalism and socialism, in quite different ways, emerged as ideologies and social movements from this revolutionary conjuncture of events. They sought to bring to fruition the core themes of modernity, and the modernist perspective is seen as the key to understanding the preoccupations and tensions of these two ideological families.

The purpose of this chapter and the following one is somewhat different: to examine the paradoxical relationship that conservatism and nationalism have had with the politics and assumptions of modernity. Both ideologies can be thought of as products of a new type of society, and as essentially creatures of the modern age. Yet both nationalism (at least in some of its forms) and conservatism were protests against and critiques of modernity, and derived much of their strength and appeal from their perception of its disruptive effects. Conservative theorists invoked the idea of an organic and hierarchical society, in which people knew their place yet were related to each other as part of a totality. However, that organic unity and the bonds that held society together were being torn apart by the relentless progress of modernity and commercial relationships. Conservatives lamented the fragmentary and disassociated character of modernity, its capacity to make all relationships ones of individual competition and instrumental calculation.

In certain respects the conservative and socialist critiques shared common themes, even if they did not agree on the solutions to the problems they diagnosed. They shared a critical stance towards the atomistic and unsettling effects of modernity, as expressed through modernity's tearing asunder the bonds of community, and its creation of a world in which disassociated individuals regarded each other only, or primarily, as means by which to satisfy their own ends. For at least some of those who contributed to the rich and diverse tradition of conservative thinking the solution lay in the return to a preindustrial society, to a community linked once more by the ties of tradition and mutual obligation that industrial society and modernity had so powerfully rent apart.

However the house of conservative, or right-wing, thought has many mansions, ranging from the resolute antimodernism of theorists such as de Maistre, with his ideas of 'throne and altar' to the 'radical right' currents that culminated in fascism. Fascist thinkers saluted the dizzy onward rush of modernity, and saw in this a sign of the feebleness of reason, the superiority of emotional and irrational attitudes towards life that denied the cold Enlightenment tradition of reason and measure. Only through the dynamic of modernity could human beings realise their true nature, that was to be controlled by an all-powerful leader who could achieve a higher form of community purged of the democratic, liberal and generally rationalistic features of the Enlightenment tradition.

Conservatism was critical of modernity while at the same time being its product. Traditional conservatism developed as a passionate protest against the disintegrating tendencies of modernity, and against the market as spreading these tendencies to the organic, hierarchical and traditional society that certain conservative thinkers saw as the ideal. It was an ideal which to them had existed in medieval society, in which people had found their identity in a God-given, traditionally fixed community. Such a society was the antithesis of modernity, with its emphasis on progress, rationality and individuality, all encapsulated in the new 'civil society' celebrated by thinkers of the Scottish Enlightenment such as Adam Ferguson. The paradox is, however, that throughout the age of ideology this anti-modernist philosophy of conservatism remained able, at least in some of its guises, to stimulate mass support, thus enabling conservatism to remain a key player in the age of ideology. The core problem therefore remains of how a philosophy that emerged as profoundly anti-modernist was able to survive and gain mass support when it viewed with fear and disdain the rise of the masses and other central features of modernity.

While thinkers of the conservative camp had a strong grasp of some of the negative features of modernity, their solutions to the problems of modernity were inadequate. Nevertheless any account of the politics of modernity has to take account of conservatism as it provided some of the most acute and insightful critiques of the process.

Defining 'the Right'

The term 'conservatism' is somewhat inadequate to describe the entire body of thought that is the subject of this chapter as it implies a wish to 'conserve' the existing order, to defend what is in place. Yet there were many who opposed modernity but did not wish to preserve the existing order and were severe critics of established institutions. The criticism of the Enlightenment tradition and the assumptions of modernity does not necessarily equate with defence of the existing order, and here the concept of the 'radical Right' comes into play. In post-revolutionary France the radical Right – the 'Ultras' or 'White Jacobins' – vehemently opposed the radical revolutionary tradition, yet were equally hostile to the existing liberal order, which was seen as a vain attempt to accept some of the ideas of 1789. Another problem with the term 'conservatism' is that it has too British a ring about it, with its connotations of one particular political party and its continuing history.

'The Right' refers in general to that complex body of thought that emerged in reaction to the changes created by the American and French Revolutions, and challenged the onward march of modernity. As described earlier, the term 'the Right' arose from the seating arrangements in the French Constituent Assembly of 1789. Those who sat on the right of the president's chair were those who wished to restrain the pace of change, to defend the existing order from the attacks of the revolutionaries (Gauchet, 1992).

'The Right' in its most general sense denotes a philosophy that was hostile to the politics of modernity, with its ideas of emancipation and rationality. In this connection 'the Right' refers to the movements and parties that shared this anti-Enlightenment and anti-modernist philosophy. 'The Right' is also used as an umbrella term for a wide range of heterogeneous perspectives, united by their rejection of Enlightenment ideas and revolutionary change but marked by strong divergences.

Much of the scholarly literature on the politics and philosophy of the Right is concerned with developing a typology of the differences and divergences within this common right-wing tradition. One example of such a typology is that developed by the French historian and political scientist René Rémond in *Les Droites en France* (1992). Rémond makes the fundamental point that there is no one Right, but several Rights. His analysis is specifically developed with reference to the French Right, and he argues that the course of French history and politics has revealed three forms of Right, a traditionalist Right, an Orleanist Right, and a Bonapartist Right. The first of these is exemplified by theorists such as de Maistre and the Legitimists in post-Restoration France. Traditionalist politics emphasised a God-given natural order that was strictly authoritarian and hierarchical, and had no truck with the revolution or the post-revolutionary society. It was quite clearly anti-modernist and wished to return to a golden age, with Church and State presiding in strict harmony over a hierarchically structured society. In the conditions of post-1815 France, Legitimists did not want to 'conserve' the existing framework. They wished rather to overthrow it through a monarchist *coup d'état*, and return to the sort of society that had existed (or they thought had existed) before what they considered as the evil days of 1789.

This current of thought was later taken up by the monarchist thinker Charles Maurras and his organisation *Action Française*, formed in 1899 in the aftermath of the Dreyfus case, which so bitterly divided France. This organisation wanted to overthrow the democratic republic and replace popular sovereignty by a monarchical regime. Its political programme was explained in the manifesto *Dictateur et Roi* of 1899, which proclaimed the desire to combine local liberty with strong centralised power (McClelland, 1970, pp. 213–38). According to Maurras, the democratic republic was marked by anarchy at the top, where firm control was needed, and through centralisation it had created dictatorship at the bottom by refusing to allow local diversity and provincial autonomy. Restoration of the monarchy would create unity of command at the seat of the state, through the monarch, and decentralisation at the local level, through provincial autonomy.

Rémond contrasts the traditionalist Right, which refused any accommodation with the post-revolutionary order, with the Orleanist Right, which was more parliamentary and liberal, more inclined to accept the gains of the French Revolution, at least in its liberal stage, and rejected any notion of violently overthrowing the existing regime in order to revert to an earlier hierarchical society. The Orleanist Right could be called with some justification a 'conservative' Right, since it wished to conserve the features of the post-1815 parliamentary state and condemned any form of extremism. While elitist in its politics, in a limited way it accepted the modernist idea of individual rights and liberty. However it firmly rejectied the socialist idea of collectivism or other attack on private property. The Orleanist Right could be likened to a Burkean style of politics, which accepted the need for limited political change in response to new demands, but was deeply opposed to radical, wholesale transformation of the political system. In this respect the Orleanist (or Burkean) type of right-wing politics was less anti-modernist than the Legitimists. Both, however, rejected the central feature of modernity: the involvement of the masses in politics.

The third form of the French Right identified by Rémond was the Bonapartist Right, which unlike the previous two forms of right-wing politics looked to the masses: while opposed to democracy and popular sovereignty, it encouraged mass participation and popular involvement. According to Rémond, this third form of the Right was exemplified by the Bonapartism of the nineteenth century. The authoritarian leader who later became Emperor Napoleon III sought popular legitimacy for his power by appealing over the head of representative parliamentary institutions directly to the masses through plebiscitary politics and referenda. Another example of this form of politics was the French fascist leagues of the interwar period, which sought to mobilise the masses against the parliamentary system of Third Republic France. Through the use of demagogic and populist rhetoric these leagues appealed to the people directly over the heads of the elites of the parliamentary order, who were accused of having usurped power from the people. This form of right-wing politics can be seen as a particularly insiduous and dangerous way of opposing modernity, in the sense that it paid lip service to the idea of popular participation and popular sovereignty, and yet used the masses to bolster authoritarian politics and personal despotism.

The Bonapartist Right had much in common with fascism, and Bonapartism and the populist leagues in 1930s France can be seen as anticipating fascism as a style of right-wing politics. Fascism can be defined as mass-based authoritarianism, using the political apparatus and devices of modernity as means of overthrowing democracy and bolstering personal power.

Thus concurrent with the onset of the politics of modernity there developed a set of ideas and movements that challenged the principles of emancipation and enlightenment that were part of that process of modernity. These ideas and movements were of a diverse nature, ranging from traditional conservatism to the more pragmatic style of

Orleanist/Burkean conservatism and the mass-based authoritarianism which culminated in fascism.

Conservatism and Modernity

What is the conservative critique of modernity? Here 'conservatism' means, at least initially, what could be called traditionalist conservatism, whose chief theorists were Burke in England, the more abrasive Joseph de Maistre in France and the theorists of the German Romantic tradition, for example Adam Müller. Not that all these 'traditional conservatives' shared the same ideas: for example the obvious contrast is between the more moderate and pragmatic form of conservatism expressed by Burke and the far more violent and irrationalist critique of the French Revolution mounted by de Maistre, who condemned the revolution as 'Satanic' and 'pure impurity'. He has been seen as anticipating the origins of fascism, rather than of conservatism, in his emphasis on the need for a violent purge of the revolution, whose sins in his opinion could only be wiped out by blood (Berlin, 1991). Nevertheless, allowing for these differences, a common critique of modernity can be discerned in the writings of traditionalist conservatives, and also elements of a common solution to the ills of modernity. This solution is couched in terms of the creation, or recreation, of the type of community that was disrupted by the onset of modernity.

The new society that was developing at the end of the eighteenth century and found its philosophical justification in the principles of Enlightenment philosophy and liberal economics, was criticised for its individualism and was seen as dissolving the bonds of society. The German Romantics in particular presented the Middle Ages or feudal period in terms of a golden age, in which all people were linked in an organic and unified – though of course unequal – community. The coming of modern society had changed all that, or so these theorists held. Revolutionary change was condemned not just as individualistic and egalitarian, but as (certainly for de Maistre) destructive of authority and social cohesion, and as leaving people 'free' in an entirely frightening sense: free from the traditions and customs that gave them their identity and morality. In Burke's indictment of the French Revolution, *Reflections on the Revolution in France*, it was deemed better to let people follow what he called 'prejudice and prescription' than to abandon them to their individual reason, which was a weak reed upon which to rely. By 'prejudice and prescription' Burke meant the traditions of the particular society, and the customary ways of doing things in that society. The onset of modernity was seen by conservative thinkers as taking away from people the guidance afforded by these customs and practices, so that they were left helpless in a world where tradition could no longer offer them any accepted guide for action.

It is clear that for conservative thinkers, reason was a dangerous enemy, and the praise of reason that they saw as inherent in the Enlightenment tradition led them to oppose that tradition. The three thinkers mentioned above (Burke, de Maistre and Müller) shared a common fear that modernist philosophy, the philosophy of the Enlightenment, would lead to a revolutionary transformation of politics, and to the spread of ideas of democracy that these thinkers saw as deeply destructive of the traditional hierarchical society they defended, or wanted to restore. Modernity was criticised as individualistic, disruptive of community, hierarchy and authority, and for opening the way to dangerously democratic ideas of equality and popular sovereignty. For all these thinkers the French Revolution, with its reign of terror, was the inevitable result of modernity. Burke in particular warned of the creation of a new style and philosophy of politics, based on abstract ideas and on rationalistic philosophy, which threatened to sweep away the institutions, customs and traditions that had built up over past generations and afforded people a sense of continuity and identity.

In his recent intellectual biography of Burke, *The Great Melody*, the scholar Conor Cruise O'Brien makes the case that Burke was not a reactionary and in some ways not a conservative. Burke's constant concern was the abuse of power, the creation of a dominating state that knew no limits (O'Brien, 1993). O'Brien's analysis takes as its *leitmotif* the following lines from Yeats:

> American colonies, Ireland, France and India
> Harried, and Burke's great melody against it.

What was the 'it' against which Burke 'harried'? According to O'Brien, the 'it' at stake in all these issues was the danger of power. On this interpretation Burke, who is commonly seen as the father of British conservatism, was not so much a conservative, or even a critic of modernity, but rather a liberal, welcoming the onset of modernity and warning of the dangers of the extreme radicalism of the French

Revolution because that revolution had created a new form of tyranny. This interpretation of Burke suggests, contrary to what is argued here, that he was not an antagonist of modernity as such, but a defender of liberty against unrestricted state power, a critic of the French Revolution and its creation of the new collective sovereignty of the people, which could only result in tyranny.

There was a definite contrast between Burke's conciliatory attitude towards the American Revolution and his harsh condemnation of the French Revolution. This can be explained by his view that the two revolutions were animated by contrasting philosophies. Burke 'was favourable to the Americans, because he supposed they were fighting, not to acquire absolute speculative liberty, but to keep what they had under the English constitution' (O'Brien, 1993, p. 427). Unlike the American Revolution, according to Burke the French Revolution was based on a philosophy of abstract metaphysical rights, that is, on a purely rationalist philosophy, which spoke of the rights of man and citizen in universalist terms, as being true of human beings everywhere, at all times and in all places, and it was this that he saw as dangerous.

Burke's attitude towards the American Revolution, and the themes enunciated in his pre-French-Revolutionary writings generally, were more moderate than his thundering denunciation of the Jacobins and the other French revolutionaries. Burke's writings on Ireland, where he opposed discrimination against Catholics, even offered a defence of popular sovereignty:

> Now as a law directed against the mass of the nation has not the nature of a reasonable institution, so neither has it the authority: for in all forms of government the people is the true legislator; and whether the immediate and instrumental cause of the law be a single person or many, the remote and the efficient cause is the consent of the people, either actual or implied; and such consent is absolutely essential to its validity (quoted in ibid., p. 41).

It seems strange that Burke, the great enemy of the French Revolution with its ideas of popular sovereignty, would propose that the consent of the people was necessary for the legitimacy of a law. However O'Brien makes the convincing case that Burke's defence of the American colonists rested on the same core ideas as his attack on the French revolutionaries, namely that circumstances must be the best guide to political conduct, and that it was necessary to avoid excessive rationalism in politics. He pointed to the dangers of basing political conduct on general and universal laws. As Burke stated in his speech of 22 March 1774, in defence of 'Conciliation with America':

> I set out . . . with a profound reverence for the wisdom of our ancestors, who have left us the inheritance of so happy a Constitution and so flourishing an empire, and, what is a thousand times more valuable, the treasury of the maxims and principles which formed the one and obtained the other (Burke, 1993, p. 240).

Thus the point at issue is whether Burke's moderate defence of the American Revolution and his undoubted 'modernity' in economic matters undermines the idea of a common conservative critique and attack on the principles of modernity. He definitely defended the new commercial society of which England (and America) were examples, as he condemned interference with free trade:

> We are going to restrict by a positive arbitrary Regulation the enjoyment of the profits which should be made in commerce. I suppose there is nothing like this to be found in the Code of Laws in any civilised society upon Earth – you are going to cancel the great line which distinguishes free government (quoted in O'Brien, 1993, p. 260).

Nevertheless Burke's attack on the French Revolution was couched in terms of certain assumptions that were common to all thinkers of traditional conservatism: the assumption of a God-given natural order of society, which had evolved gradually over the ages, and whose continuity and traditions gave it a divine legitimacy that individual reason could never attain.

Conservatives saw the onset of modernity as the manifestation of a rationalist attitude towards politics. Burke was suspicious of and de Maistre downright antagonistic to reason, in particular the reason of the individual. They saw this as subversive of the traditional hierarchy of society, which offered individuals a clearly defined position in the world, linked to others in society in a 'great chain of being' (which extended beyond the human world to include God above and animals below).

de Maistre went much further than Burke in his excoriation of individual reason, which he thought was quite incompatible with authority in social matters. He saw political sovereignty as requiring absolute authority, which would be impossible if individuals could apply their critical reason to political matters. Indeed de Maistre insisted that government was a dogma, like theology it needed its own priests and the imposition on individuals of fixed beliefs. To this end the nascent critical reason of individuals had to be submerged into what he called 'the national mind':

> Man's nascent reason should be curbed under a double yoke; it should be frustrated, and it should lose itself in the national mind, so that it changes its individual existence for another communal existence, just as a river which flows into the ocean still exists in the mass of water, but without name and distinct reality (Maistre, 1965, p. 109).

The cradle of the infant should be surrounded by dogma so that the emerging adult would not come to question the structure of authority. In the thoughts of de Maistre the critique of reason reached a level never attained by Burke, and this is perhaps why de Maistre has been seen as the anticipator of fascism rather than belonging to the school of traditional conservatism. de Maistre welcomed violence and praised the role of the executioner in holding society together. He thought the blood and suffering that had accompanied the French Revolution were providential, God's way of punishing the presumption of human beings in taking seriously the Enlightenment view that human beings could construct a rational and organised society. This idea of 'constructivism' was a central pillar of the politics of modernity. Both Burke and de Maistre, admittedly to significantly different degrees, were opponents of this assumption; they thought that only God could create, and that attempts by human beings to bring into being new constitutions and new political institutions were as doomed as attempts to build a house on sand. Only divine foundations were secure, and for de Maistre these were manifested in the traditional institutions of society, backed up by the Catholic Church, which had endured for a long period of time. He saw the proliferation of legislation in the French revolutionary period and the succession of constitutions after 1789 as signs of the fragility of human constitution-building and of the absurdity of attempts to create a rational society on Earth.

In this respect the conservative critique manifested itself as an attack on some of the most fundamental assumptions of the politics of modernity. The whole thrust of modernity was to insist on the supremacy of reason, and the ability of human beings to recreate their society, to throw off the weight of tradition and as Kant put it in his essay 'What is Enlightenment?', 'dare to know', to emerge from the tutelage of the established authorities and traditions and stand on their own feet in matters of belief. The conservative counter-attack held that this was an impossibility, and that the wisdom built up over the past through continuity and tradition, accumulated over generations, was far greater than that which any particular individual could attain, or than could be laid down in any code of laws or statement of abstract rights.

This, then, was the critique of modernity as enunciated by conservative thinkers who sought to cut human reason down to size. Modernity was criticised because it set human beings adrift from each other, from the traditional bonds between them, and from those very rules and habits that gave them some orientation in a rapidly changing world.

The Organic Community

If such were the main lines of the traditional conservative critique of modernity, and all its works, two questions arise: what solutions did conservative thinkers offer to the dilemmas of modernity, as they saw them, and how did the Right, in its different manifestations, survive the age of modernity?

In general terms the solution offered by thinkers of classical, or traditional, conservatism was the goal of community, some kind of organic unity that had to be restored in the face of the disintegrative tendencies of modern market society. In some of its forms this vision of an organic society was reactionary, a wish to revert to a (mythical) golden age of community and hierarchy. For de Maistre, faced with the reality of post-Revolutionary France, community could only be restored through a coup d'état, by putting the monarch back on the throne and recreating the order and hierarchy that revolutionary ideas had so rudely destroyed. Burke's vision of community was less reactionary and backward looking. He shared much of the more positive liberal attitude towards modernity, as indicated by the quotation given above attacking restrictions on commerce. Indeed Marx mocked Burke for claiming that 'the laws of commerce were the laws of God', and for being a defender of (highly modern) *laissez-faire* (Marx, 1977, p. 711).

Yet basic to Burke's thought, as to that of de Maistre, was the subordination of human reason to the requirements of tradition and defence of a hierarchical society. For Burke this was not backward looking, it was not a question of restoring the prerevolutionary hierarchy. The style of politics which he defended was a profoundly empirical one, seeking reforms when necessary, rejecting *a priori* principles and intellectual abstractions, and insisting on the need for reform rather than revolution. In his great polemic of 1790 against the French Revolution, *Reflections on the Revolution in France*, Burke inveighed against the revolutionaries for being intellectuals, 'for knowing nothing of politics except the passions they excite', and above all for being concerned with abstract metaphysical rights rather than particular rights gained and recognised under a particular legal and political system. Hence his distinction between the American and the French Revolutions, and indeed also his contrast between the revolutions in 1688 in England and 1789 in France. The American Revolution and that of 1688, which indeed Burke denied was a revolution at all, appealed, he argued, to rights recognised in the English system of law, based on precedent and circumstances, whereas the French Revolution invoked the general 'rights of man and citizen', which Burke called 'metaphysical' rights.

Traditional conservatism therefore operated in line with an idea of organic community, which could take more or less backward-looking forms. This suggests the idea of unity, of cohesion, and the appeal of conservatism in its various forms was precisely this idea of a community with particular traditions, built up over time to form a nation with its own history, language and culture. This is not to say that conservatism and nationalism are the same, and the following chapter explores the ambiguities of nationalism. However conservative thinkers made powerful critiques of modernity and the costs of modernity.

The continuing appeal of conservative parties, their survival in the age of modernity and mass politics, and the effectiveness of conservatism had much to do with the emphasis on community. The German Romantic variety of conservatism also promoted the idea of a national community, and rejected the Enlightenment ideas of reason and science. As noted by Hans Reiss, 'It [German Romanticism] sought to approach social and philosophical problems not, as the *Aufklärung* did, by the method of scientific analysis, by testing a hypothesis in the light of experience, but rather through the working of intuitive insight and of the imaginative faculties' (Reiss, 1955, p. 4).

Reiss also notes that the German Romantics in the period after the French Revolution 'were opposed to all abstractions, they also attacked the School of Natural Law which, in the last stage of its development, had as its distinguishing mark an abstract rationalism'. The ideas of natural law appeared to the German Romantics 'to be the harbingers, if not the creators, of the political radicalism of the American and French revolutionaries which the German Romantics condemned absolutely' (ibid.).

The ideas of Burke, de Maistre and the German Romantics cannot easily be lumped together under the single heading of 'conservatism'. Yet they all stressed the need for organic unity, community and social cohesion, sometimes through quite authoritarian means, such as the throne and altar hierarchy of de Maistre, and the need for an ordered structure of authority. The paradox is that this reaction against modernity was itself a product of modernity: where tradition had been attacked, in an epoch when the revolutions in America and France had overturned the traditional structure of authority, then the need was felt to defend or show the desirable features of the organic unity and community that had been lost. The search for community and social cohesion to counter the disintegrating effects of modernity was common to both socialists and conservatives of various sorts. However the latter thought this could be achieved by restoring a vanished medieval world of authority, or, for Burke, by accepting the economic structure of modernity but tempering it with tradition and an imposed hierarchy to mitigate the divisive and atomistic effects of modernity.

The strength of conservatism, its ability to survive in the modern age, resided in this vision of community and integration, resting on a different view of human nature from the ones that grounded the politics of modernity. As a reaction to the spread of industry, the upheaval of the industrial revolution and the growth of uniformity, conservatism held out the prospect of individual communities, each with its own traditions, history and character. As Ronald Beiser has shown in his study of German Romantic thought, the concept of historicism, which was fundamental to the German Romantics, involved the unique and organic nature of distinct national cultures, which made individuals what they were (Beiser, 1992). Rather than the glib assumptions of some crude versions of Enlightenment thought that the world could be started afresh from scratch, that human nature was infinitely perfectible, conservative thinkers instead referred to the weight of the past and the danger of setting people loose from familiar traditions and contexts, to the weakness of rationality and the need to form bonds in society.

Yet while the various thinkers offered a vision of social cohesion, they had a profoundly inegalitarian and hierarchical view of community that went against the democratic and egalitarian strands of modernity. In their different ways, all the thinkers considered in this section (Burke, de Maistre, German Romantics such as Fichte and Müller) presented society as naturally hierarchical, with a traditional aristocracy (a monarch in the case of de Maistre and Burke) presiding over a society in which everyone knew his or her place. Hence it was a static society, at odds with the dynamic of modernity and often backward looking.

Thus conservative thinkers may have been adept at painting a picture of the costs of modernity and the downside of progress, but they were unable to offer a compelling solution to the problems of modernity, other than recreating the hierarchy that had been irrevocably swept away by the onset of the revolutionary period.

The Revolutionary Right

Traditionalist criticisms of the Enlightenment tradition and their insistence on the limits of reason could turn into extreme forms and become highly abrasive under changed historical circumstances. The conservative notion that human beings were moulded by the traditions and history of their particular society could easily slip into the much more extreme view that those who did not belong – by birth, history or tradition – to the society in question were outsiders, 'other', and had to be expelled from that society and denied citizenship rights. Examples of this position include the writings of the right-wing French nationalists at the time of the Dreyfus case in late-nineteenth-century France, writers such as Barrès and Maurras. Barrès preached a doctrine of nationalism as a form of determinism, claiming that those who did not have French blood were not 'real' Frenchmen (Barrès, 1902). In this category he included the writer Emile Zola, who criticised (in his famous letter 'J'Accuse') the victimisation of the Jewish army captain Dreyfus. For Barrès, Zola's arguments could be simply disposed of because he was of Italian extraction, hence not a 'true' Frenchmen. Furthermore he shared the intellectual and rationalistic misapprehension of those who believed that social and political problems could be solved through reason. In other words, he was an intellectual, a '*déraciné*' or rootless person, not truly a member of the national community (McClelland, 1970). This attitude is much closer to fascism than to traditional conservatism.

A similar example is provided by the French thinker Charles Maurras and his organisation Action Française, a nationalist organisation that sought to overthrow the republican regime. Maurras' followers identified 'the other' as those who belonged to of one of the 'four estates' – Jews, freemasons, foreigners and Protestants – none of which were seen as sharing the common history and traditions (classical, Catholic, monarchist) of what Maurras and his followers called '*le pays réel*', the real France, which was defined in quite arbitrary terms.

Thinkers in the conservative tradition were unable to cope with the most crucial aspect of the politics of modernity: the rise of the masses. The traditional Right tried to exclude the masses from politics, seeking to preserve or recreate the traditional hierarchy. However, what has been called the radical or even the revolutionary Right differed in two respects: it did not seek to defend the existing order, but wanted to overthrow it; and it tried to bring the masses into politics as a way of achieving the destruction of the liberal-democratic order. On both counts the radical Right, of which fascism can be considered the most extreme, must be clearly distinguished from the traditional or conservative Right. The radical Right represented an adaptation of the forces of the Right to the pressures and characteristics of modernity, but this adaptation was purchased at the expense of moderation. Among the radical Right movements, conservative politics became considerably more abrasive.

The various movements and ideologies of the radical or revolutionary Right grew up in the nineteenth century. They made use of the new style of politics opened up by the era of the French Revolution, the political methods of modernity, but not for the purposes of enlightenment and emancipation. Rather the tools and rituals of mass politics were used to distort and oppose the emancipatory thrust of modern politics and democratic movements. They represented a particularly dangerous orientation of modern politics in the sense that they appeared to espouse mass democracy, in line with the politics of the modern period, but instead used mass support for authoritarian purposes, totalitarian ones in the case of fascism.

The political scientist Zeev Sternhell has provided various examples, in the French context, of the revolutionary Right (Sternhell, 1986), including the Boulangist movement in France. Boulangism

arose in 1888 to mobilise support for the republican General Boulanger, who in 1889 was accused of plotting a *coup d'état* against the
Third Republic. The Boulangist movement is seen by many scholars
as anticipating the fascism of the twentieth century in a number of
ways: it directed slogans against foreign workers and immigrants; it
called for a revision of the constitution of the Third Republic in order
to strengthen its executive elements and weaken its representative and
parliamentary institutions; and it used themes of nationalism and
national renewal to call for 'revenge' (*La Revanche*) against Germany,
to stimulate a cross-class mass movement of national unity and
reassertion.

The Boulangist and other such movements were '*ni droite ni
gauche*' – they spanned the Right–Left divide (Sternhell, 1986). They
were right-wing in that they wanted to overthrow the democratic
regime and substitute authoritarian institutions for the (in their eyes)
discredited parliamentary system. Yet at the same time they aped the
style of the Left by appealing to the masses, albeit through right-wing
slogans of racism, xenophobia and nationalism. They practised the
politics of fear, exploiting the resentment and insecurity of people
faced with economic and social dislocation. They made full use of the
façade of democratic mass politics, the mechanisms of politics
developed since the French Revolution: mass rallies, mass demonstrations, the use of public space to stir up the people. As George
Mosse (1989) has pointed out, while twentieth-century fascist movements opposed the ideas and development of the French Revolutionary tradition, they too used the style of politics associated with
the French Revolution in terms of the rituals and mechanisms of
mass politics.

Thus right-wing politics in the period after the French Revolution
adapted to modernity in ways that traditional conservatism never
could. This adaptation consisted in opposing the democratic and
emancipatory elements of modernity by using or manipulating some
of the key elements of the revolutionary tradition, namely ideas of
popular sovereignty or democracy, nationalism, and a form of
socialism.

The movements of the radical Right and fascism claimed to be
promoting a superior form of democracy by bringing the people into
direct contact with the heroic leader. In the nineteenth century
Boulanger's attempt ended in failure, but in the next century the
existence of more advanced technology, deeper social conflicts and
fear of the Russian Revolution, together with the severe economic

crisis that characterised interwar Europe meant that fascist movements were able to seize power by exploiting mass discontent and
insecurity. Eric Hobsbawm has usefully characterised the optimal
conditions for what he calls 'the triumph of the crazy ultra-Right':

> The optimal conditions for the triumph of this crazy ultra-Right
> were an old state and its ruling mechanisms which could no longer
> function; a mass of disenchanted, disoriented and discontented
> citizens who no longer knew where their loyalties lay; strong
> socialist movements threatening or appearing to threaten social
> revolution, but not actually in a position to achieve it; and a move
> of nationalist resentment against the peace treaties of 1918–20
> (Hobsbawm, 1994, p. 127).

These fascist movements claimed to be able to realise a higher form of
democracy, on the plebiscitary model, by invoking a form of socialism that was confined to the inhabitants of the nation ('national
socialism'). In particular they exploited the grievances and insecurities
of the middle class or petty bourgeoisie.

In summary, the radical Right adapted the politics of modernity to
its own ends. Whereas the traditionalist conservative Right developed
criticisms of modernity in terms of its disintegrating effects, the newer
movements of the radical Right exploited people's insecurities and
resentments and set up scapegoats against whom these resentments
could be directed. This found expression in the disasters of fascism in
the twentieth century.

The Future of the Right

While the fundamentally premodern idea of an organic and God-
given society is crucial to traditional conservatism, it would not be
difficult to show the irrelevance of this concept to the world of
modernity, defined as a world based on reason, individuality, progress and the overthrow of tradition. It is true that traditional
conservatism, in the form of de Maistre's defence of throne and altar,
has long vanished as a potent political force. Nevertheless conservative or rather right-wing theories had a crucial significance for
modernity in the following way. The strength of the tradition of the
Right was some vision of community, of individuals held together

despite the divisions of market society. While traditional conservatism has ceased to be an effective force in its own right, as long as the disruptive effects of modernity continue there will be a search for the ideas of community that the tradition of the Right has long cultivated. This is not to say that the idea of 'community' is the exclusive preserve of the Right, but the socialist tradition aspires to a community in which there are no class divisions.

It should be made clear that the concept of community is a highly malleable one and can take many different forms. Even within the camp of the Right there are a plurality of contrasting types. For example the German fascists held out the prospect of an extended *Volksgemeinschaft*, or people's community: a racially defined authoritarian, or rather totalitarian, community, whose unity involved the annihilation of all those not of pure Aryan blood – Jews, Bolsheviks, gypsies and so on. This type of community was obviously not based on democratic rights, but was unified politically through submission to the *Führer*, who supposedly articulated the will of the racially homogeneous people and led them on a crusade against the 'alien' scapegoats mentioned above.

Of course this type of fascist or Nazi community was totally distinct from the kind of community envisaged in traditional conservative thought. For example the British Conservative Party, which has long had a strand of communitarian thinking within it, has expressed the idea of a unified if hierarchical nation. 'One nation' conservatism, in the British tradition, had as its goal a nation based on common traditions, a shared history and literature, unified across social divisions by this common legacy. The strength of right-wing theorising has been that it started from an 'organic' view of society which emphasised that individuals are not atomistic, but are moulded in various ways by the society of which they form part, and also by the history and traditions of that particular society. Against a *tabula rasa* view of humanity and society of Enlightenment thought, conservative theorists offered some highly necessary correctives and warnings. Enlightenment thought, as noted by Horkheimer and Adorno in their classic study, *Dialectic of Enlightenment*, knew no bounds to human reason and its ability to dominate society and natural environment:

From its origins Enlightenment, in the broadest sense of progressive thought, pursued the aim of freeing people from fear and installing them as masters (Horkheimer and Adorno, 1995, p. 9).

Horkheimer and Adorno further noted the emphasis in enlightenment thought on the idea of a unified system: 'The Enlightenment recognised initially as object and event only what could be grasped as a unity; its ideal is that of a system, from which the whole and its parts follow' (ibid., p. 13).

In protest against the uniformity and pretensions of reason, conservative theorists from the onset of modernity issued both protests and warnings, defending traditional and established institutions against system-building, and suggesting that individual reason was not an adequate basis for the construction of society. Conservative thought is highly topical in its protest against a sweeping universalism indifferent to national particularities and local differences. The Enlightenment tradition offered, as de Tocqueville noted in his study of the French revolution, a vision of universal liberation, seeking to liberate human beings everywhere. Conservative thought in contrast has always highlighted the idea of the particular traditions, customs and shared history specific to a nation or a people. This was exemplified by de Maistre's famous assertion that he had seen Frenchmen, Italians, and Russians, 'but I must say, as for *man*, I have never come across him anywhere, if he exists, he is completely unknown to me' (Maistre, 1965, p. 80).

This leads to quite a nuanced judgement on the contribution of conservatism to the politics of modernity. Modernity was marked by its universalising sweep, and its vision of global or international emancipation, freeing people from the grip of tradition and of the weight of the past. The tradition of right-wing theorising has been to oppose this through ideas of community and the limits of reason. In some of its forms, as in radical-right or fascist movements, this call for community and praise of irrationalism has assumed the most dangerous shape, and depends for its survival on the constant mobilisation of the masses and the creation of a scapegoat or target against whom all energies can be directed.

Resolutely anti-modernist in its traditionalist form, yet itself a product of the modernist revolution whose results it deplored, the tradition of the Right has in some of its guises offered powerful critiques of the universalism of the modernist and Enlightenment tradition. In some respects this tradition of the Right has been able to adapt to the crisis of modernity, to the emergence of postmodern times, for two reasons. In the first place, forms of conservatism or the Right have been able to claim as their forte the idea of community,

associated with ideas of identity, which can function as defences
against the onward sweep of modernity.

The relevance and survival of the philosophy of the Right in
contemporary society stem from its ability to accept the relativism
of postmodern developments, to criticise the universality and the
commitment to emancipation typical of the modernist tradition. This
critique can be expected to have renewed appeal in a period which has
come to exalt the particular, to be sceptical of promises of universal
emancipation, and to give more emphasis to long-established (or
reinvented) traditions which offer identity and (apparent) solace from
modernity and its upheavals. All of these are themes well articulated
in the tradition of conservative thought. This scepticism about reason
and emancipation has taken widely varying forms in the tradition of
right-wing thought, ranging from Burke's critique of the intellectual
leaders of the French Revolution through to Barrès' denunciation of
the intellectuals at the time of the Dreyfus case:

> Intellectual: an individual who convinces himself that society
> should be founded on a basis of logic; and who fails to see that it
> rests on past exigencies that are perhaps foreign to the individual
> reason (McClelland, 1970, p. 175).

Two points can then be made in conclusion. The first is that right-
wing theorising, while arising within the age of ideology, originating
as a critique of the totalistic transformation engaged in by the French
Revolution, has functioned as a critique of ideology and ideologi-
cally-inspired transformation, stressing the recalcitrance to such
transformation of local and long-established traditions and their
importance in providing people with a sense of identity and continuity. Such warnings can be heeded, and the strength of the
conservative critique acknowledged, without drawing the conclusion
that ideologies as frameworks for democratic discourse are necessarily to be rejected as leading to domination and the imposition of a
straitjacket on to society.

The second concluding point is that the conservative 'valorisation'
of tradition and continuity, its praise of the particular in opposition
to the universal, is often taken in conjunction with nationalism, as
heightening the value of national traditions and the nation as that
organic community which gives individuals their necessary context
and identity. Hence the conservative scepticism of the project of

modernity links up with nationalism. Both nationalism and conservatism share an emphasis on organic unity, which for nationalists makes the nation the supreme focus for human loyalty, the expression of modernity as well as a barrier against its most disruptive effects. The conclusion as far as conservatism is concerned is that a philosophy which arose in reaction to modernity has provided acute criticisms of some of its effects, and has functioned as a warning sign against excessive commitment to ideological politics. This conservative reaction to modernity has come into renewed life in a postmodern age of scepticism, relativism, stress on the local and the particular.

6

Nationalism and its Ambiguities

Of all the ideologies that have marked the age of ideology, nationalism seems to have been one of the most successful, if the criteria of success are the capacity to mobilise people, and to influence the course of world politics and political events. At the end of the Second World War nationalism was tarnished by its association with fascism and national socialism, but with the recent collapse of communism, nationalism has enjoyed a resurgence not only in Western and Eastern Europe, but throughout the world:

> Since the war, Europe has been built on a liberal project, civil society at the expense of the nation. This project is today out of breath, and the nationalist passions, with their infinitely more powerful capabilities of mobilization, are again at work (Rupnik, 1996, p. 71).

This in itself may seem rather surprising, and certainly would have been a cause for reflection among those adherents of the ideologies and political traditions dealt with above that took the Enlightenment promise seriously. Both liberalism and socialism, in their different forms, accepted the fundamental premises of Enlightenment thought: liberation and emancipation. Stemming from this was a view of emancipation and progress that tended to dismiss nationalism for its attachment to localism and particularity. In different ways both socialism and liberalism shared the view that the progress of humanity and the very process of modernity itself would lead to the weakening of nationalism and the forces of national identity. The idea of the nation would be replaced by other, wider affiliations as the power of reason and enlightened consciousness grew and developed. For liberalism, free trade and the rational individual were seen as universal, transnational forces. While it is true that liberals such as John Stuart Mill were convinced defenders of the principle of national

self-determination, what Mill had in mind were larger, more progressive nations, which, he suggested, should absorb nations that were not
sufficiently enlightened and modern:

> Nobody can suppose that it is not more beneficial to a Breton, or a
> Basque of French Navarre, to be brought into the current of the
> ideas and feelings of a highly civilised and cultivated people – to be
> a member of the French nationality, admitted on equal terms to all
> the privileges of French citizenship, sharing the advantages of
> French protection, and the dignity and prestige of French power
> – than to sulk on his own rocks, the half-savage relic of past times,
> revolving in his own little mental orbit, without participation or
> interest in the general movement of the world. The same remark
> applies to the Welshman or the Scottish highlander as members of
> the British nation (Mill, 1975, p. 385).

This passage – in its dismissive attitude towards the smaller nations of
Europe, writing off what would nowadays be called the force of sub-
state nationalism – seems in some ways astonishingly similar to
Engels' famous, or notorious, rejection of the national claims of those
he quite wrongly and unhistorically called 'the historyless peoples'.
Indeed some of the same nations consigned by Mill to the category of
'half-savage relic of past times' appear in Engels' list of losers:

> There is no country in Europe that does not possess, in some
> remote corner, at least one remnant-people, left over from an
> earlier population, forced back and subjugated by the nation which
> later became the repository of historical development. These rem-
> nants of a nation, mercilessly crushed, as Hegel said, by the course
> of history, this *national refuse*, is always the fanatical representative
> of the counter-revolution and remains so until it is completely
> exterminated or de-nationalized, as its whole existence is in itself a
> protest against a great historical revolution.
>   In Scotland, for example, the Gaels, supporters of the Stuarts
> from 1640 to 1745.
>   In France the Bretons, supporters of the Bourbons from 1792 to
> 1800.
>   In Spain the Basques, supporters of Don Carlos.
>   In Austria the pan-Slav South Slavs, who are nothing more than
> the *national refuse* of a thousand years of immensely confused
> development (Marx, 1973a, p. 221).

In the nineteenth century, leading representatives of both Marxism and liberalism saw the demand for national self-determination on the part of some of the smaller nations of Europe as going against the trend of modernity. Progress for both Engels and Mill lay in the formation of larger national units, and not in the principle of nationality as such. Indeed even the formation of larger nations was seen as a step on the way to a world that was truly international rather than based on different nation-states. Mill wanted smaller nationalities to come together under a common government: 'Whatever really tends to the admixture of nationalities, and the blending of their attributes and peculiarities in a common union, is a benefit to the human race' (Mill, 1975, p. 385). Mill and Engels both put forward views whose implication seems to be that nationalism, and in particular the demands for national self-determination by small nations, would be a feature of declining significance. The bearers of progress would be the large nations of Western Europe. As A. D. Smith says,

> Underlying both the socialist and the liberal evolutionist viewpoints has been the assumption that the large-scale nation or 'great nation' (always a national state) was the sole vehicle of social and political progress and that, once it had performed its world-historical role of bringing all peoples into the civilising process, it would be superseded by even larger and more powerful units of human association (Smith, 1995a, p. 16).

The Paradoxes of Nationalism

However, in defiance of these predictions nationalism has remained a powerful force, and a key player in the age of ideology. The persistence of nationalism seems to highlight the failure of all the ideologies that stemmed from the Enlightenment, precisely because of their universalist nature. According to Gray, writing in somewhat apocalyptic terms,

> The world-historical failure of the Enlightenment project – in political terms, the collapse and ruin, in the late twentieth century, of the secular, rationalist and universalist political movements, liberal as well as Marxist, that that project spawned, and the dominance in political life of ethnic, nationalist and fundamentalist

forces – suggests the falsity of the philosophical anthropology upon which the Enlightenment project rested. In this philosophical anthropology, cultural difference was conceived as an ephemeral, even an epiphenomenal incident in human life and history (Gray, 1995, p. 65).

The implication of this statement seems to be that nationalism offers insights that other ideologies are unable to grasp, since those ideologies such as socialism and liberalism are based on a universalist view of emancipation. These ideologies are condemned by Gray for being abstract in the sense of neglecting the human need for community and bonding. They are criticised for assuming the possibility of a rational foundation for ethics and the possibility of a universally valid scheme of social improvement and reconstruction. Nationalism's appeal is that it stresses the traditions and culture of a particular community, or nation, and thus avoids the facile universalism of the Enlightenment project. Hence the victory or continuing prominence of nationalism is seen as testimony to the failure of these more global ideologies. While these have crumbled, nationalism in its diverse forms has triumphed precisely because of its superior 'philosophical anthropology'.

However this is too superficial a view of the matter. Nationalism stands in an ambiguous relationship with both the Enlightenment project and the very processes of modernity. Nationalism is both modern and anti-modern, it combines elements of Enlightenment and modernity with appeals to tradition and, at least in some of its forms, to the idea of an ethnic community. Tom Nairn's portrayal of nationalism as a 'Janus', facing two ways, points out the ambiguities of nationalism, the paradoxes that need to be understood before its contradictory relationship with modernity can be grasped (Nairn, 1977).

The first paradox lies in the fact that it combines political effectiveness and durability with philosophical and theoretical simplicity, even crudeness. There is also a fundamental ambiguity with regard to the relationship between nationalism and modernity. Nationalism can be defined as a belief system that prioritises or gives special significance to the nation as a focus of loyalty. As a political doctrine or ideology it sees the world as 'naturally' divided into nations, each with its own distinctive national character. Nationalists, those who adhere to some variety of nationalism as a political doctrine, agree that national identity is a central plank or strand of people's character and identity, and that individuals need to be part of a nation if they are to find freedom and a sense of community.

This does not mean that nationalism necessarily entails the belief that national identity is or ought to be the sole or most important focus of individual loyalty. However, certain abrasive and extreme forms of nationalism have indeed led to this position: what has been called 'integral' nationalism has taken the prioritising of nationalism to the extreme, positing loyalty to the nation as an absolute value that must be accepted without question and placed before all other loyalties, which are seen as subsidiary and subordinate. The phrase 'integral nationalism' was coined by the French nationalist Charles Maurras at the end of the nineteenth century: for him the nation was the supreme political body, and a nationalist was someone who put the nation first. This involved a commitment to tight national cohesion, to a concept of national unity that for Maurras could be guaranteed only by a monarch. Describing the nation as the basic political unit, Maurras wrote: 'We maintain that the nation forms the highest point in the hierarchy of political ideas. Quite simply, it is the strongest among all the institutions of the real world' (Girardet, 1966, p. 198). Hence if national allegiance came into conflict with other loyalties, the latter would have to give way to the commands and interests of the nation: 'Since the nation transcends all other great common interests, which depend on the nation, it is quite obvious that, *in case of conflict,* all these other interests must by definition yield to the nation. In so doing, they also give way to something more general' (ibid.) In the prevailing circumstances of the Third French Republic, installed after military defeat by Germany in the Franco-Prussian war of 1870–71, and after the revolutionary upheaval of the Paris Commune of March–May 1871, nationalists such as Maurras thought that the only guarantee of social cohesion lay in integral nationalism, and the republican regime was seen as leading to the further dissolution and decay of society.

More recently the term 'integral nationalism' has been taken up by scholars and analysts of nationalism such as Peter Alter to suggest a general form of nationalism that makes the nation the be all and end all of all loyalties and identities (Alter, 1989). Moreover this form of integral nationalism is hostile to democracy and does not see the nation as a community of choice, open to newcomers and constituted by the consent of its citizens. Alter contrasts this with what he calls 'Risorgimento' nationalism, whose aim is to liberate the nation from foreign rule. This type of nationalism, which takes its name from the nineteenth-century movement for Italian unification and liberation, is centred on the value of national autonomy and self-determination.

Certainly the idea of self-determination is a central part of the politics of nationalism in general: nationalists of all kinds usually demand that their nation should have its own state. The reason for this demand for 'nation' and 'state' to coincide is that the state is seen as the best possible means of protecting and defending the nation, its culture, its shared history and traditions. Without an apparatus of political control – the state – the nation will be left defenceless in a harsh world of aggression and competition.

The political theorist David Miller suggests that what he calls 'the principle of nationality' does not necessarily require full nation-statehood, a separate state for each nation, though he does acknowledge that 'an independent state is likely to provide the best means for a nation to fulfil its claim to self-determination' (Miller, 1995, p. 81). There may be cases in which a national group can achieve its ends by securing autonomy or some degree of self-government that falls short of total secession from a larger state.

Nationalism, initially defined as a doctrine that attributes special significance to the unit of the nation, has taken many different forms in modern politics. Nationalism is a product of the modern world, one of the central ideologies that emerged during the epoch marked by the founding revolutions of modern times in America and France. Nationalists hold that individuals find, or ought to find, fulfilment in their nation, and that national identity is central to the individual. Theorists such as Ernest Gellner have shown that there is nothing natural in the nation, in the sense that for hundreds, indeed thousands of years human beings lived in communities that were not nation-states. So contrary to nationalist myth, there is nothing inherent or natural about identifying with a national unit.

Some historical accounts of the development of nationalism put its genesis at a somewhat earlier date than the late eighteenth century. For example Liah Greenfeld suggests the first example of nationalism arose in England in the sixteenth century with the idea of the nation as constituted by the people, along with the related concept that each nation has a special and specific character (Greenfeld, 1992). In the English case it was a view of England as a land of freedom, marked by the particular importance given to personal liberty along with the Protestant tradition in religious matters. Thus nationalism in six-teenth-century England was not only the first nationalism, it was marked by the absence of certain *ressentiments* that characterised later nationalism.

These later manifestations of national identity developed in a context where those asserting it were conscious, and resentful, of a gap between their nation and more advanced rivals. Examples of this could include France's awareness in the eighteenth century of its commercial rivalry with England, and the need to shake off the yoke of tyranny; or the Russian consciousness at the time of Peter the Great that huge changes would be necessary if Russia was to take its place in the modern world. Nationalism, as enunciated by intellectual groups proclaiming the nationalist message, has often been bound up with a collective inferiority complex, and in order to overcome this exaggerated attention has sometimes been given to a particular aspect in which the apparently (or actually) backward nation was in some way 'forward', special, having characteristics that were unique to it, characteristics that were proclaimed by nationalist intellectuals who wanted to spread a message of national rebirth and renewal.

Nationalism and Modernity

Nationalism and the inculcation of ideas of national identity were modern in the further sense that they represented 'roads to modernity', or even as one writer says 'the religion of modernity' (Llobera, 1994). The creation of nation-states, internally unified in economic terms and culturally homogeneous, was a necessary precondition of modernity and its continued development. Nationalism in this sense was seen as necessary if people were to harvest the fruits of modernity. Nationalists in a wide variety of countries and historical situations have spread a message of national renewal, of people becoming aware of their national identity and acting to realise it, because this gospel of nationalism was seen as the way for a society to move forward into modernity and reap its benefits.

The *ressentiment* described in the previous section could become extremely abrasive and hostile when articulated by groups of people who wanted to take over state power in order to accelerate the nation's development, to overtake hated rivals. The classic case is clearly the use of nationalism by fascists and national-socialists. The Nazi and Italian fascist ideologues used nationalism for particular purposes: firstly to mobilise people and implant dreams of national renewal; and secondly to create a scapegoat, a target, a category of 'the other', or non-member of the nation, who could then be blamed for the decline of the nation and its problems. In this respect Nazism went to extremes by invoking 'the Aryan myth' and demonising the Jews in order to gain mass support for a closed national community, the *Volksgemeinschaft*. According to Tom Nairn, Italy, Germany, and Japan were all

> societies with a relatively recent experience of 'backwardness' – a deprivation and impotence suddenly made humiliatingly evident to them by the impact of outside powers. All three reacted to this dilemma with particularly strong, compensatory ideological me-chanisms – mechanisms which, as far as the two Western members are concerned, comprise virtually the whole panoply of nationalist beliefs and sentiments (Nairn, 1981, p. 346).

Hence Nairn's conclusion that, 'Seen in sufficient historical depth, fascism tells us far more about nationalism than any other episode' (ibid., p. 347). This is not to suggest that modernist nationalism was the same as fascism, or even intrinsically linked to fascism. The argument is that fascism brought out in clear and exaggerated form a central element of nationalism:

> it is through nationalism that societies try to propel themselves forward to certain kinds of goal (industrialisation, prosperity, equality with other peoples, etc.) *by a certain sort of regression* – by looking inwards, drawing more deeply upon their indigenous resources, resurrecting past folk-heroes and myths about them-selves and so on (ibid., p. 348).

This illustrates the fundamental ambiguity or paradox of nationalism, that involved a transition to modernity, yet it was a transition that was accomplished through a sort of regression or retreat from modernity. The creation of the nation-state and the mobilisation of people through nationalism involved an appeal to myths, the invoca-tion of history and tradition. It was often the state (and the state elite) that created nationalism, created 'nations by design'. The state and its agents instilled a mood of nationalism, a sense of national identity, as a means of solidifying the legitimacy of the state.

An example of this is the case of nationalism and republican patriotism in the Third French Republic from 1871 onwards. This is a classic example of a process in which the republican regime sought to bolster its legitimacy by using a rhetoric of nationalism and republican patriotism. There was a policy of creating a new consciousness, above all through the education system. Schoolteachers were to be the agents of this new republican and patriotic consciousness. Eminent historians such as Ernest Lavisse wrote textbooks that presented the republican regime as the culmination of France's history, so that the core values of the French Revolution (liberty, equality, fraternity) would hold society together as a single nation. The republican regime, these authors claimed, was the only way in which national cohesion could be achieved. In this respect their view of the republic was the exact opposite of that of the 'integral nationalists' cited above, as writers such as Barrès and Maurras asserted that the republican regime was a system of 'dispersion, diversity, and evil'.

Advocates of the republican tradition asserted that through a common republican and national consciousness based on shared democratic values France would be able to assert its role as a nation with a special part to play, a messianic mission to show other nations the road to liberation. The state elite consciously created a national awareness, a national identity of a particular type: an idea of civic nationalism based on the democratic republic and republican equality. This was designed to stimulate a sense of national cohesion and prepare the citizens to defend the republic should it come under attack. Hence the French socialist Jean Jaurès' idea of a new citizens army, a militia, ready to defend the national territory. However this army could not be used by a would-be authoritarian leader, nor would it engage in foreign adventures or aggressive wars (Jaurès, 1932).

As discussed above, the paradox of nationalism was that it involved a transition to modernity while appealing to past tradition and historical memories that were anything but modern. In this sense Nairn's idea of nationalism as a Janus phenomenon is extremely apt. Janus was a two-faced Roman god, and in the case of nationalism one face looks to the past and the other to the future. Nationalists have often sought to mobilise people for the task of economic modernisation and progress, yet nationalism and nationalist movements have also emphasised the weight of the past, the glorious traditions of the nation and its history, and nationalists have even invented such traditions when they cannot authentically be found. Indeed, as Renan's famous lecture '*Qu'est-ce qu'une nation?*' ('What is a nation?') makes clear, a capacity for getting one's history wrong is a necessary condition for the existence or development of a national consciousness and national identity (Renan, 1992). Hence the important role of intellectuals in creating and sustaining myths of national identity and past history, in creating languages or developing them where they did not exist, such as occurred with the Czech language. Under the reform-minded Emperor Joseph II,

> Chairs of Czech language were established at the Military Academy and the universities of Vienna and Prague; school textbooks, agricultural manuals and religious works were published in Czech; and officials in regions of Czech speech were officially encouraged to learn Czech. Thus spontaneous forces and official policy combined to favour a revival and development of the Czech language, and this in turn produced a growing identification of nation and language (Seton-Watson, 1977, p. 151).

David Miller notes that, 'National identities are, in a strong and destructive sense, mythical' (Miller, 1995, p. 33). However they are not entirely mythical since they rest on a genuine past history of ethnic and historical community, however that history may be interpreted, or even manipulated.

The answer to the question of nationalism's durability lies in its paradox: its ability to be both modern and premodern. It has appealed to ideas of a common community and of catching up with more advanced areas. Nationalists have often spoken a discourse of *ressentiment*. They have pointed out the gap between the great history of their nation and its present situation, overtaken by and backward in comparison with its more advanced neighbours. An example of this is provided by Russia:

> From the days of Kantemir, it was the political reality of Russia which Russian patriots found most embarrassing: the lack of liberty, equality, respect for the individual. It was this difference in the fundamental relation to Man, not economic or cultural under-achievement, which militated most conspicuously against the moral canon of the West, which Russia, eager to be incorporated in this luminary family of nations, nonchalantly embraced (Greenfeld, 1992, p. 255).

Greenfield also notes that 'It was *ressentiment*, not social concerns, that fuelled Russian national consciousness, and it was *ressentiment*, not sympathy for the peasantry, that made the peasant a symbol of the Russian nation' (Greenfeld, 1992, p. 258).

The Malleability of Nationalism

Contrary to the expectations of adherents of more modernist ideologies, nationalism has been a powerful force throughout the age of ideology, although its nature has changed over time. Classical nineteenth-century nationalism involved the idea of large nations, certain minimum thresholds that would provide the necessary criteria for nationhood: a certain size, a certain scale of the economy, a certain wealth of culture and tradition, historical continuities and identities. These criteria did not include ethnic identity. Hence 'ethno-nationalism' is a relatively recent phenomenon. While it is obviously the case that ethnic affiliation and ethnic identity are very ancient forces, the idea that ethnic group alone should determine membership of a nation-state has only come to the fore in the twentieth century. An extreme example of ethno-nationalism was German national socialism, which made citizenship, indeed life itself, dependent on membership of the *Volksgemeinschaft*, the racially defined people's community. 'Ethnic cleansing' is an equally extreme manifestation of this form of social closure.

There is an important distinction between an 'open' and a 'closed' nation: the former involves civic nationalism, while the latter is ethnically or linguistically based (Winock, 1990, ch. 1). Classical nineteenth-century nationalism was bound up with the idea of large units, a bringing together of people from different ethnic groups, perhaps from the more backward nations, as suggested in the earlier quotation from Mill. However the criteria that governed citizenship were not in any way ethnic or linguistic. Some threshold criteria did have to be met if a nation was to be a practical entity, but these related to size, economic viability and the ability to sustain and develop a high culture. National groups that could not meet those criteria would be absorbed by the more advanced nations, and both Mill and Engels endorsed this view.

In contrast late-twentieth-century nationalism is separatist, fragmentary and much more emphatic of language and/or ethnic identity as the criteria for membership of the nation. This form of nationalism is very prevalent in modern politics, especially in Eastern and Central Europe in the aftermath of the collapse of communism. If membership of the political community depends on ethnic identity, or ability to speak the language of the dominant national or ethnic group, this undermines the conditions necessary for democratic citizenship. It creates new conditions of inclusion and exclusion that are much more rigorous and inflexible than the old ones.

The contrast, then, is between the continuing pulling power and resilience of nationalism and the relatively uncertain fate of the other ideologies of the age of ideology. Nationalism is part of the modernist project in that it involves the idea of a people, a nation, a political and cultural community that is animated by ideas of autonomy and self-determination. In this sense it is right to speak, as David Miller does, of nationalism as involving an activist component, the idea of a people forming itself into a nation (Miller, 1995). This does not mean that this is an arbitrary process, that any group can become a nation, and that the power of nationalism is totally the work of an elite imbued with nationalist ideas. The argument is rather that there have to be certain ethnic markers and a historical background, some basis from which to create the myths and symbols of national identity. In this sense nationalism and its power derive from a combination of these two factors and the conscious wish to form a nation, whether this is articulated by a nationalist *avant-garde* of intellectuals or the people as a whole.

One can trace the development of nationalist movements through a number of stages. Hroch's model of stages A, B and C is useful here (Hroch, 1985, 1993). The early stage of a nationalist movement, stage A, is confined to scholarly or intellectual investigation into the history and culture of a particular nation. This is an elite stage, pre-political, in which the cultural roots of nationalism are explored. In Stage B which is much more political, groups of intellectuals move from purely scholarly investigation to the formulation of nationalist demands and articulation of the message of national self-determination. In this stage the nationalist elite is active and the politicisation of cultural nationalism takes place. Finally, in phase C the nationalist message mobilises some degree of mass support, and a mass movement begins to develop. Nationalist movements can therefore be seen as the initiative of an elite group of intellectuals who are seeking to mobilise the masses and use their support as a means of nation building and gaining political power for a newly constituted nation-state.

However the forces of modernity, in particular economic forces, seem to have developed in such a way as to bear out some of the Marxist, and indeed liberal, predictions of an international rather than national world order. The move towards globalisation suggests that we now live in a world where economic exchanges and the international division of labour are weakening national boundaries and that the nation-state is much less relevant, at least in the context of industrial production and manufacturing. Thus at the economic level the idea of a world system in which nations are increasingly irrelevant seems to have been realised.

However, and this is yet another paradox in the analysis of nationalism, alongside the growing interdependence and globalisation of the world economy, which would appear to point to the declining significance of nationalism and a weakening desire for the formation and maintenance of the nation-state, there seems to be a resurgence both of nationalism and the related (though not identical) forces of ethnic identity and conflict: 'The idea that the global market and the universal *Homo economicus* are dissolving ethnic particularities is not true' (Rupnik, 1996, p. 50). One way of explaining this paradox is that nationalism as a broad ideology is particularly appealing in uncertain times of rapid social change, 'when all that is solid melts into air'.

Hence the rapid progress of modernity and its sweeping away of national boundaries and national cultures may be seen as giving rise to a defensive counter reaction. The assertion of national identity and the erection of boundaries of inclusion and exclusion, metaphorically and literally, is an understandable process in a world being changed by forces that people feel are beyond their control.

The first wave of nationalism followed the American and French Revolutions, the second took place in the late nineteenth and early twentieth centuries, when small nations began to demand their liberation from the multinational empires of Central and Eastern Europe (the Russian, Austro-Hungarian and Ottoman Empires). To these could be added the somewhat later rise of anticolonial or Third World nationalism. As various writers (for example Alter, 1989) have noted, after the Second World War it was confidently predicted that nationalism would decline in significance. This was partly because of the association of nationalism with fascism and national socialism, and partly because of the expectation of increased international cooperation and exchange. Modernity was seen as having dealt a death blow to the influence of nationalism.

The Resurgence of Nationalism

In contrast to the expectations of the core modernist ideologies of liberalism and socialism, the late twentieth century has witnessed a third wave of nationalism, which has both continuities and disconti- nuities with the two waves discussed in the previous section. In this instance the emphasis is on the ethnic or linguistic character of nations, as opposed to the political criteria of nationhood stressed in the nationalism of the nineteenth century. In fact this new nationalism seems completely to disregard, as Hobsbawm (1990) has pointed out, the 'threshold' criteria of size and economic viability that were crucial to European nationalism in the nineteenth century. Clear examples of the new wave of nationalism are Scottish nation- alism, Basque separatism and other instances of 'sub-state national- ism': the break-up of what used to be large and seemingly unified nations into smaller units, as in Eastern and Central Europe since the collapse of Communism.

Nationalism, whether of the civic or the ethnic kind, provides a sense of community, and in times of dislocation and uncertainty it offers security and personal identity. Nationalism was able to develop in the age of modernity precisely because it offered a link between state and society: the society was a national one, nationalism was the force that bound society together, and because of the political component (the idea of national self-determination) it provided a basis for the state as well. Nationalism offered an image of an ideal community, the nation-state, which was highly 'functional' in the process of economic development and modernisation. This 'function- ality' as far as the economic sphere is concerned has now been weakened by forces of economic development cutting across the unit of the nation. However this does not mean that nationalism has no future in a world increasingly unified by links of globalism, especially in terms of economic exchange but in cultural matters too. On the contrary, as discussed above it has been given a new lease of life by people's reaction to the effect that modernity and modernisation have had on their sense of self-identity and culture. Nationalism offers a refuge against the continuing progress of modernity because of the importance that nationalists place on to the specific, the particular, the national culture.

It is true that civic nationalism may be just as exclusive as ethnic nationalism, and may favour one group over others. It may have a hidden agenda that means it is less open than it at first appears. In any model of civic nationalism there has to be some common accord, some point of contact, a public sphere in which citizens can set aside their particular affiliations, cultural and religious, otherwise there can be no agreement or sense of common citizenship. The danger is that if membership of the nation, and hence citizenship, is defined in ethnic terms, then this denies citizenship rights to those who are not of the same ethnic identity. This is much more exclusivist than civic nationalism.

Nationalism in Postmodern times

The final section of this chapter serves as a bridge to the following chapters, which discuss whether the ideologies of the French Revolution tradition, which grew up in response to the revolution of modernity and shared the agenda of modernity, have any relevance to a world in which modernity itself has been transformed, leading, some would argue, to a 'postmodern' society. While the details of these changes are examined in Chapter 7, it can be said here that nationalism occupies a special place in contemporary politics. Nationalism seems to be both modern and postmodern: it is not only one of the 'victors' of the age of ideology, the period since the revolutions of 1776 and 1789, but it also seems uniquely able to accommodate itself to, even to be the expression of, a postmodern society in which many of the pillars and institutions of modernity seem to have been transformed or undermined.

Nationalism as an ideology can be described in terms of mass appeal, malleability and modernity. Despite or perhaps because of its philosophic simplicity, its lack of sophisticated theorists, as Gellner (1983) observes, it has secured mass backing, with greater or lesser degrees of spontaneity: sometimes it has been enforced by the state, sometimes infused into the masses through the efforts of an intellectual elite who seek to heighten national awareness. Indeed nationalism has often been more successful than its ideological rival – socialism – in securing popular support. While it is wrong to see the outbreak of the First World War in August 1914 in simplistic terms as the victory of 'nation' over 'class', it seems hard to deny that the collapse of the Socialist International and its failure to mobilise the masses against war did reveal the integration of the working class into 'their' nation. The mobilising power of nationalism seems to show no sign of declining, *pace* Hobsbawm, in contemporary times.

Hobsbawm claims that 'the phenomenon [of nations and nationalism] is past its peak' (Hobsbawm, 1990, p. 183), and that the world history of the late twentieth and early twenty-first centuries will, as he puts it, 'have to be written as the history of a world which can no longer be contained within the limits of "nations" and "nation-states" as these used to be defined, either politically, or economically, or culturally, or even linguistically' (ibid., p. 182). However this is contestable in the light of the national and ethnic struggles in the recent war in Yugoslavia, the continuing power of nationalism in Eastern and Central Europe, and the appeals to nationalism of various kinds by politicians both of Left and Right.

To this characteristic of mass appeal can be added that of malleability, the different ways in which 'the nation' can be defined and characterised. 'Civic' and 'ethnic' nationalism conceptualise the nation in contrasting ways: is the nation an ethnic grouping or an association of citizens; is the basis of the nation linguistic, religious or racial? Thus the way in which the nation is constructed or invented can have different political implications. As A. D. Smith notes, such ideas have been taken up by postmodernist accounts of nationalism to suggest that 'the nation' can be constructed or invented from more or less any ingredients, rather as a chef constructs a meal: 'For the post-modernists, the nation has become a cultural artefact of modernity, a system of collective imaginings and symbolic representations, which resembles a pastiche of many hues and forms, a composite patchwork of all the cultural elements included in its boundaries' (Smith, 1995b, p. 7). According to what Smith terms 'the gastronomic theory of the nation', 'nations are composed of discrete elements and their cultures possess a variety of ingredients with different flavours and provenances' (ibid., p. 4).

The crucial factors in this are what Gellner calls the 'national awakeners', the intellectuals or political leaders who invent the national community, plus the 'ingredients' they use and the cultural mix that results. The elements may be of a civic kind, for example those that went towards the creation of the national-democratic consciousness of Third Republic France. Or they may be more akin to *völkisch* myths of an *Ur-Volk*, an original people, along the lines of Fichte's picture of the German people speaking a language uncontaminated by foreign elements, and tracing their lineage to the heroic days of their defeat of the Roman legions.

Such 'gastronomic' theories of the nation can be taken to excessive lengths. Smith is no doubt right to argue that there has to be some genuine basis for the nation: 'The nation is not a purely modern creation *ex nihilo*, much less a *mélange* of materials constantly reinvented to suit the changing tastes and needs of different elites and generations' (ibid., p. 13). However the nation can undoubtedly be defined in a variety of ways, and invented, or reinvented, with different elements being given priority according to the political ideals of the national awakeners. The inevitably subjective element in the definition and consciousness of national identity means that nationalism has certain features that will enable it to survive well into the postmodern age, in which different identities compete in a much more fluid and pluralistic way for people's allegiance.

The fact that national identities are constructed, and that national history and criteria of national identity are being constantly redefined, with important political implications in each case, suggests that nationalism has a chameleon like quality that enables it to adapt to situations of crisis, and to do so with more success than other ideologies of the age of modernity, for example socialism, which took as its basis the much more fixed and socially given identity of class.

The flexibility of the concept of the 'nation' also means that nationalism can be exploited by political elites of various kinds for its mobilising power. One account of the break up of Yugoslavia notes of Serbian leader Slobodan Milosevic's visit to Kosovo in April 1987 that 'the whole episode had provided him with a ready formula for rousing nationalist sentiments' (Silber and Little, 1995, p. 37). On that occasion Milosevic delivered a speech full of nationalist rhetoric to the Serbs of Kosovo in opposition to the ethnic Albanians: 'You should stay here for the sake of your ancestors and descendants. Otherwise your ancestors would be defiled and descendants disappointed' (ibid.). This is not to suggest that Milosevic brought such sentiments into being merely by articulating them, they were already there, waiting to be ignited by the right leader.

Therefore, to anticipate some of the arguments developed below, in a situation in which modernity itself is in crisis nationalism seems more likely to survive this crisis than the other ideologies of modernity, for two reasons. First, because of the way in which nationalism has built into it a critique of the universalism that characterises the other main ideologies, a universalism that in recent times has been subjected to strong criticism. Second, because nationalism offers a sense of inclusion and citizenship at a time when national borders are in flux, both literally and metaphorically, especially in the newly democratised societies in Eastern and Central Europe.

It was stated at the start of this section that nationalism can be defined by three key words: mass-appeal, malleability and modernity. Bound up with the modernity of nationalism is its universalism, in the sense that the message of democratic nationalism in the late eighteenth century was that all peoples everywhere should form their own nation-state. Nationalism has always involved the idea of the particular, the special qualities of the nation, and this has sometimes formed the basis for resentment that these qualities have been neglected by more 'advanced' nations. Sometimes, perhaps always, nationalism has sought to combine the universal with the particular, endowing the special, historically given qualities of the nation with universal significance.

Thus while standing on the general terrain of modernity, nationalist theory has appealed to a sense of the particular, the relative, the local, the special virtues or characteristics of nationhood. This has enabled nationalism to survive while other ideologies have fallen, because it is precisely the relative, the particular that have come to be exalted in the face of what is seen as the dangerous universalism inherent in modernity, which offers one future, one goal for all of humanity and, in line with the Enlightenment tradition, sees attachment to local traditions as a sign of backwardness and parochialism.

To conclude, nationalism has remained a powerful force, yet it has taken highly different forms in the modern world. The concluding section of this book seeks to investigate the relevance of the different ideologies considered so far in the present conditions of postmodernism, in conditions where the values of the Enlightenment tradition have come under severe attack from a variety of sources. The aim is to review the different ideological traditions considered so far, and to discuss their relevance in an age when the three pillars of modernity are in crisis, when there is a double crisis, that of modernity and that of ideologies which developed in the conditions of modernity.

Part III
The Crisis of Ideologies

7

The Crisis of Modernity

The ideologies that became central to the political life of Western societies after the American and French Revolutions shared a common agenda, the agenda of modernity. They all responded to the common set of problems thrown up by the new society that emerged at the end of the eighteenth century, and whose development formed the context in which the ideologies themselves unfolded during the nineteenth and twentieth centuries. That new society of modernity was one in which industrial production and the exploitation of what seemed to be the unlimited resources of the natural world were central features. It was a society in which the nation-state provided the framework for political and cultural identity, as well as economic activity and (later) the impetus for imperial and colonial conquest. Finally, it was a society riven by class conflict arising from the capitalist mode of production, a conflict that socialists and Marxists saw as leading to a different type of society, to socialism or communism, which alone would be able to harness the fruits of modernity.

It is the contention here that in the conditions of the late twentieth century modernity has experienced a set of crises, and that because of this the ideologies that have dominated the age of ideology (1776–89 to the present day) have themselves suffered a crisis. The purpose of this chapter is to explain this double crisis and probe its implications. Are the ideologies discussed in Part II of this book irrelevant in the light of the profound changes in modernity, which some people see as leading to a postmodern society? Is the very concept of 'ideology' – with its framework for political discussion and critique, ideals and views of agency – problematic in a postmodern society in which there are so many sources of identity that they cannot be accommodated in one overarching picture of society, such as those provided by the 'classical' ideologies of modernity? And does the more pluralistic and diverse postmodern society render obsolete the familiar Left–Right spectrum of ideologies that have formed the basis of political life and ideological debate over the last two centuries? These questions form the subject matter of this and the following chapters.

Theoretical Critiques of Modernity

Modernity is seen as being linked to the idea of enlightenment and continued progress towards individual and social emancipation, a goal that was taken for granted by liberalism, socialism and (through the route of national liberation) nationalism, but regarded sceptically by conservative theorists. However in our own time the notions of enlightenment and emancipation have been criticised not just by conservative and reactionary theorists, but also by those who see the project of modernity as instrinsically bound up with elements of domination and power. The modernist project of rationality, organisation and control has been put under a critical microscope to reveal the hidden aspects of domination, leading to a critique of the Enlightement aim of emancipation.

For example Foucault's essay 'What is Enlightenment?' takes as its starting point Kant's essay of the same title, yet the implications of Foucault's answer to this question are quite different from Kant's (see Norris, 1993). For Foucault, the growth of capacities of human reason and command over nature conflicts more strongly with the aim of freedom and emancipation than the thinkers of the Enlightenment assumed: 'The relations between the growth of capabilities and the growth of autonomy are not as simple as the eighteenth century may have believed' (Rabinow, 1987, p. 47). For Foucault, the new technologies and capacity for organisation unleashed by the Enlightenment gave rise to 'disciplines' and processes of 'normalisation', that is, power relations:

> We have been able to see what forms of power relations were conveyed by various technologies (whether we are speaking of production with economic aims, or institutions whose goal is social regulation, or of techniques of communication): disciplines, both collective and individual, procedures of normalisation exercised in the name of the power of the state, demands of society or of population zones, are examples (ibid., p. 48).

In other words, the processes of organisation, the acquisition of knowledge and scientific method that characterised modernity and underpinned modern ideologies, notably liberalism and socialism, were themselves suspect, because they gave rise to new forms of domination and thwarted rather than promoted freedom. The modern state moved from an association of citizens, democratically determining their own destiny, to a rationalising and controlling force, whose reality is best captured by Foucault's understanding of Bentham's Panopticon, a prison in which all the inmates are under constant surveillance from the controlling guards. Worse, at any particular moment they do not know if they are being controlled or not (Foucault, 1980, p. 147). Hence the crucial question for Foucault, as posed in his essay 'What is Enlightenment?', was 'How can the growth of capabilities be disconnected from the intensification of power relations?' (Rabinow, 1987, p. 48). The Enlightenment tradition of modernity allowed the growth of capabilities, described by Foucault as a complex of 'elements of social transformation, types of political institution, forms of knowlege, projects of rationalisation of knowlege and practices, technological mutations that are very difficult to sum up in a word' (ibid., p. 43). The critique of modernity here seems to be that the growth of capabilities can stunt human freedom rather than extend it, as the modernist Enlightenment tradition uncritically assumed.

This critique of what could be called, following Horkheimer and Adorno (1995), the 'dialectic of Enlightenment', is also a critique of ideologies in general, as well as of the modernist tradition. All ideologies offer a general view of society and (especially in times of revolution) a perspective not just of social and political transformation, but of the transformation of human nature, the realisation of 'the new man'. The idea of 'the regeneration of man' has been seen by Mona Ozouf as a central theme of the French revolutionaries (Ozouf, 1989, p. 116). Yet this aim of total transformation is seen by some critics as opening the way to totalitarianism, politics unlimited, in which the goal becomes the abolition of difference, the imposition of one identity and total uniformity on society, whether in terms of the Jacobin vision of the good patriot, the fascist or communist visions of the new man, or the nationalist idea of an ethnically pure nation with one identity linking everyone in a tight community. This critique of the modern ideologies seems to be implied in Foucault's preference for 'specific transformations' rather than the more dangerous idea of 'the new man', and possibly 'new woman' too:

I prefer the very specific transformations that have proved to be possible in the last twenty years in a certain number of areas that concern our ways of being and thinking, relations to authority, relations between the sexes, the way in which we perceive insanity or illness; I prefer even these partial transformations that have been made' in the correlation of historical analysis and the practical attitude, to the programmes for a new man that the worst political systems have repeated throughout the twentieth century (Rabinow, 1987, p. 46).

Hence it is the ideological mode of thinking that is condemned as leading to dangerous abstractions, and the elevation of one category (whether the individual, class or the nation) to be the be all and end all of social transformation. It is better to aim for partial transformation that does not affect all of society at once, than to achieve the goal of 'the new man', as at least this prevents a single all-embracing vision being imposed on a complex society. Modernity for Foucault was both an attitude (or ethos) and a period of history. Modernity as an attitude is seen as giving rise to the totalising (which can become totalitarian) aspects of ideology, and the acquisition of new knowledge is seen as providing new means of human domination. Similarly the new institutions of modernity – the rational republic, the organised nation-state educating its citizens in the common language of the nation – can too easily be used to manipulate and indoctrinate the citizens in a Panopticon-like situation of total control. The French Revolutionary ideals of autonomous citizens forming the nation-state (Hobsbawm: nation = state = people) turn into a means of annihilating diversity and provincial autonomy in a situation in which the state, however democratic it might be, is able to control and manipulate its citizens, and modern ideologies provide the intellectual rationalisation for this control.

Hence there are two sides to the crisis of modernity and the ideologies stemming from it. In the first place, on the philosophical and theoretical level the ideas of modernity, including emancipation and progress, are now being met with greater scepticism about their validity and there is a suspicion of a hidden agenda of domination and control. This has led to an undermining of the ideologies that shared the modernist agenda of liberation, and by extension to a suspicion of *all* ideologies (even those critical of modernity) because of their dangerously totalising implications. Secondly, the crisis of modernity and modernist ideology is also due to a number of changes in 'the real world' that are seen as totally transforming the world of modernity, leading to a 'postmodern' society that poses questions and problems to which the old ideologies and Left–Right spectrum can offer no answers.

Before explaining what the crisis of modernity and ideologies involves in this second dimension, it is worth extending the analysis of the philosophical and theoretical aspects of this crisis. One dimension of modernity that was highly relevant to the unfolding of political ideologies was the idea of specialisation, the differentiation of society into separate spheres, each with their own 'language' and approach. The various ideologies of politics sought in their different ways to offer a way of reintegrating or 'totalising' the fragmented modern world. However the problem this posed for modern ideologies was what Habermas, a defender of the modernist project, calls 'the pathology of modernity', the danger of instrumental reason, or economic and administrative rationality, seeking to invade all spheres of life. For Habermas, modernity is an 'unfinished project' that depends on separating out the different spheres of human activity:

> The project of modernity as it was formulated by the philosophers of the Enlightenment in the eighteenth century, consists in the relentless development of the objectivating sciences, of the universalistic foundations of morality and law, and of autonomous art, all in accord with their immanent logic (Habermas, 1996, p. 45).

The hope of Enlightenment philosophers such as Condorcet was that 'the arts and sciences would not merely promote the control of the forces of nature, but also further the understanding of self and world, the progress of morality, justice in social institutions, and even human happiness' (ibid.) However for Habermas, as a defender of modernity and its contened progress and development, there seem to be a number of problems with modernity that pose a danger of its 'pathology'. Firstly, the continuing separation of natural science, morality and law, and art, will prevent rational communication across these separate spheres. Secondly, the continuing divorce of the specialists in each of these spheres from the general public means that the latter will find it increasingly difficult to grasp specialist areas of knowledge. Finally, the opposite danger arises that if instrumental reason, the idea of scientific knowledge, is applied to all areas of social and political life, this could lead to manipulation and excessive rationalisation:

> Many different occasions for discontent and protest arise whenever a one-sided process of modernisation, guided by criteria of economic and administrative rationality, invades domains of life which are centred on the task of cultural transmission, social integration, socialisation and education, domains oriented towards quite *different* criteria, namely those of communicative rationality (ibid., p. 44).

The contrast seems clear with the view of '*bürgerliche Öffentlichkeit*' put forward by Habermas in his earlier book, *Strukturwandel der Öffentlichkeit* (1993), and discussed in Chapter 1 above. There, the original ideas of modernity seemed to rest, according to Habermas, on an informed general public acquiring and discussing in the public sphere the new knowledge of science and public affairs, and using this knowledge to exert control and impose rational ends on the holders of political power. This was the promise of modernity – showing the way to a rational society – conceptualised by the different ideologies of politics. However in a later analysis by Habermas, a picture emerges of a society where the promise of an enlightened public sphere has not been met, where society is split up into separate spheres of activity, where people become specialists in their own 'iron cage' from which there is no escape. At the same time criteria of scientific rationality are applied throughout society to impoverish and restrict critical thought and the free development of what Habermas calls 'the lifeworld'. In his words, the hope must be that 'the life world [can] develop institutions of its own in a way currently inhibited by the autonomous systemic dynamics of the economic and administrative systems' (ibid., p. 53).

The critical implications for the ideologies of modernity seem to be as follows, though it should be made clear that these suggestions have not been developed by Habermas himself. They are offered here as further dimensions of the double crisis of modernity and modernist ideologies. First, the task of ideologies is to provide unity in a deeply fragmented society by offering some overall vision of how society could be organised, and how a defective society could be transformed to a better one (critique, ideal, agency). However this task is all the harder in a society fragmented by the separation of spheres, in which 'scientific discourse, moral and legal enquiry, artistic production and critical practice are now institutionalised within the corresponding cultural systems as the concern of experts' (ibid., p. 45). Secondly, what Habermas calls 'many different occasions for discontent and protest' (ibid., p. 44) arise as protests against the rationalising and homogenising tendencies of modernity (the extension of the sphere of economic and administrative rationality to other spheres). However these protests can and often do emphasise particularity, tradition and difference, and thus undermine the universalism of the Enlightenment and the modernist ideologies (liberalism and socialism) that took their cue from that universalism. Ideologies of ethnic and fundamentalist nationalism arise as protests against modernity, yet these seem unable to complete the task of emancipation and move towards the goal of universal liberation, which was and remains at the heart of the modernist project.

To these problems must be added that stemming from the real world of modernity: the crisis of ideology which is itself a reflection of the broader crisis of modernity. In what ways and for what reasons are the broad frameworks of political debate and action analysed in Part II of this book in difficulty when it comes to providing critique, ideals and a theory of agency relevant to present-day politics? Is this crisis a terminal one, leading to the conclusion that the tradition of the French Revolution has run its course, and that the ideologies of modernity have nothing to offer to a world that has fundamentally changed in nature?

The Transformation of Modernity

The first stage in answering these questions is to point to the fundamental transformations that have provoked the crisis of modernity and, by extension, rendered more problematic the ideologies of politics that were based on it (socialism, liberalism, conservatism and nationalism). If the ground on which these ideologies developed has irrevocably changed, then it is not surprising that all are being challenged by new problems, both practical and philosophical. The question remains (to be answered below) of whether the ideological tradition of modernity can adapt itself to the changed social, political and economic context of the contemporary world.

In the introduction to this book it was noted that modernity had three main features, relating to industrial production and the conquest of nature; to the nation-state, democratically organised, as the framework of political action; and to class politics, the struggle of large and well-organised classes as central (though not the only) features of modern politics. More generally, the agenda of modernity (shared to varying degrees by all the ideologies considered so far) has been one of universality, meaning that a common ideal would be held by all human beings, who would form communities of democratic citizens and determine their own destiny. However challenges to these core ideas of modernity have arisen because of fundamental changes in the political, economic and social structure of the contemporary world. These changes have not merely transformed the nature of modernity, but pose totally new problems for the hitherto-dominant ideologies.

The Crisis of the Nation-State

The theorists of modernity – liberal and socialist – envisaged that its dynamic would span national borders and ultimately create an international order. However the age of modernity from the French Revolution onwards was the age of nation-state formation and nationalism, expressed as the wish to form and preserve large, internally unified nation-states. The democratic nation-state was the classical political unit of modernity, with France as the chief example. As the nineteenth century progressed, the demands of nations that were part of the multinational empires (Russian, Austrian, Ottoman) began to grow, and sometimes ethnic or linguistic homogeneity became more salient than the idea of democratic community. However the idea of the nation-state as offering economic unity, cultural homogeneity and political protection to its self-governing citizens was a basic assumption of modernity. This model of the democratic nation-state is in crisis today for a number of reasons that relate both to the ideal of internal homogeneity and to the aspiration for sovereignty and self-determination.

The ideal of the nation-state as a political and cultural unit was of 'one nation, one state', whose citizens would be unified through a common civic spirit and shared democratic rights. This was what A. D. Smith has called the 'standard Western model' of the nation-state (Smith, 1991). This was challenged by more *völkisch* and ethnically based models of the nation, but while these differed in who would make up the nation, they shared with more civic forms of nationalism the assumption that a unified and autonomous national community would form the basis of the nation-state.

In the contemporary world nationalism has assumed a more ethnic form, and as a consequence national homogeneity has become much more difficult to realise, especially in the multicthnic and multinational societies of Eastern and Central Europe. Likewise the idea that the nation-state can command the loyalty of its citizens through cultural homogeneity and common education has become difficult to sustain in nation-states where multiculturalism is a feature (for example Canada), as well as in those with a significant proportion of national minorities. These minorities sometimes resist the process of what R. Brubaker calls 'nationalising states', and are sometimes the objects of what he calls 'external homelands', which develop irredentist policies to attract them (Brubaker, 1996).

Along with the internal problems of cultural and ethnic unity come the problems globalisation poses for the nation-state. In this context 'globalisation' means the spreading of economic production to a number of centres throughout the world, and the consequent loss of control by national governments of the process of production and determination of the welfare and employment prospects of their citizens. As a result of this the modernist assumption of control by a central agency (the democratic nation-state) over the lives of its citizens has become less tenable. Modernity pictured a society in which citizens would live in culturally homogeneous, politically and economically self-determining nation-states, linked by symbols of civic union. This aspiration has been shattered by the rise of global markets, internal fragmentation, cultural diversity and the growing ethnic, as opposed to civic, pull of nationalism.

While some authors assert that in the economic sphere the extent of globalisation has been exaggerated (Hirst and Thompson, 1996), it seems clear that the politics of modernity, with the nation-state as one of its main pillars, is being challenged by what has been called 'hybridisation', stemming from the contradictory relationship between global flows and national particularities. In the words of one social scientist,

> Introverted cultures, which have been prominent over a long stretch of history and which overshadowed translocal culture, are gradually receding into the background, while translocal culture made up of diverse elements is coming into the foreground. This transition and the hybridization process themselves unleash intense and dramatic nostalgia politics, of which ethnic upsurges, ethnici-

sation of nations, and religious revivalism form part (Pieterse, in Featherstone *et al.*, 1995, p. 62).

The bringing together, through global processes of economic moder-nisation, of different cultures and traditions is certainly 'subversive of essentialism and homogeneity' (ibid., p. 58), but what some authors call 'globality' contains both 'homogenising' and 'heterogenising' features, a confusing blend of the universal and the particular: 'Globality is the general condition which has *facilitated* the diffusion of "general modernity", globality at this point being viewed in terms of the interpenetration of geographically distinct "civilizations" (Featherstone *et al.*, 1995, p. 27). The result of these contradictory processes is that the modernist idea of citizen identity being largely moulded by the nation-state is no longer valid in postmodern society, where the process of globalisation offers a 'framework for the amplification and diversification of "sources of the self" ', a situation of 'global intercultural osmosis and interplay' (Featherstone et al., 1995, pp. 52, 54).

Problems of State and Citizenship

In similar vein, developments in the political sphere of the state render problematic certain features of modernity, and hence core assump-tions of its ideologies. These ideologies saw the state and democratic citizenship as basic elements of modernity. True, they differed over the extent and scope of state involvement, the degree to which the state should be based on the nation, and indeed whether (as con-servative theories maintained) the state should be left in the hands of a predemocratic traditional aristocracy, a wish expressed by Burke and clung to by leading conservatives such as Lord Salisbury in Britain. But the centrality of the state as a focus of collective life, and the need to capture state power in order to realise political projects, were ideas that were shared by all the ideologies of modernity.

The present crisis of the state and citizenship renders problematic these assumptions. The crisis is a result of a number of transforma-tions that seem to have weakened the state and undermined its role as the central focus of loyalty and cohesion, and as an instrument of political and social progress. As a result the state is undergoing both 'retreat and redefinition' (Müller and Wright, 1994). In liberal-democratic societies the ability of the state to look after the welfare of all its citizens and articulate collective purposes has come under sustained attack. This attack has intellectual roots in the work of liberal theorists such as Hayek, and its practical origins lay in the growing demands made on liberal-democratic states to provide health care for an ageing population, education and training for a society facing higher levels of unemployment, and retraining in new skills in line with technological developments. The fact that the state in liberal-democratic societies is seen as unable to cope with these demands, or that the state is unsuited to these tasks even if the resources are available, has weakened the central idea of modernity that the state will provide all its citizens with the care, education and security in the market society. Thus economic privatisation and marketisation have led to fragmentation of the modernist idea of common citizenship and democratic community.

There is also a crisis of the state in many of the former conmmunist societies, as the current elites seem unable to secure legitimacy for their new political systems, and hence to provide a focus for common citizenship by unifying the fragmentary tendencies of modern society. As a result modern states (whether established liberal democracies or those seeking to establish such a state) have willingly or otherwise abdicated much of their responsibility to private, decentralised centres of decision making, leading to greater fragmentation and loss of collective purpose. This poses a large problem for the ideologies of modernity.

Crisis of Civil Society

Civil society was a central strand in the politics of modernity. In the world of contemporary politics, civil society, with its range of associations and groups, is seen as the true source of democratisation, as the proper arena in which citizens can develop their capacities and express their varying interests and diverse identities. Hence this crucial idea has recently been given a new lease of life, especially in the context of post-communism and the contribution of civil movements to the overthrow of the single-party system. However civil society too seems to have become more problematic as a result of the transformations of late modernity. Civil society, as Gellner points out, rests on certain assumptions of 'modularity': citizens can move from one group to another, expressing a range of different interests through membership of a number of groups and associations (Hall, 1995). This pluralist picture however carries with it the problem of fragmentation and diversity: how can a common interest be realised in the face of the specialised and partial interests that find expression in civil society?

In the case of ex-Communist societies, while mass demonstrations and popular movements contributed to the democratisation of those regimes, the cooptation of the leaders of these movements into the ranks of the political elite raises the question of whether the groups that supported them can keep an appropriate distance from the state, whether they can maintain the right balance between autonomy from the state and awareness of their wider responsibilities as citizens in a democratic order – an old problem in democratic theory. Hence civil society and its popular movements, often hailed as the salvation of modern society, can become too fragmented and diverse, making it difficult to develop ideas of common citizenship.

There is a further problem in that some contemporary political theorists suggest a decline in civic awareness and participation, which is seen as indicating that fragmentation and individualism are eroding the appeal of the ideologies of modernity, and perhaps of democracy itself. The current debate about civil society suggests a lack of civic involvement, and points to concern about what has been called the declining 'social capital' of supposedly mature liberal democracies. While this debate has not yet embraced the consequence of this for the ideologies of modernity, there are some implications to be drawn.

This debate focuses on evidence of diminishing citizen involvement in the groups and associations that typify civil society. Here the chief reference point is the work of Robert Putnam, with his study of Italian democracy and his emphasis on the connection between a healthy democracy and the quality, and extent, of people's involvement in a network of groups and associations. In an often-cited article, Putnam noted an increase in the number of Americans tenpin bowling alone, rather than in teams, and saw this as symptomatic of a wider decline in social capital and social engagement, and indicative perhaps of the weakening of civil society. This has important implications for the stability and health of democracy, since it is through what Putnam calls 'networks of civic engagement' that citizens learn the give and take that is necessary for democratic politics: these groups and associations 'foster sturdy norms of generalised reciprocity and encourage the emergence of social trust' (Diamond and Plattner, 1996, p. 292).

There are also some implications here for the ideologies of modernity, since it is through the formation of a rational informed public opinion, itself the product of interaction in civil society, that critical discussion is fostered, as indicated in Habermas's study of the public sphere. If citizens are 'bowling alone', and not engaging in civic interaction, this suggests the decline of public space, of forums for the formation of public opinion. The consequences of this could be the greater atomisation or individualisation of society, with the prospect of greater manipulation of individuals by the mass media, and difficulty in sustaining an informed public among whom to disseminate ideologies as broad frameworks for political and public discussion. This should not be taken as advocating a golden age of citizens discussing social and political change in informed discussion circles. However the perceived decline of civil society does have certain implications for the ideologies of modernity.

Liberalism, socialism and nationalism all rested on the idea of a public sphere of citizen activity and some degree of rational interaction, as conjured up by the term 'civil society'. For example de Tocqueville, in *Democracy in America,* saw in diverse groups and associations, especially at the local government level, the pluralistic source of healthy democracy. The danger for contemporary society, with consequent implications for the entire modernist project, is that the decline of public space and areas of civic interaction means that ideological alternatives to the existing order will be more difficult to sustain. The ideological dimension of political life will shrivel away, to result in what Barber (1984) calls 'thin democracy', where politics will be a matter of individual or group interest representation, and ideas of critique, ideal and agency, the fundamental concerns of ideological discussion, will be lost. Thus one of the pillars of modernity, a rationally informed and active civil society, seems to be in some degree of crisis because of excessive individualism or fragmentation of society, leading individuals to 'bowl alone' instead of in groups, functioning as separate individuals rather than engaging in the social interaction that is basic to ideological politics.

The conclusion seems to be that civil society, for all its importance in recent discussion of politics, is itself in crisis: in the context of liberal-democratic systems, the network of groups and associations may become too interest-specific to generate any general social concern on issues of common citizenship. The decline in membership of the institutions of civil society may destroy some of the underpinnings or preconditions of the informed and active public opinion that theorists of the ideologies of modernity, in their more optimistic moments, relied on to articulate the general views of society, in other words to express and evaluate ideologies as frameworks for political discussion.

Putnam claims that 'By almost every measure, Americans' direct engagement in politics and government has fallen steadily and sharply over the last generation . . . Every year over the last decade or two, millions more have withdrawn from the affairs of their communities' (Diamond and Plattner, 1996, p. 293). If this is true, and if such findings apply to other contemporary liberal democracies, the implications for ideological debate as an index of a healthy democracy are considerable. It would suggest that the space necessary to sustain a broader conception of politics is lacking in modern liberal democracies, and that the ideologies of modernity – which rest on public opinion – are losing their grip on public life. Declining civic participation, greater privatisation in the sense of heightening the importance of the private as opposed to the public sphere, does seem to herald the danger of excessive fragmentation and division, which some of the more perceptive analysts of the new civil society that emerged at the end of the eighteenth century saw as central features of modernity. Both Adam Ferguson and de Tocqueville issued warnings of the dangers of excessive individualism and lack of concern with the public sphere.

The Decline of Class Identity

Modernity, it was claimed earlier, rested on industrial production, the capacity of human beings to conquer and exploit nature, and the centrality of class divisions to modern politics. All these have now become problematic, with large implications for the foundations of the ideologies of modernity. Environmental movements and theories question the whole idea of the conquest of nature and the continuing expansion of production. They point out that natural resources are not infinite, and highlight the devastating effects of unrestrained industrial production, devastating both with regard to the remaining natural resources and to the disasters that can be unleashed by the relentless pursuit of profits (for example the Exxon Valdez and Bhopal disasters). Likewise Ulrich Beck's idea of 'risk society' (Beck, 1992) points to the unintended risks that are created by continued production and the search for yet more commodities. These critiques naturally lead to a certain scepticism about the modernist stress on the primacy of industry and the development of new needs that can be satisfied without irrevocably disturbing the balance between humans and their environment.

A central strand of the politics of modernity was the significance of class divisions. Obviously this was at the heart of Marxism and more generally of socialist theorists, but even doctrines that rejected the Marxist view of the emancipatory potential of class struggle thought that antagonism between the social classes defined the era of modernity. It is true that Marxism did not see the class divide as a feature limited to modern society, since earlier societies had been stratified along class lines, with resultant antagonisms. As the *Communist Manifesto* proclaimed, 'All history is the history of class struggles'. Nevertheless the era of modernity, defined in Marxist terms as the era of capitalism, brought class divisions to a head and reduced other lines of conflict to a position of minor significance. The other ideologies of modernity did not share the view that class struggle would lead to emancipation, but it is hard to deny that even liberals saw the rise of the masses as posing the threat of revolution. This threat could be allayed, as Mill put it, by educating the masses in order to improve literacy and tax-paying qualifications for the franchise, to prevent what he saw as the danger of 'class legislation'. Conservative and nationalist writers saw class politics as a problem to be met by stressing the rallying power of the nation, a cohesive entity reconciling in one national unit the conflicting social classes.

The social transformations of postmodernity seem to have eroded the significance of class divisions in two ways. First, the power of 'class' as a collective subject in its own right, of a group of people acting collectively in pursuit of shared class interests, has been eroded by the economic and social developments of postmodernity. The productive processes of modernity were typified by 'Fordist' production lines, mass production in large-scale units by a homogeneous proletariat, albeit one always stratified by intraclass divisions of skill and industry. In contrast the contemporary world of advanced technology, 'flexible accumulation', smaller productive units employing people with a wider range of skills is a marked departure from the industrial structure that created the large industrial armies, to use the Saint-Simonian expression (Harvey, 1989).

Second, while not suggesting that the politics of modernity was ever dominated by class politics to the exclusion of other lines of division, such as religion, nationalism, and regional and local affiliations, there is no denying the historic centrality of class identity and the salience of class division to large sections of the population. From this emerged mass parties – classically represented by the German SPD in the period before 1914 – that wished to seize state power. The aim of such parties was to use the 'rules of the game' (Bobbio, 1994) of democratic politics to come to power legally, though holding the threat of violent revolution in reserve in case the property-owning classes felt tempted to abandon democracy. This was the scenario held out by Engels in his famous 1895 preface, pointing to the fact that the time of street-fighting *à la* 1848 was over, and suggesting that the steady advance of the German SPD was proceeding as 'irresistibly, and at the same time as tranquilly, as a natural process' (Marx and Engels, 1973, Vol. 1, p. 201).

In the conditions of contemporary politics, this 'forward march of labour', as Hobsbawm (1989, Ch. 1) put it, has long ceased to be seen as a central feature of reality. It is not that class politics has disappeared, but as a result of the economic and social transformations mentioned above, the centrality of class conflict has diminished and other identities have arisen to challenge class as a fundamental reference point. These other identities are gender, ethnic affiliation and cultural group, all of which are less firmly centred at the 'point of production' than class identities. Whether as a result of this or as a self-fulfilling contribution to this process, the leaders of social-democratic parties (for example Tony Blair of the British Labour Party) have more or less abandoned the language of class and instead appeal to a range of different affiliations and criteria of identity. These may take individualist forms (voters as consumers) or more group-based ones (national interests, one-nation themes). This new discourse of politics undermines one of the central pillars of modernity, namely the centrality of class division and the idea of politics as the expression of class struggle and the need for redistribution, or, in the classical Marxist view, politics as part of a wider process of class struggle involving the eventual removal of class differences.

The transformations described above are obviously central challenges to socialist theories with their emphasis on class division and class struggle. However, more is involved, as these changes in class structure pose a problem for modernity itself, and for all the ideologies arising out of it. If the familiar class map of capitalist societies has changed beyond recognition, with a host of criss-crossing identities and plural affiliations competing for citizens' loyalties, then where, if anywhere, is the social basis for a majoritarian movement of social transformation and emancipation that could overcome the inequalities inherent in any market society and create a genuine community spanning such economic divisions? If the answer to this question is that there is no social basis for such a movement, one pessimistic conclusion would be that ideas of emancipation will have to be jettisoned as archaic remnants of a modernist age whose defining features no longer apply. None of this suggests that class politics has totally disappeared from the map of the postmodern world, but class as a collective subject of politics is much less salient, more fragmented and less dominant than in the era of modernity. Hence traditional class analysis of the Marxist sort seems less able to analyse the conflicts and tensions of contemporary society, partly because conflict arising at the point of production is just one of many sources of difference and antagonism. In the words of the French thinker André Gorz,

> It is not through identification with their work and their work role that modern wage-earners feel themselves justified in making demands for power which have the potential to change society. It is as citizens, residents, parents, teachers, students or as unemployed; it is their experience outside work that leads them to call capitalism into question (Gorz, 1994, p. 42).

This has important implications not just for socialist thought but for all the ideologies of modern politics, which now have to deal with a much more complex and less clearly delineated social structure.

In the conditions of contemporary politics, these changes have totally transformed the context in which the 'traditional' ideologies of politics are situated, and thrown up new problems for the protagonists and theorists of those ideologies. The problematic nature of the nation, the crisis of the state, the ambiguities of civil society, and the quite new structure of economy and industry, have provoked the crisis of modernity and of its ideologies. In particular these changes make more problematic the *universalism* inherent in modernity and its political ideas. The challenges facing the nation-state because of growing ethno-nationalism, leading to the possible undermining of the idea of a nation of democratic citizens; the difficulty of the state maintaining its role as a unifying body and the ceding of some of its powers to processes of market allocation and criteria of distribution; the crisis of civil society with the danger of excessive fragmentation and concentration on issues of particular interest representation and the underestimation of common civic interests; and the transformed social and industrial structure that splits up large industry and cohesive classes into small productive and more specialised units – 'all these changes are leading to a more fragmented and divided society marked by particularism and loss of the idea, dear to the Enlightenment and modernist traditions, of a common agent of change and common emancipatory interests.

The increased complexity of society, and the emergence of several competing 'subjects' or agents of collective action and sources of community and identity have undermined the idea of universalism and emancipation. The 'politics of difference', with its emphasis on heterogeneity and fragmentation, both responds to the changed nature of reality and offers a critique of the traditional ideologies of politics, with their emphasis on a single subject, be this the liberal emphasis on the individual, the socialist idea of class, the nationalist appeal to the nation or the conservative invocation of tradition. In addition the fragmented nature of contemporary society is fuelling scepticism about the modernist assumption that society can be controlled and transformed by the state. The traditional ideologies of politics believed that capturing state power was the necessary prerequisite for social transformation. Contemporary scepticism about the role of the state leads to doubt about the levers of power, the practicability of any attempt at social transformation, and the dangers of the exercise if it were possible. The emergence of ethno-nationalist movements and growing awareness of their mobilising and destructive power are also causing doubt to be cast on the rationalist and optimistic assumptions of the modernist tradition, evident of course in liberal and socialist theories.

The Challenge of Postmodernism

This section seeks to explain what is meant by the challenge of postmodernism, and the implications of this for the political ideologies discussed in this book. The ideologies of modernity all rest on three assumptions, couched in very general terms as follows:

- There is a set of basic and coherent principles upon which society should be constructed, and in principle it is possible for rational and enlightened citizens to reach a consensus on these principles.
- No insurmountable obstacles exist to prevent the transformation and reconstruction of society on the basis of these principles.

• There exists an agency – a force or set of forces, a subject – that is
adequate to the task of social transformation, and hence this task is
a practicable one. This subject is differently constituted according
to the ideology in question, whether it is the working class for
socialism, the rational self-interested individual for liberalism, or
'the nation' for the ideologies of nationalism.

These three assumptions are crucial to the politics of modernity, and
they are summed up concisely in Marx's famous statement that
'Therefore mankind always sets itself only such tasks as it can solve,
since looking at the matter more closely, it will always be found that
the task itself arises only when the material conditions for its solution
already exist or are at least in the process of formation' (Marx and
Engels, 1973, vol. I, p. 504).

Postmodernist theorists offer a challenge to the traditional canon of
the ideologies of Left and Right. But what exactly is meant by
postmodernism in this context? In the words of H. Bertens (1995,
p. 3), 'postmodernism is an exasperating term, and so are postmodern, postmodernist, postmodernity, and whatever else one might
come across in the way of derivation'. Postmodernism has been
summarised as involving the following propositions (White, 1991,
pp. 4–12).

First, there are no 'grand narratives' any more, and the idea of
progress towards 'the good society' is rejected. Since there is no
Archimedean point from which to attain agreement on the principles
of the good society, any attempt to reach agreement will only lead to
dictatorship and the elimination of those who think differently.

Second, no single party or movement can encapsulate everybody's
vision of the good society, hence the idea of a single force creating a
free society is irrelevant in a context of pluralism and diversity.

Third, as a result of the above the future of politics lies in a variety
of new social movements that contribute to, but can not dictate, the
global (ideological) view of the good society. Today everything is
fragmented and polarised, and this finds political expression in new
social movements rather than the old bureaucratised parties. These
associations are often seen as the bearers of diverse identities and
separate issues that are appropriate to the postmodern age, since 'the
possible number of social movements is limited only by the potential
range of collective identities people are willing to adopt (for example,
as women, rate payers, animal lovers, inner-city dwellers, etc.)' (Scott,
1990, p. 3).

Postmodernism as a broad set of theories has important implications for the ideologies of modernity. The postmodern critique
focuses on the three main elements of the modern ideologies, namely
critique, vision and agency. The postmodern perspective is that
ideologies in general are examples of 'grand narratives' that cannot
successfully claim the universal legitimation they seek, and that any
total view of an alternative society, such as those offered by those
ideologies, is bound to be partial and incomplete. Similarly the
critique of existing society offered by the various ideologies is seen
as limited, stemming from a perspective that cannot command
universal allegiance. Postmodern critiques also suggest that the
ideologies of modernity lack a coherent subject or agency of change
to realise the transformations they call for, thereby attacking the
conceptual roots of all these ideologies.

The term 'grand narrative' comes from one of the chief theorists of
postmodernism, Jean-François Lyotard, who cites what he calls 'the
emancipation of the rational or working subject' as an example of a
'grand narrative'. The postmodern age, he suggests, began at the end
of the 1950s. In the postmodern era knowledge has become a
principal force of production, and there can be no consensus on
shared principles, on a common 'language game', and hence no
coherent agent of emancipation, no 'social subject':

> The social subject itself seems to dissolve in this dissemination of
> language games. The social bond is linguistic, but is not woven with
> a single thread. It is a fabric formed by the intersection of at least
> two (and in reality an indeterminate number) of language games,
> obeying different rules (Lyotard, 1992, p. 40).

This perspective has a number of implications for the ideologies of
modernity. If there is no coherent 'social subject', whether this is seen
as 'the people', 'the working class', 'the nation', then the ideologies of
modernity lack any means of putting their critique of existing reality
into practice. Furthermore Lyotard seems to suggest that partial,
small-scale transformations are all that one can hope for in the
postmodern age, since broader views of emancipation and total social
transformation have no purchase – there can be no general agreement
or consensus on such ideologies:

> We no longer have recourse to the grand narratives – we can resort
> neither to the dialectic of Spirit nor even to the emancipation of

humanity as a validation for postmodern scientific discourse . . . the little narrative (*petit récit*) remains the quintessential form of imaginative invention, most particularly in science (Lyotard, 1992, p. 60).

This is similar to Foucault's preference, cited earlier, for 'very specific transformations' in contrast with 'the programmes for a new man' (Rabinow, 1986, p. 46). It also seems to suggest that, quite apart from there being no general agreement or consensus on any ideology, the whole notion of progress and emancipation – which underpins at least some of the central ideologies of modernity, certainly liberalism and socialism – cannot hope to survive the postmodern 'incredulity towards metanarratives'. Modernity involved the idea of a new 'subject' of politics, the people, who swept away the remnants of the old order, but Lyotard suggests that this is just an example of a 'narrative of emancipation' that has lost its credibility in the postmodern age. The modern idea was that

the representatives of the new process of legitimation by 'the people' should be at the same time actively involved in destroying the traditional knowledge of peoples, perceived from that point forward as minorities or potential separatist movements destined only to spread obscurantism (Lyotard, 1992, p. 30).

However, in his view,

In contemporary society and culture – post-industrial society, post-modern society – the question of the legitimation of knowledge is formulated in different terms. The grand narrative has lost its credibility, regardless of what mode of unification it uses, regardless of whether it is a speculative narrative or a narrative of emancipation (ibid., p. 37).

This critique serves to undermine the basis of the ideologies of modernity. It suggests that there is no coherent agent or subject, that there can be no consensus or agreement on the critical perspectives and alternative visions presented by the ideologies of modernity, and that the emancipatory perspectives proposed by them (conservatism excepted) have no foundation.

Indeed the postmodern critique suggests that notions of the agent or 'subject' are themselves constituted by or internal to a particular ideology, that they have no general validity, that they are constructed by a particular discourse (or language game as Lyotard would say). Foucault asked the question 'How are we constituted as subjects who exercise or submit to power relations? How are we constituted as moral subjects of our own actions' (Rabinow, 1986, p. 49). If the notion of the 'subject' or agent of change is constructed by the particular ideology in question, then it need not be accepted by those who do not share the premises of that ideology, it is an intellectual construct with no necessary purchase on reality. Hence the difficulty experienced by, for example, the French Jacobins in constructing the 'subject' of 'the patriot' or 'good citizen'. The Jacobins did manage to construct such a figure, but as the search involved an ever more restricted circle of persons, Jacobinism became a discourse of exclusion, since only a small number of people were seen as really good patriots, the virtuous few who were supposedly the agents of history and committed to the revolution (Ozouf, 1989; Jaume, 1989). Postmodern critiques problematise the notion of the subject or agent, which was a central, relatively unproblematic element of all the ideologies of modernity.

Part of the challenge of postmodernism lies in its insistence on multiple sources of 'self' (Taylor, 1991) and of authenticity. The idea is that there are a variety of sources of identity, and these find expression in social and political action in innumerable ways:

> It [postmodernism] attempts to expose the politics that are at work in representations and to undo institutionalised hierarchies, and it works against the hegemony of any single discursive system – which would inevitably victimise other discourses – in its advocacy of difference, pluriformity and multiplicity (Bertens, 1995, p. 8).

Hence to reduce politics to a basic Left–Right division is seen as a reductive and false way of conceptualising political life. To the extent that the ideologies of the modern period sought to do this, and to the extent that conceptual maps of the politics of modernity perpetuated this division, they are both false to reality and neglect the multiple divisions that surface in society. The ideas of difference and of identity are seen as fundamental concepts that blow apart some of the old ideologies and proclaim their irrelevance. Postmodernists declare that traditional identities have lost their primacy, hence the negative implications for the long-established ideologies of Left and Right. The accusation is that the main ideologies of the modern

period are unable to account for the plural affiliations that characterise the contemporary period, and therefore the whole agenda of the
age of ideology needs to be discarded.

What then is the challenge of postmodernism with regard to the
ideologies of modernity? If postmodernism is right, then all ideologies
share a common structure that suppresses or fails to realise the variety
of sources of identity and indeed of power. The argument is that the
very structure of an ideology and its basic ground principles negate
pluralism. Ideology and pluralism are mutually incompatible, and the
political consequences or implications of the age of ideology are that
one view of 'the good society' is created or imposed by each ideology,
and that the binary opposition between Left and Right, as well as the
imposition by each ideology of its own particular truth, suppresses
freedom and variety.

Pluralism and Diversity

Pluralist perspectives in this sense go along with the politics of
postmodernism. Because there are so many identities – gender, ethnic,
national, class, individual, regional, perhaps supranational – then
none of the ideologies of modernity, which sought to impose one
identity above all others, can be valid any more, if they ever were. In
other words the continued development of modernity created the
conditions for the dissolution or disintegration of the ideologies that
arose in response to it, and the dialectic of modernity undermined the
bases, intellectual and social, of the ideologies that were the initial
expression of modernity.

There are thus two sets of arguments that suggest a 'crisis of
ideologies' and offer an alternative in terms of the kind of pluralism
sketched out above. The first argument is an empirical or explanatory
social-scientific one, concerning the changed nature of postindustrial
or postmodern society. The second is a more normative one concerning the desirability of heterogeneity or pluralism. The structure of
contemporary society means that overriding importance is not given
to one particular identity, so theories that emphasise a single identity
(class in the case of Marxism) have failed to come to terms with the
diverse sources of identity and difference in a complex postmodern
society. From a society in which different social classes did indeed
lead quite different styles of life, concentrated in particular geographical communities, each with its own codes, there has been a

transition to a much more inclusive type of society, in which new skills are called for and former divisions are if not exactly removed, then rivalled by other distinctions. Hence new terms of social and political discourse have emerged to reflect this heterogeneity. Concepts of 'citizenship', 'identity' and 'difference' and a revived interest in the idea of pluralism have emerged, along with the resurgence of ethno-nationalism, to suggest a new interpretation of reality. The idea of citizenship now suggests the inclusion in the affairs of society of an exceedingly heterogeneous variety of groups and individuals, who can no longer, if they ever could, be adequately categorised by class affiliation. In this sense the renewed significance of the idea of citizenship and community reflects a concern to bring together in some political association, however loosely defined, the plurality of individuals that typify modern society.

The language of the old ideologies has been challenged as no longer appropriate to a world whose contours have changed, hence the traditional Left–Right spectrum and the individual ideologies ranged along it cannot, for different reasons, adequately cope with the features of this new society. In the new society there is competition between a variety of identities and perspectives, none of which are captured sufficiently by the old ideologies, with the possible exception of nationalism.

The new words of pluralism – 'identity', and 'difference' – seek to 'break the mould' of the traditional ideologies. 'Identity' suggests the need for group affiliation to achive a sense of belonging. Pluralism offers the idea of membership of a multiplicity of groupings, such as national and regional, ethnic, professional, class, gender, cultural, generational, environmental and religious, to mention only the most obvious ones. These identities go along with, as their corollary, a whole set of differences: the politics of identity and difference is a new topic to which the traditional ideologies of Enlightenment politics were blind.

8

Critiques of the Enlightenment Ideologies

The politics of modernity and the ideologies that express the modernist perspective have suffered badly in the twentieth century. The experiences of fascism, the barbarism of Nazism, and the mass terror and violence of Stalinism have severely dented belief in the power of reason, in the capacity of humanity to construct a good society and eradicate violence and political tyranny (Miliband, R. 1994, p. 58). Nor has the experience of the years since the end of fascism, as humanity advances towards the end of the twentieth century, been very encouraging in terms of realisation of the Enlightenment project of a world ruled by reason. Critics of that project point to the emergence of religious and ethnic fundamentalism, to desperate appeals to national identity, to illustrate their view that the idea of a society controlled by rational cooperation between human beings is further away than ever, that what has been called the politics of identity and difference can take abrasive and antagonistic forms in the world of modern politics, making the politics of modernity an unrealisable project. The very process of modernity has 'hollowed out' the community, and the seeming decline of liberalism and socialism has left a void that can all too easily be filled by irrational and emotive ideologies, such as extreme forms of ethnic nationalism. Hence modernity has led, in the view of critics such as John Gray (1995), to 'disenchantment' with the process of rationalisation, and hence to the privileging of movements and ideas that exalt emotivism and myth, for example extreme-right forms of nationalism.

This chapter seeks to marshall the arguments that consign to irrelevance the main ideologies of modernity and propose new ideologies or different attitudes towards politics that modernity's critics see as more suited to the new age. The critique of modernity and its ideologies is thus a double critique. It is a critique of particular

175

ideologies, of particular views of 'the good society' and the ways of achieving it, and it is also a critique of the very nature of ideology itself, of the impossibility of a holistic or totalistic view of the good society.

Critique of Liberalism

Starting with the critique of liberalism, on the surface it seems as though that liberalism has been a decided winner in the age of ideology, and it is therefore strange to argue that it is in crisis. Indeed one version of liberalism, free-market liberalism, seems to have been adopted as a panacea by the countries of the ex-Soviet Union (Szacki, 1994). Liberalism offers a desirable model in its vision of a society governed by the rule of law, the market as the method of allocating scarce resources, and the more limited role of the state as an arbiter. However there are deep problems for liberalism in the contemporary world.

Early liberalism held out the promise that humanity would be emancipated from tradition and the deadweight of the past. Later liberals saw the pressure of democracy as something that could not be halted, but were aware that it threatened individual liberty as they conceived it. This was the burden of de Tocqueville's analysis of democracy. However contemporary liberalism seems to have abandoned its emancipatory vision, to have problems with the idea of community, and to have elevated the market to the supreme end to which all else is sacrificed.

The first problem is the classical one of the ontological basis of liberal thought: commitment to the rational individual. The rational individual, knowing his or her interests, emancipated from tradition, from the weight of the past, and also protected from pressures of democratic conformity and mediocrity, was the highest goal of liberalism.

What does this vision have to offer in the postmodern age? There are two core problems here. The first is growing scepticism about the possibility of individual rationality. For liberals of all hues the individual is capable of rational conduct, and the aim is to free individuals from constraints that fetter their rational self-determination. However the problem is whether this is a realistic picture of humanity, whether it overestimates the human capacity for self-determination and rational conduct at the expense of underestimating the capacity of human beings to be manipulated and controlled by hidden or not-so-hidden sources of power.

For example fascism stressed the irrational and emotive side of human nature that caused human beings to be part of a mass, capable only of being led and directed by a superhuman figure, who would mould them as the raw clay of history. There are plenty of examples in the rhetoric of fascism of the view that people are not self-determining, but rather are passive recipients of the will of the heroic leader. Of course this view does not have to be seen as accurate, but it serves to illustrate one critique of liberalism, namely its optimistic view of human nature. From the socialist point of view, the liberal view of the individual abstracts from the class forces and economic structure of society that restrict individuals' capacity for autonomy and self-determination in a class-divided society.

Criticism of the excessively rational and optimistic nature of the liberal view of the individual has gained force in the postmodern age, since the opportunity to manipulate individuals and control information about them is much greater. The implications of new technology and sources of information point to greater empowerment of individuals and groups but also to greater control by powerholders (Bryan, 1996). Throughout its history liberalism has been criticised for taking too cerebral a view of the individual, too atomised a view of what has been called 'the disembodied self'.

The second core problem with liberalism is its failure to understand the idea of community. Liberal theory neglects the social structures, the communities – national or regional, intellectual or religious – that mould individuals and give them their identity, which is particularly necessary in times of rapid change. The charge that liberalism has been blind to the social determinants of the individual comes from a variety of sources, with quite contrasting political implications. The Right stresses the organic unity of society, and the need for individual rights and identity to be circumscribed by communities, usually ones that give little autonomy to the individual. Postmodern theorists stress that individuals exist in a variety of social contexts that shape their often conflicting identities, make them different, and hence the idea of the abstract rational individual is a fiction, inapplicable to any actual society.

To give one topical example of the problem of liberalism as a contemporary ideology, the introduction of market liberalism in the ex-communist countries, quite apart from its purely economic consequences, seems to have led to a resurgence of nationalism, which

offers the sense of solidarity and community that liberalism is unable
to provide on its own. Similarly it has often been remarked in
analyses of the 'New Right' in Europe and America, that the
imposition on societies of 'strict' liberalism has gone hand in hand
with values of a different type, emphasising national union or the
importance of 'family values' (King, 1987). The Enlightenment
principles of individual rationality and sovereignty are challenged
by ideas that criticise liberalism for its artificial and impoverished
view of what individuals are or what human nature is. These ideas
stress the need for ideologies that offer answers to the question of
identity, of community and solidarity, and of difference. Liberalism
cannot offer a convincing answer precisely because of its incomplete
view of human nature and the social contexts that give individuals
their identity.

Explaining human identity in terms of affiliation to different
communities, with particularistic loyalties, deals a severe blow to
the universalism that is basic to the liberal, as to the socialist,
tradition. The theme of particularism is central to critiques of
ideologies in the Enlightenment tradition. These ideologies presup-
pose a basis of universalism, and have a view of human nature and
human identity that transcends any particular local or national
context.

This critique thus emphasises the diversity and fragmentation that
characterise the present situation, in which the politics of modernity
and the processes of modernity have given rise to a rationalisation or
'disenchantment' of the world. If the politics of modernity, whose
premises were shared by liberalism and socialism, emphasised uniformity, or at least common processes that were sweeping the globe,
then movements based on ideologies that emphasise difference and
local traditions can be seen as a reaction to this process of modernisation. This is where nationalism scores highly as a protest and
reaction against the uniform sweep of modernisation.

One of the most celebrated statements of the rationality and
uniformity of capitalism comes from the pages of *The Communist
Manifesto*, where the progress of capitalism is represented as undermining national differences:

The bourgeoisie has through its exploitation of the world market
given a cosmopolitan character to production and consumption in
every country. To the great chagrin of reactionists, it has drawn
from under the feet of industry the national ground on which it

stood. All old-established national industries have been destroyed or are daily being destroyed . . . National one-sidedness and narrow-mindedness become more and more impossible, and from the numerous national and local literatures, there arises a world literature (Marx, 1973a, p. 71).

But what liberals and socialists such as Marx and Engels saw as 'national one-sidedness and narrow-mindedness' was seen by others in a much more positive light – as national cultural traditions that gave people a distinct identity, a particular way of life that was in danger of being swept away by modernisation and globalisation – then this explains the resurgence of the particular. The defence of particularism challenges the universalism of the Enlightenment tradition, and thus the basis of both liberalism and socialism. The challenge is that both liberalism and socialism are unable to understand the rise of particularistic movements that give people a sense of identity in an increasingly homogeneous world.

The Dissolution of Socialism

With socialism the issues are different. The starting point for socialism is the collective, the social, the primacy of the whole (society) over its component parts, the individuals who comprise it. Socialist theories emphasise one kind of difference, one sort of antagonism, namely class conflict. The postmodernist criticism of socialism, and more broadly of the whole tradition of ideas stemming from the revolutionary era, is that socialist theory makes certain teleological assumptions. Marxism is criticised for operating with too deterministic and schematic a schedule, for seeing history as moving towards a predetermined end: the liberation of humanity, the proletariat as the agent of this emancipation. The charge levelled by critics of the Enlightenment tradition is that socialist theory is a prime example of 'grand narrative'. Marxism is 'tainted' by its Hegelian origins and its consequent view of human history as going through certain fixed stages to arrive at a final goal: the overcoming of scarcity and human liberation from exploitation and domination. However, the evolution of capitalism has not followed the path laid down in Marx's great work *Capital*, and the attempt to force history into a straitjacket has led, as with all ideologies, to justification of tyranny and domination.

The critique of socialism is that it has no realistic or scientific basis. In defence of this critique one could bring into play certain ecological perspectives. It could be suggested that Marxism aimed to conquer nature, and in this respect it shared certain features with Enlightenment theory and nineteenth-century scientism. Marxism, along with the whole Enlightenment tradition, had a productivist and rather manipulative attitude towards the environment and nature. The aim was the 'Promethean' one of conquering nature and exploiting its unlimited resources as a necessary part of human and social emancipation. It is strange that Marx's writings were very alive to the dialectic and interaction between individuals and their social context, but the interaction between the social and natural worlds was given much less importance, so the new theories of environmentalism seem a necessary corrective to the productivist emphasis in Marxism. 'Productivism' here means a view of society that stressed the fundamental importance of material production, that the development of the forces of production was a precondition for human liberation, and that the natural world possessed enough resources to allow this to happen.

The implication of this for socialist theory is that socialism has come to share some of the deficiencies of the whole Enlightenment philosophy. Modernity is seen as relatively unproblematic in the socialist and Marxist tradition. Indeed the socialist project, in its most general and abstract sense, was to bring the politics of modernity to completion, both philosophically and practically. In the philosophical sense the socialist project was a universalist one. This does not mean that socialist and Marxist theory neglected nationalism and its appeals, as recent studies make clear (Benner, 1995; Schwarzmantel, 1991). However the socialist perspective was that human emancipation was a process that required certain universal preconditions. Chief among these was the worldwide development of productive forces to enable international cooperation and emancipation on a world scale.

The bourgeoisie were unable to make full use of the productive powers that they themselves had harnessed and developed, so it was up to the socialist movement to carry on the project of modernity and develop it for the benefit of humanity as a whole. In socialist and Marxist analysis, the property-owning classes took only a short-term view. Politically (and this comes out very clearly in Marx and Engels' writings on 1848 in Germany) they feared that creating a democratic republic and removing the monarchy and aristocracy would lead to their own overthrow. Hence in Germany in 1848, as in France in 1851, the bourgeoisie compromised with the established order and gave their support to an authoritarian leader in order to repress insurrection from below. Thus the bourgeoisie could not be relied on to be the agents of political modernity and progress. True, the *Communist Manifesto* talked of the bourgeoisie having attained 'exclusive political sway' in the form of the modern representative state. And indeed the whole perspective of the *Manifesto* is of the bourgeoisie as the remorseless agents and instigators of modernity. Yet in the political writings of Marx and Engels 'the bourgeoisie' are depicted as hesitant agents of modernity, especially in the political sphere, being unwilling to advance democracy because of the danger of popular power and the consequent threat to bourgeois economic and social power.

The core idea of socialism was collective control (however achieved) over the social apparatus of production and distribution was necessary to realise the full benefit of advanced production, of the capitalist mode of production, for all the members of society. Indeed in some respects this idea seems highly relevant to present-day societies as they confront the problems of the late twentieth century.

The main dilemma for socialism is that the continued advance of modernity has led to the dissolution or fragmentation of society along individualist lines rather than to class unity and the collectivist outcome expected by socialist theories of all types. Furthermore, where there have been attempts at unity or collective action these have taken place not along class lines, but along various lines of identification and affiliation that ignore class division. On this question of agency, the French writer André Gorz makes some pertinent points: 'The question as to the 'subject' that will decide the central conflict, and in practice carry out the socialist transformation, cannot . . . be answered by means of traditional class analysis' (Gorz, 1994, p. 69). Given the changing nature of workplace activity in contemporary capitalist societies and the growing number of people unemployed or employed on a part-time basis, work cannot provide the basis for the satisfaction of the individual and the focus for general emancipation:

In present conditions . . . neither the material possibility nor the subjective capacity for a transformation of work into autonomous activity exists. The labour process and the nature of the tasks performed in work develop the capacity to engage in

autonomous activities only for an ever smaller number of employ-
ees (ibid., p. 57).

Hence for Gorz the socialist idea of 'binding . . . capitalist rationality
within a democratically defined framework' involves the need 'to
promote the development of a sphere of lived sociality . . . made up of
forms of self-organised, voluntary cooperation and of non-commod-
ity, non-monetary exchange' (ibid., p. 84). However the agency or
means of attaining such a goal in contemporary conditions cannot be
the traditional labour movement, but what Gorz calls 'a multidimensional social movement that can no longer be defined in terms of class
antagonisms' (ibid., p. 89). The term socialism, then, cannot refer to a
completely alternative model of society along the lines of traditional
socialism, but to a movement that would 'focus on cultural, inter-
personal, community life as intensively as it does on working life'. Its
'bearers' would be a 'post-industrial proletariat', and those in short-
term, part-time work, as well as those without work, whose

> criticism of capitalism and socialist sensibility are not to be derived
> from their working lives or their class consciousness but, rather,
> from the discovery they make as citizens, parents, consumers,
> residents of a neighbourhood or town, of capitalist development
> dispossessing them of their – social and natural – lifeworld (ibid.,
> p. 72).

The implication of this is that changes in the nature of work in
contemporary society throw into doubt both the classical agency of
socialism (the traditional labour movement), and its vision of an
alternative society. Gorz does not conclude that socialism is dead,
indeed he suggests that it can revive itself 'if, in keeping with its
original meaning, it understands itself as striving to carry through the
emancipation of individuals begun by the bourgeois revolution' (ibid.,
p. 39). However this would involve a redefinition of both agency and
the traditional view of socialism as offering an alternative system
based on a scientifically validated view of history.

   Hence the shape of postmodern society has diminished the prospect
of traditional socialism and those movements, whether reformist or
revolutionary, that sought to realise its ideals. The evidence is that
modernity has stimulated individualism and difference, and that the
politics of identity has taken forms that no longer involve class
distinction and division. These forms emphasise national and ethnic

identity, gender, consumerism and what Giddens calls 'life style politics'. These have reduced the importance of the discourse of socialism and led to a need to 'reinvent the Left' in ways that respond to the transformations in contemporary society (D. Miliband, 1994).

There is one further problem that contemporary socialism has to confront: the question of democracy, which has become the core legitimating ideal of the modern world. In some of its manifestations socialism has had trouble with the concept of democracy, above all in East European socialism and in relation to Lenin's idea of the vanguard party. The revolutions against communism, against the Soviet-style system, were revolutions in the name of democracy and 'power to the people' was their slogan. In a sense the anti-communist revolutions from 1989 onwards were in Habermas' words '*nachholende Revolutionen*', revolutions that were not backward-looking but sought to bring to Eastern and Central Europe civil liberty, the right to free association and assembly, independent civil society, and plurality and representation outside the grip of the single party – in fact all these rights that had long been taken for granted in the liberal–democracies of the West.

In the course of these revolutions the discourse of socialism, the idea of proletarian power became discredited, even though these movements were protests against the communist or Soviet power structure, and not against the theory of socialism as such. However the fact remains that the language of democracy was mobilised against regimes that, in however perverted a way, were speaking the language of Marxism and socialism. Furthermore there was little evidence of such revolutions holding a commitment to any other type of socialism. Indeed the idea of collective control over the productive resources of society was rejected as giving rise to new sources of power that could be captured by a politico-economic elite.

To summarise, socialism in the postmodern world is faced by three serious challenges it seems unable to meet. First, because of its championship of modernity it does not seem able to recognise the individualist and fragmentary thrust of contemporary society. Second, the collectivist emphasis of socialism privileges one particular type of collective identity, class, which seems less important as a mobilising force in postmodern times than the many other identities that exist today. Finally the recent upsurge in demand for democracy, people power, and the whole phenomenon of the revolutions of 1989 to 1991 were carried out in opposition to communist regimes. Those regimes employed, albeit in distorted ways, the language and discourse of Marxist socialism, so the democratic challenge was a challenge to Marxism and socialism. Socialists were accused of having paid too little heed to democratic rights and to the importance of people choosing their representatives and deciding what they thought best, not guided by the representatives of a single ruling party.

Nationalism and Identity

Unlike liberalism and socialism, nationalism derives its continuing strength from its appeal to the particular rather than the universal, to the idea of a particular nation endowed with its own special features – be these related to language, culture, history or religion – that enable people to bond together and feel a sense of unity.

Nationalism in its various manifestations has tried to heal the wounds of modernity by offering people a refuge against the remorseless universalism and uniformity it espouses. If modernity is defined at least in part as the ceaseless desire for economic development, irrespective of time, place, culture, language and shared history, nationalism with its focus on precisely those features is able to serve as a bastion against the unceasing levelling process of modernity.

There is a second way in which nationalism has 'scored' over liberalism and socialism: it has been able to ally itself with democracy, at least on a superficial level, in some quite surprising ways. Nationalism has, so to speak, a *prima facie* democratic legitimacy, even though in many cases it has actually functioned to undermine democracy and make it more difficult to achieve. Nationalism's link with democracy is both historical and conceptual, and the two have joined together as expressions of the modernist principles discussed earlier. The relevance of this for contemporary politics is that nationalism's claim to democratic legitimacy has enabled it not only to survive but also to gain strength as the age of ideology draws to a close. The idea that a group of people aware of their common identity and shared historical, cultural and perhaps religious or linguistic background should be self-determining has been taken up in many parts of the world. The postmodern stress on fragmentation and diversity, and the associated ideas of identity and difference, is not shaking the hold of nationalism, but rather is grist to its mill, because nationalists are able to endorse the idea of national differences and share in the rejection of what is seen as false universality.

Nonetheless the problems that nationalism faces in the modern world are no less intractable than those facing liberalism and socialism. In the first place, the link between democracy and nationalism is seen by many as highly tenuous, and this is undermining the credibility of nationalism in a world that is supposedly moving towards the universal acceptance of democracy. It is also undermining nationalism's strongest claim: the desire for genuine community. Nationalism can be both inclusive and exclusive, depending on how 'nation' is defined. Nationalism has all too often undermined democracy by denying citizenship to those who do not share the state-defined characteristics of the rest of the nation, whether these are based on ethnicity, language or religion.

Hence critics of the Enlightenment ideologies may spare nationalism because it allows for particularism and does not operate with an abstract concept of universalism. However the purchase of particularism sometimes comes at a very high price: the demonising or exclusion of those who do not share the defining characteristics of the nation. This serves to undermine the democratic credentials of nationalism.

As discussed earlier, a strong feature of the postmodern age is fragmentation and the diffusion of different identities. While nationalists are strong in their insistence on the importance of national identity, they are often reluctant to recognise the plurality of identities within a particular nation, and in this respect nationalism can often be highly backward looking and hostile to the politics of modernity. Indeed 'integral' nationalism shares with certain kinds of conservatism a defensive and aggressive traditionalism, that aims to avoid or repress plurality and diversity within the nation. Even civic nationalism, while much more inclusive, has problems in this direction.

This chapter has examined three of the central ideologies that emerged from the Enlightenment tradition – liberalism, socialism and nationalism – and subjected them to certain themes of the postmodern critique: those that emphasise diversity (the variety of different identities in the modern world), community, democracy and particularism. Liberalism seems unable to cater to the desire for community; socialism offers a view of community, but one that seems less appealing when compared with much more powerful sources of community and identity in the modern world; while nationalism is unable, at least in some of its most powerful forms, to offer a stable basis for democracy, or to avoid slipping into abrasive and extreme forms that purchase identity through hostility to a scapegoat and abandoning rational politics.

The concluding chapter investigates whether any elements of the Enlightenment tradition are relevant to the contemporary political world. In other words, whether ideology has a future.

9

The Future of Ideology

Does ideology have a future? The question is whether the hopes for any transformative politics have been destroyed by the new features of the postmodern world sketched out in Chapter 7. The answer offered here is that different ideologies are necessary to identify broad features of contemporary reality and suggest ways in which social transformation is possible. Ideological thought is a necessary part of the process of democratic politics. Political parties, if they are not to degenerate into power-hungry groups with no principles or guiding aims, must adhere to an ideology. In this sense the end of ideology could mean the end of democratic politics, and of principles in political life.

The argument that will be put forward here is that the ideologies of modernity do have a future, but that they need to be developed and made more flexible to take account of the undoubtedly changed contours of the postmodern world. However, before defending the ideologies of modernity it is worth summarising the lines of attack to which ideological discourse has been subjected. Ideologies have been criticised on the following three grounds:

- The assumptions they make about a coherent and conscious agent of political and social change.
- Their unitary assumptions and failure to recognise diversity.
- Their connection with totalitarianism.

Each of these problems is briefly reviewed below.

Problems of Subject and Agency

The theorists of postmodernity suggest that the shape of modern society is one of fragmentation and diffusion, and that as a result any attempt at ideological politics is fundamentally misguided. All ideologies are seen as politically dangerous because they seek to impose a single set of principles, a political masterplan, on a complex and pluralistic society that is resistant to social engineering.

The ideologies of modernity assumed a core division in society, broadly along the lines of the conflict between Left and Right, between the forces of progress and those opposed to change. The issues of popular power, democracy and then socialism were the chief focus of this conflict. The demand for popular power arose first in the political sphere (political democracy) and then in the social sphere (economic and social democracy or socialism). Nationalism fits somewhat uneasily in to this Left–Right spectrum because of its malleable character, but certainly can be said to have originated because of the demand for popular sovereignty and democracy.

The postmodern critique is correct in the sense that the polar opposites of modernist politics are not equipped to deal with the more complex reality of contemporary society. The key words here are pluralism, difference and identity. The politics of postmodernism emphasise, and rightly so, the existence of different subjects of politics, and this has been taken up by some of the 'new' ideologies of politics, notably feminism. Feminist theory has suggested not just the importance of gender in political theory, but has highlighted the idea of a fragmented subject, in some cases doing away with the notion of a subject. In the words of one defender of postmodern feminism, such a theory

> would dispense with the idea of a subject of history. It would replace unitary notions of 'woman' and 'feminine gender identity' with plural and complexly constructed conceptions of social identity, treating gender as one relevant strand among others, attending also to class, race, ethnicity, age and sexual orientation (Ross, 1989, p. 101).

Feminists have criticised established ideologies because of their 'essentialism', for operating with the idea of a supposedly universal and coherent subject or agent of emancipation. One of the main tasks of feminism as a theory has been to 'deconstruct' this idea of the subject. The charge has been that beneath ideas of 'the citizen', 'the democrat' and 'the working class' there is a less universal and more particular figure constructed on the basis of certain masculinised assumptions. Some versions of feminist theory insist that to talk of 'men' and 'women' is to be blind to the differences within these categories, for instance race, class or nationality. The idea of a single agent of modernity neglects the plurality of identities that exist in modern politics, identities that are much more a matter of choice than hitherto.

Some postmodernist critiques deny the possibility of a 'subject' at all. This 'death of the subject' would, if valid, undermine the idea of agency, of a conscious subject transforming society through political and social action. For example, following Foucault's analysis of power, the subject seems to disappear as an agent of liberation and emancipation. If 'the subject' is constituted by a field of power, if, for example, in the Panopticon the inmates are constrained by the structure or system in which they live, they may come to internalise this disciplinary structure and police themselves. In Foucault's words,

He who is subjected to a field of visibility, and who knows it, assumes responsibility for the constraints of power; he makes them play spontaneously upon himself, he inscribes himself in a power relation in which he simultaneously plays both roles; he becomes the principle of his own subjection (Dews, 1984, p. 85).

Thus there may be 'subjects' or 'agents', but they are defined by a particular structure of power, whose norms they internalise. The idea of emancipatory agency fades completely away, doing away with one of the main strands of the modern ideologies.

Even if this idea of the disappearance of the emancipatory agent is not accepted, the ideologies of modernity stand accused of operating with too deterministic or essentialist an idea of identity and of the subject. For example some types of nationalism have emphasised the fact that people's fate is largely determined by a single identity (their nation), which they cannot choose and which structures their life chances. Barrès proclaimed nationalism as a form of determinism (McClelland, 1970, p. 159). However the significance of postmodernism is its emphasis not just on the variety of identities in the modern world, but on the extent to which they are self-chosen labels that people affix to themselves. The idea is of individuals selecting for themselves a set of varying identities that need not be mutually exclusive, such as consumer, or member of an ethnic or religious group, with people determining for themselves the relative significance of each of these identities in their own lives. Thus an ideology that emphasises the dominance of one particular factor, for example nation or class, as structuring the lives of the individual, fails to recognise both the plurality and the degree of self-choice of each of the various identities that are possible in the politics of the modern world.

Furthermore, in a criticism of the idea of collective human agency, ecologically inspired criticism suggests that the modernist belief in the conquest of nature and the inexhaustibility of the resources of the natural world is an illusion. The ecological critique recommends a more balanced view of the relationship between humanity and nature. This leads to more modest expectations of the possibility of social transformation, and to recognition of the costs of social and political progress. Transforming nature may have consequences that will elude human control.

None of this invalidates the modernist project and the ideologies stemming from it, though they need to be reinterpreted in the light of these critiques. The attempt to put any ideology into practice has its dangers if it is done in such a way as to give unlimited power to those using the force of the state to remould society. Stalinism and fascism bear witness to this: 'Neither the Nazi nor the communist vision jarred with the audacious self-confidence and the hubris of modernity; they merely offered to do better what other modern powers dreamed of, perhaps even tried, but failed to accomplish' (Bauman, 1991, p. 29). However there is no need to fall into a binary opposition that contrasts a dogmatic and plurality-denying 'ideological' view of politics with a postmodern perspective that rejects any overall view of society and the possibility of social transformation. The need is to temper the ideological style of politics by recognising the greater diversity and plurality postmodern perspectives rightly signal. New social movements such as the ecology movement, can be seen not as replacements for movements that articulate the ideologies of modernity, but as means of adaptating and rejuvenating those ideologies and the parties that express them: 'By articulating new issues and by forming the new middle class into a political public, ecology has provided left-of-centre parties with an opportunity to modernise their political programme' (Scott, 1990, p. 152).

Assumptions of Unity

'Pluralism' is meant in part to suggest the idea of multiculturalism, but more generally the diversity of perspectives that pose problems for any attempt at 'ideological politics'. These difficulties stem from the incomparability of the different communities and values that coexist in modern societies. Any attempt to construct a blueprint of how society should be organised will come up against this hetero-geneity. Hence the emphasis on diversity in modern politics poses a challenge to the potentially unifying force of all modern ideologies.

The experience of the French Revolution is illustrative here. Through rites and ceremonies such as the *Fête de la Fédération* the revolutionaries attempted to create a sense of unity and to give shape to the new citizen. They wished to build up a united and indivisible republic and create a common political culture, a community of citizenship. The political dynamic of this community and the ability of political leaders to impose it on the mass of the people was restrained by the primitive technology and limited propaganda opportunities open to the Jacobins compared with political elites of later times. Later attempts at nation building that sought to invent traditions, whether of a democratic or an authoritarian kind, were backed up by more extensive resources for political socialisation, provided by a powerful state.

The whole tradition of ideological politics stemming from the French Revolution took over certain assumptions of a unified society. If consensus and common citizenship did not exist, then the aspiration was to create it, to develop notions of shared fraternity through political rituals and the newly developed forms of mass politics (Mosse, 1989). The greater heterogeneity of modern politics and society renders these assumptions less sustainable and less defensible. The development of more diversified societies, in which Enlightenment universalism is challenged by greater particularism, renders much more problematic the assumptions of all the ideologies of the age of modernity. These ideologies all took for granted a society in which the common will could find expression, once certain obstacles had been removed and this unity would lead to the transformation of society in a rational direction. These assumptions were always problematic, but seem much more so in contemporary circumstances. How then can the core ideologies of modernity cope with this problem of pluralism and diversity? Do these problems not render the whole notion of ideology not only suspect but irrelevant?

Ideology and Totalitarianism

A further charge against the ideologies of modernity is that they can be used to promote totalitarian politics rather than pluralistic democracy.

This critique points to the historical record of those societies in the twentieth century that were most explicitly 'ideological', elevating ideology to the status of a creed that had to be accepted by all members of society, and which was imposed by monopolistic state parties through their permeation of civil society. The reference here is clearly to the communist and fascist regimes, both of which sought to impose their ideology on society and mobilise the population to pursue the collective goal. Those regimes were the extreme ends of the political spectrum that included non-totalitarian but highly authoritarian states such as Franco's Spain. These states all proclaimed their adherence to a particular ideology, one of strong leadership and (with regard to fascism) national cohesion, combined in some cases with the concept of economic development strictly controlled by the state. In short there seems to be plenty of evidence that, far from being a necessary condition for a healthy democratic society, ideology, with the emphasis firmly on its singular and non-pluralistic nature, is an essential part of totalitarian or at least authoritarian society. In such a society all aspects of life are oriented towards the collective goal, proclaimed and interpreted by a single leader, and enforced by the state party and its support organisations throughout society.

On this account ideologies are viewed as a crucial element of totalitarianism, as justifying the unrestricted power of a supreme leader whose aims can be expressed in vague terms such as 'the building of communism', 'the construction of a *Volksgemeinschaft*' (people's community) or whatever. Defining the nation's goals is left to the leader, who orchestrates the permanent revolution that is the norm in these societies. Ideology, then, can be politically dangerous.

The fall of communism can be seen as exemplifying the inevitable fate of those ideologically inspired politicians who sought to impose a masterplan on a diverse society, a society that was growing even more complex as a result of modernity. Because of the continued development of modernity and the consequent growth of sophistication and diversity in civil society, ideological projects became increasingly difficult and eventually impossible to sustain. Citizen movements rose up to smash the ideological mould and restore diversity, the precondition of the healthy liberal-democratic society to which all the world aspires.

The implication of these arguments is that the very processes of modernity, culminating in the postmodern society of difference and fragmentation, undermined the unitary and 'holistic' thrust of all the ideologies of the post-French Revolution period, so that ideology has no future in the contemporary world. Indeed, to continue this argument, the idea of a free society, in which people express their different identities and interests, is quite incompatible with all forms of ideology, as they seek to impose a fixed pattern on society. Ideology is thus an anachronism that must be shed as soon as possible, and which in fact is doomed because of the transformed realities in the political, economic and social spheres.

Modern criticisms of the French Revolution and Jacobinism level similar charges. Jacobinism is seen as the first but by no means the last ideology seeking to stamp on to society a view of 'the good citizen'. Jacobinism is seen as characterised above all by its insistence on unity and its refusal to accept aspects of reality that did not conform to this goal. This found expression in repeated purges, the narrowing down of the circle of 'virtuous citizens' to ever smaller circles. In turn this involved an increasingly desperate attempt to regenerate the republic and preserve its unity. Robespierre was one of the first ideologues to rise to power, with disastrous results.

The Bolshevik revolution shows the same incompatibility between ideology and democracy, and the futility of imposing a single goal on society.

Ideology and Common Citizenship

These factors together amount to a formidable critique both of ideology in general (ideologies as relatively coherent frameworks for political debate and action) and of these ideologies that are central to the tradition of modernity. The conclusion seems to follow that ideology is dead as a general category of understanding and analysis, and that the ideologies of the Left–Right spectrum have no relevance in a contemporary society whose conflicts are too multidimensional to be subsumed in this conceptual map.

This book rejects these arguments and maintains that ideology is necessary to democratic politics and the concept of progress, albeit couched in more modest terms than some of the aspirations of the Enlightenment (for example the hopes Condorcet sketched out at the end of his *Esquisse*). It is also maintained here that the Left–Right spectrum is still fundamental to an understanding of contemporary politics throughout the world. But how can these bold claims be supported, particularly against the charge of the totalitarian implications of ideological discourse and the ideological mode of thought?

The importance of preserving the central ideologies of modernity is that, while recognising the different identities and values that are held concurrently by individuals in the modern world, the need remains for some integrating belief systems to hold together a fragmented and divided society. The politics of identity and difference are indeed crucial correctives to the single 'subject' or collective agent that marked the central ideologies of the modern era. But these 'correctives' cannot become absolute goals in themselves, because society would then lose sight of all ideas of common citizenship and common focuses of action. Ideologies are needed to make sense of democratic politics, to provide broad frameworks that enable us to understand the forces that make up the modern world.

The postmodern emphasis on difference and heterogeneity ignores the common links and bonding devices that are necessary to establish a political community. Postmodern critiques end up with a sort of relativism, in which each and every type of community is credited with its own value. The ideologies associated with modernity, notably socialism and nationalism, and in some of its forms liberalism, sought to develop common citizenship and social inclusion, based on the development of industrial society. These are still core concerns in our era.

The ideologies of modernity are now attempting to offer general solutions to the core problem of contemporary politics: the need to create a social order that combines the separateness and distinctiveness of individuals and groups with a shared tradition of citizenship and community. In this sense the tradition of modernity and the ideologies that developed from it are still relevant and important to contemporary politics. That tradition also involved a belief in the possibility of social progress and a commitment to emancipation from social and natural constraints.

The intellectual tools of the ideological tradition are also necessary to cope with the question of inclusion and exclusion. In the headlong rush towards globalisation, communities are being 'hollowed out' with alarming rapidity, and the central value of the Enlightenment tradition, the idea of common rational control of the affairs of society, is becoming less attainable. One consequence of this situation is the abandonment of universalism, as people exalt particular traditions and values as boundary markers to cement the unity of the group, often at the expense of the outsider or outgroup. This can take the form of national exclusiveness, as in Latvia and Slovakia, which use linguistic competence as a test of citizenship; ethnic exclusiveness, as in Bosnia during the recent war; or religious exclusiveness and intolerance, of which there are many examples. In all these the move is away from universalism and inclusiveness towards particularism and exclusion. The obvious implication here is not only that heterogeneous citizenship and human rights are being undermined, but also that national tensions are being created that could lead to war.

The need to create bonds of common citizenship provides a defence of key elements of the tradition of modernity, encapsulated in three central strands: the idea of basic human rights and their inviolability, as represented by liberalism; the idea of social equality, as represented by socialism; and, more hesitatingly in this case, the idea of cultural autonomy and national self-determination, as represented by nationalism. The last element is included somewhat tentatively because of the tendency of nationalism to foster exclusion rather than inclusion, and to emphasise the particular rather than the universal However civic nationalism offers the possibility of recognising the particular history and culture of a national group while welcoming newcomers, irrespective of ethnic affiliation. It is only through these central strands of the modern ideologies that the problem of social inclusion can be tackled in ways that combine recognition of diversity with some degree of community and universalism. This argument is couched in normative terms in order to highlight the desirability and continuing relevance of this tradition of thought.

The politics of modernity and the ideologies that constitute that tradition have not been made irrelevant by the arrival of postmodern society, or shown to be incoherent by that broad and vague body of thought called 'postmodernism'. The need to defend the rights of individuals in the face of greater intolerance and group pressure; the huge need to prevent the pressures of market society from creating further inequalities that undermine common citizenship and democratic participation; the need to respect national identity and the right to self-determination, especially on the cultural level; the need to preserve some degree of social cohesion in the face of fragmentation and diversity – all these are central issues in contemporary politics as well as core elements of the politics of modernity.

Ideology and Democratic Politics

Political ideologies are still a necessary element of any genuine democracy despite the far-reaching social and political transformations of the present age. They are needed to set collective goals for the democratic community, to reunite citizens of fragmented postmodern society, and to offer broad guidelines for progress and emancipation. This is the argument of this concluding section, which highlights the danger of 'ideologylessness', of the evolution of democratic politics into a competition for power that is bereft of overarching ideas and social goals. The rapid and unsettling contemporary developments mean the need is all the greater for general concepts of society, for ideologies as central organising frameworks for political debate and democratic action, and the modernist agenda is still of relevance to the politics of contemporary societies throughout the world. It is argued here that the ideologies discussed in this book can ensure the continuation of open democratic debate and collective dialogue, or its introduction in countries where this is yet to occur.

Ideology and ideological thinking have been criticised for leading to revolutionary and monolithic politics, for imposing a single view on society with terrible results. But this is only the perverted version of ideological politics that results from extremist ideologues taking over state power and exercising it in monopolistic ways. Ideological politics can be pluralistic, permitting the necessary coexistence of different views of the world within the same political system. Moreover ideologies such as socialism, nationalism and conservatism are necessary in that they offer general goals for the whole of society, even if those goals are spelled out by each ideology in quite general ways. Without these broad frameworks of thought and action political activity takes place in a void. Political parties competing for power in a democracy need the broad 'hinterland' of these ideologies of politics – as the basis for specific policies, as criteria by which to evaluate those policies and as ideals to which 'day-to-day' politics can aspire.

Without the competing frameworks for debate and action offered by political ideologies, democratic politics becomes in Burke's phrase a 'low-level concern' (Burke, 1969), concerned purely with interest representation, with advancing particular sectoral demands. The struggle to defend particular interests is certainly a legitimate part of politics. However it can only be a part, not the whole, otherwise democracy risks becoming what Benjamin Barber (1984) calls 'thin democracy', involving 'politics as zoo-keeping', a struggle of different interests against each other. Without some competing concepts of 'the good society' no critical perspective on politics is possible. Democratic politics becomes 'a war of all against all', carried out within the framework of certain 'rules of the game' (Bobbio, 1996), a not unimportant fact, but insufficient to offer anything more than purely procedural democracy.

Hence ideologies are necessary to set general goals, to orientate the programmes and policies of political parties, and to create frameworks for action and debate that unite citizens as members of democratic societies across sectoral divisions. Ideologies provide criteria against which social progress, or the lack of it, can be measured. The prescriptive theories derived from various ideologies provide benchmarks for assessing society, its aims and objectives, and the success or failure of governments in meeting those objectives. For example liberalism provides certain indices in terms of the degree of freedom individuals have to follow their own interests, think their own thoughts and determine their own lives. These of course are not the only criteria by which to evaluate a society, but they have been central to the European tradition and provide some core values by which policies can be judged and progress evaluated.

This raises the question of whether the ideological standpoints of liberalism and the other ideologies of modernity are truly universal, as they claim to be, or just culture-relative, the product of localised West European traditions that have no justifiable claim to universality, and hence cannot be applied in societies that reject them. Can, for example, Western notions of human rights and gender equality be applied to, say, Asian societies, which may reject them as irrelevant to their own traditions and as showing no understanding 'of the way we do things here'? While this is a vast issue, the stance taken here is that these concepts rest on notions of choice and self-determination that apply to all human beings irrespective of their particular community. Communities that deny such choice and autonomy are denying the opportunity for emancipation and progress. The hollowing out of communities lamented by John Gray (1995) may not be a cause for regret in societies where repressive and stifling customs prevent individuals from choosing their own way of life and developing their capacities, however comforting adherence to the traditional way of life may be.

Political ideologies, with their triple focus of critique, goal and agency, are essential to democratic politics and need not take the form of totalitarianism. What then of the content of these ideologies? If we need ideologies for democratic politics, which are most relevant to the vastly transformed world of postmodernity? It might be the case that ideology in general is necessary to democratic politics, but that the ideologies of modernity, with their universalist assumptions and core ideas developed on the ground of modernity, are not up to the task, that new ones are needed. The final task, then, is to establish the continued relevance of the ideologies of modernity.

It is contended here that the ideologies necessary to make sense of the contemporary world remain those that originated with modernity. The tradition represented by the Left–Right spectrum is still significant, and new ideologies such as feminism and environmentalism are necessary correctives or additions to this spectrum, not replacements for it. Ideas of emancipation and social transformation, the critical evaluation of social realities and discussion of alternatives to the existing structure of society are all made possible by ideological discourse and the ideas of critique, agency and goal that these modernist ideologies proclaim. If a single ideology is mobilised and imposed on a diverse society, and competing perspectives are denied, then this is clearly totalitarianism. However there is no reason to reject the necessity of ideologies just because they have sometimes been taken to extremes and imposed in a monolithic way to legitimate repressive and totalitarian regimes. Nonetheless they will have to be modified, and some important insights can be provided by the newer ideologies. Feminism, pluralism and environmentalism emphasise difference, identity and complexity, all of which are necessary to ward off ideological monolithicism.

What then do the traditional ideologies provide, why are they in particular, as opposed to ideologies in general, necessary to the understanding and mastering of a complex and changing social reality? The common agenda of modernity, as taken up by socialism and liberalism, was one of rational control over a changing society where localised agrarianism was being pushed aside in the interests of large-scale industrialisation. Both socialism and liberalism sought to take advantage of this colossal transformation for the benefit of humanity by applying rationality to the collective purpose. A similar agenda is highly relevant today as equally large-scale changes are taking place in the social and economic structure. Like the process of modernity, postmodernity requires conscious human control and rationality. In the same way that vast social transformations brought about the transition to modernity, and were to some extent controlled and harnessed under the impetus of the grand ideals of liberalism and socialism, the same projects are relevant now, in radically changed conditions. What liberalism and socialism have to offer is the possibility of rational control, and this part of their legacy needs to be preserved in contemporary ideological discourse.

This does not mean that liberalism and socialism have to be preserved in their nineteenth-century form. One contemporary author, discussing the problem of democracy and civil society, suggests that 'We need to develop a complex division of labour in democratic governance, bridging state and civil society, in order to cope with the complexity of an organisational society that tends to blur the two spheres' (see Hirst, in Hirst and Khilnani, 1996, p. 106). His argument is that neither classical liberalism nor collective socialism can provide the answer, which in his view is to be found in a form of 'associative democracy'. However what is being argued here is that both liberalism and socialism remain of value in asserting those key values of modernity: the rational fashioning of society and the appeal to reason. Furthermore liberalism, whatever its weaknesses, has one central strength: its espousal of individual rights and diversity as basic elements of democracy. Without the core freedoms of speech, belief and assembly, and the right to think differently and express one's opinions openly, no democracy is possible (Beetham, in Held, 1993).

By the same token, belief in the separate worth and value of the individual is a central element of modernity. Similarly, in spite of what has been said about the weaknesses of liberalism with regard to community, it remains true that communities can be stifling and repressive, and that liberalism's insistence on the right to be different, the right to assert one's individual reason and autonomy are essential bulwarks against the rush towards community politics and identity that is a feature of contemporary politics – but one that may have more dangerous features than excessive ideological zeal.

Socialism, for its part, has the core value of equality – in particular social equality – to offer as a benchmark against which to assess the rapid changes that have accompanied the move from modern to postmodern times. Just as early socialism and Marxism held out to a world transfixed by the transition to modernity the idea of collective control and the aspiration to harness these changes for the benefit of humanity as a whole, involving the vision of an organised and harmonious society, these goals and ideals remain no less important in a world riven by the economic and social changes involved in the transformation of modernity to postmodernity.

Bibliography

Alter, P. (1989) *Nationalism* (London: Edward Arnold).

Aron, R. (1976) *Essai sur les libertés* (Paris: Calmann-Lévy).

Babeuf, F.-N. (1976) *Textes Choisis* (Paris: Éditions Sociales).

Bailyn, B. (1992) *The Ideological Origins of the American Revolution*, enlarged edition (Cambridge, MA, and London: Harvard University Press).

Baker, K. M. (1990) *Inventing the French Revolution: essays on French political culture in the 18th century* (Cambridge: Cambridge University Press).

Barber, B. (1984) *Strong Democracy: participatory politics for a new age* (Berkeley, CA and London: University of California Press).

Barrès, M. (1902) *Scènes et Doctrines du Nationalisme* (Paris: Émile-Paul).

Bauman, Z. (1991) *Modernity and Ambivalence* (Cambridge: Polity Press).

Beck, U. (1992) *Risk Society: towards a new modernity*, translated by Mark Ritter (London/Thousand Oaks/New Delhi: Sage).

Beer, S. H. (1993) *To Make a Nation: the rediscovery of American federalism* (Cambridge, MA and London: Belknap Press of Harvard University Press).

Beetham, D. (1984) 'The Future of the Nation-State', in D. McLennan *et al.* (eds), *The Idea of the Modern State* (Milton Keynes and Philadelphia: Open University Press).

Beetham, D. (1991) *The Legitimation of Power* (London: Macmillan).

Beiser, F. C. (1992) *Enlightenment, Revolution and Romanticism. The Genesis of German Political Thought 1790–1800* (Cambridge, MA and London: Harvard University Press).

Beissinger, M. R. (1996) 'How Nationalism Spread: Eastern Europe adrift the Tides and Cycles of Nationalist Contention', *Social Research*, vol. 63, no. 1, pp. 97–146.

Benner, E. (1995) *Really Existing Nationalisms: a post-communist view from Marx and Engels* (Oxford: Clarendon Press).

Bentham, J. (1988) *A Fragment on Government*, edited by J. H. Burns and H. L. A. Hart, with an introduction by Ross Harrison (Cambridge: Cambridge University Press).

Berlin, I. (1991) *The Crooked Timber of Humanity: chapters in the history of ideas* (London: Fontana).

Berman, M. (1983) *All That is Solid Melts into Air: the experience of modernity* (London: Verso).

Bernstein, E. (1993) *The Preconditions of Socialism*, edited and translated by Henry Tudor (Cambridge: Cambridge University Press).

Berry, C. J. (1994) *The Idea of Luxury: a conceptual and historical investigation* (Cambridge: Cambridge University Press).

Bertens, H. (1995) *The Idea of the Postmodern: a history* (London and New York: Routledge).

Bidet, J. (1990) *Théorie de la Modernité (suivi de) Marx et le marché* (Paris: Presses Universitaires de France).

Bobbio, N. (1996) *Left and Right: the significance of a political distinction* (Cambridge: Polity Press).

Bottomore, T. B. and Goode, P. (eds) (1978) *Austro-Marxism* (Oxford: Clarendon Press).

Brubaker, R. (1992) *Citizenship and Nationhood in France and Germany* (Cambridge, MA: Harvard University Press).

Brubaker, R. (1996) *Nationalism reframed: nationhood and the national question in the New Europe* (Cambridge: Cambridge University Press).

Bryan, C. (1996) 'Manchester: Democratic Implications of an Economic Initiative?', *The Public* vol. III no. 1, pp. 103 16.

Burke, E. (1969) *Reflections on the Revolution in France*, edited and introduced by Conor Cruise O'Brien (Harmondsworth: Penguin).

Burke, E. (1993) *Pre-Revolutionary Writings*, edited by Ian Harris (Cambridge: Cambridge University Press).

Calhoun, C. (ed.) (1992) *Habermas and the Public Sphere* (Cambridge, MA, and London: MIT Press).

Calhoun, C. (1995) *Critical Social Theory: culture, history and the challenge of difference* (Oxford and Cambridge, MA: Blackwell).

Carr, E. H (1945) *Nationalism and After* (London: Macmillan).

Cohen, J. L. and Arato, A. (1992), *Civil Society and Political Theory* (Cambridge, MA and London: MIT Press).

Condorcet, J.- A.- N. C. (1988) *Esquisse d'un tableau historique des progrès de l'esprit humain* (Paris: Flammarion).

Constant, B. (1988) *Political Writings*, edited and translated by BiancaMaria Fontana (Cambridge: Cambridge University Press).

Deutscher, I. (1970) *The Prophet Outcast: Trotsky: 1929–1940* (Oxford: Oxford University Press).

Dews, P. (1984) 'Power and Subjectivity in Foucault', *New Left Review* vol. 144, pp. 72–95.

Diamond L. and M. F. Plattner (eds) (1996) *The Global Resurgence of Democracy*, 2nd edn (Baltimore and London: The Johns Hopkins University Press).

Dunn, J. (ed.) (1992) *Democracy: the unfinished journey 508BC to AD1993* (Oxford: Oxford University Press).

Dunn, J. (ed.) (1994) 'Contemporary Crisis of the Nation State?', *Political Studies*, vol. XLII, special issue.

Featherstone, M. *et al.* (eds) (1995) *Global Modernities* (London: Sage).

Fehér, F. (ed.) (1990) *The French Revolution and the Birth of Modernity* (Berkeley/Los Angeles/Oxford: University of California Press).

Ferguson, A. (1995) *An Essay on the History of Civil Society*, edited by Fania Oz-Salberger (Cambridge: Cambridge University Press).

Fichte, J. G. (1968) *Addresses to the German Nation*, edited by G. A. Kelly (Boston: Harper Torchbooks).

Fontana, B. (ed.) (1994) *The invention of the modern republic* (Cambridge: Cambridge University Press).

Foucault, M. (1980) *Power/Knowledge*, edited by Colin Gordon (Brighton: Harvester-Wheatsheaf).

Furet, F. (1989) *Penser la Révolution française*, Collection Folio/Histoire (Paris: Gallimard); English translation, *Interpreting the French Revolution*, translated by Elborg Forster (Cambridge: Cambridge University Press; Paris: Éditions de la Maison des Sciences de l'Homme, 1981).

Furet, F. (1995) *Le passé d'une illusion: Essai sur l'idée communiste au XXe siècle* (Paris: Robert Laffont/Calmann-Lévy).

Gauchet, M. (1992) 'La Droite et la Gauche', in P. Nora (ed.), *Les Lieux de la Mémoire*, vol. III, *La France: 1. Conflits et Partages* (Paris: Gallimard).

Gauchet, M. (1995) *La Révolution des pouvoirs: La souveraineté, le peuple et la représentation 1789–1799* (Paris: Gallimard).

Gautier, C. (1993) *L'invention de la société civile: Lectures anglo-écossaises, Mandeville, Smith, Ferguson* (Paris: Presses Universitaires de France).

Gellner, E. (1979) *Spectacles and Predicaments: essays in social theory* (Cambridge: Cambridge University Press).

Gellner, E. (1983) *Nations and Nationalism* (Oxford: Blackwell).

Gellner, E. (1996) *Conditions of Liberty: civil society and its rivals* (Harmondsworth: Penguin).

Giddens, A. (1994) *Beyond Left and Right: the future of radical politics* (Cambridge: Polity Press).

Girardet, R. (ed.) (1966) *Le Nationalisme français 1871–1914* (Paris: Armand Colin).

Gorz, A. (1994) *Capitalism, Socialism, Ecology* (London: Verso).

Gray, J. (1995) *Enlightenment's Wake: politics and culture at the close of the modern age* (London and New York: Routledge).

Greenfeld, L. (1992) *Nationalism: five roads to modernity* (Cambridge, MA, and London: Harvard Univesity Press).

Greenfeld, L. (1996) 'Nationalism and Modernity', *Social Research*, vol. 63, no. 1, pp. 3–40.

Habermas, J. (1987) *The Philosophical Discourse of Modernity: twelve lectures* (Cambridge: Polity Press).

Habermas, J. (1993) *Strukturwandel der Öffentlichkeit. Untersuchungen zu einer Kategorie der bürgerlichen Gesellschaft* (Frankfurt: Suhrkamp); English translation, *The Structural Transformation of the Public Sphere: an inquiry into a category of bourgeois society*, translated by T. Burger and F. Lawrence (Cambridge, MA: MIT Press 1989).

Habermas, J. (1996) 'Modernity, an unfinished project', in M. P. d'Entrèves and S. Benhabib (eds), *Habermas and the Unfinished Product of Modernity* (Cambridge: Polity Press 1996).

Hall, J. A. (ed.) (1995) *Civil Society: theory, history, comparison* (Cambridge: Polity Press).

Hall, J. and Jarvie, I. C. (eds) (1992) *Transition to Modernity: essays on power, wealth and belief* (Cambridge: Cambridge University Press).

Harvey, D. (1989) *The Condition of Postmodernity: an enquiry into the origins of cultural change* (Oxford: Blackwell).

Hegel, G. W. F. (1966) *The Phenomenology of Mind* (London: Allen & Unwin).

Held, D. (ed.) (1993) *Prospects for Democracy: North, South, East, West* (Cambridge: Polity Press).

Heller, A. and F. Feher (1988) *The Postmodern Political Condition* (Cambridge: Polity Press).

Hirst, P. and Khilnani, S. (eds) (1996) *Reinventing Democracy* (Oxford and Cambridge, MA: Blackwell).

Hirst, P. and G. Thompson (1996) *Globalization in Question: the international economy and the possibilities of governance* (Cambridge: Polity Press).

Hobsbawm, E. J. (1989) *Politics for a Rational Left* (London and New York: Verso).

Hobsbawm, E. J. (1990) *Nations and Nationalism since 1780: programme, myth, reality* (Cambridge: Cambridge University Press).

Hobsbawm, E. J. (1994) *Age of Extremes: the short twentieth century 1914–1991* (London: Michael Joseph).

Hobsbawm, E. J. and T. Ranger (eds.) (1992) *The Invention of Tradition* (Cambridge: Cambridge University Press).

Holmes, S. (1984) *Benjamin Constant and the Making of Modern Liberalism* (New Haven, CT, and London: Yale University Press).

Honneth, A. (1985) 'An aversion against the universal: a commentary on Lyotard's "Postmodern Condition"', *Theory, Culture and Society* vol. 2, no. 3.

Horkheimer, M. and T. W. Adorno (1995) *Dialektik der Aufklärung, Philosophische Fragmente* (Frankfurt: Fischer Verlag).

Hornsey, R. (1996) 'Postmodern critiques: Foucault, Lyotard and modern political ideologies', *Journal of Political Ideologies*, vol. 1, no. 3, pp. 239–59.

Hroch, M. (1985) *Social Conditions of National Revival in Europe: a comparative analysis of the social composition of patriotic groups among the smaller European nations* (Cambridge: Cambridge University Press).

Hroch, M. (1993) 'From National Movement to Fully-Fledged Nation', *New Left Review*, vol. 198, pp. 3–20.

Hume, D. (1994) *Political Essays*, edited by Knud Haakonssen (Cambridge: Cambridge University Press).

Huntington, S. P. (1996) 'Democracy for the Long Haul', *Journal of Democracy*, vol. 7, no. 2, pp. 3–13.

Iggers, G. G. (ed.) (1972) *The Doctrine of Saint-Simon: an exposition – first year, 1828–1829*, translated and introduced by Georg G. Iggers (New York: Schocken Books).

Ionescu, G. (ed.) (1976) *The Political Thought of Saint-Simon* (Oxford: Oxford University Press).

Jaume, L. (1989) *Le discours jacobin et la démocratie* (Paris: Fayard).

Jaurès, J. (1932) *L'Armée Nouvelle*, edited by Max Bonnafous (Paris: Rieder).

Kant, I. (1991) *Political Writings*, edited by Hans Reiss (Cambridge: Cambridge University Press).

King, D. S. (1987) *The New Right: politics, markets, citizenship* (London: Macmillan).

Kymlicka, W. (1995) *Multicultural Citizenship: a liberal theory of minority rights* (Oxford: Clarendon Press).

Lamberti, D.-C. (1989) *Tocqueville and the Two Democracies*, translated by Arthur Goldhammer (Cambridge, MA and London: Harvard University Press).

Leroy, M. (1946), *Histoire des Idées sociales en France: De Montesquieu à Robespierre* (Paris: Gallimard).

Llobera, J. R. (1994) *The God of Modernity: the development of nationalism in Western Europe* (Oxford and Providence, RI: Berg).

Lucas, C. (ed.) (1988) *The French Revolution and the Creation of Modern Political Culture, Vol. 2: The Political Culture of the French Revolution* (Oxford: Pergamon Press).

Luke, D. (ed.) (1964) *Goethe, Selected Verse* (Harmondsworth: Penguin).

Lyotard, J.-F. (1992) *The Postmodern condition: a report on knowledge* (Manchester: Manchester University Press).

Madison, J. *et al.* (1987) *The Federalist Papers*, edited and introduced by Isaac Kramnick (Harmondsworth: Penguin).

Maistre, J. de (1965) *The Works of Joseph de Maistre*, selected, translated and introduced by Jack Lively (London: Allen & Unwin).

Mann, M. (1993) *The sources of social power. Volume II: The rise of classes and nation-states, 1760–1914* (Cambridge: Cambridge University Press).

Marx, K. (1973a), *The Revolutions of 1848: Political Writings Volume 1* (Harmondsworth: Penguin).

Marx, K. (1973b), *Surveys from Exile: Political Writings Volume 2* (Harmondsworth: Penguin).

Marx, K. (1973c) *Grundrisse: Foundations of the Critique of Political Economy*, (Rough Draft) (Harmondsworth: Penguin).

Marx, K. (1974) *Capital: a critique of political economy*, vol. III (London: Lawrence and Wishart).

Marx, K. (1977), *Capital: a critique of political economy*, vol. I (London: Lawrence and Wishart).

Marx, K. and F. Engels (1973) *Selected Works in Three Volumes* (Moscow: Progress Publishers).

McLelland, J. S. (ed.) (1970) *The French Right (from de Maistre to Maurras)* (London: Jonathan Cape).

Miliband, D. (ed.) (1994) *Reinventing the Left* (Cambridge: Polity Press).

Miliband, R. (1989) *Divided Societies: class struggle in contemporary capitalism* (Oxford: Clarendon Press).

Miliband, R. (1994) *Socialism for a Sceptical Age* (Cambridge: Polity Press).

Mill, J. S. (1975) *Three Essays: On Liberty, Representative Government, The Subjection of Women* (Oxford: Oxford University Press).

Mill, J. (1992) *Political Writings*, edited by Terence Ball (Cambridge: Cambridge University Press).

Miller, D. (1995) *On Nationality* (Oxford: Clarendon Press).

Mosse, G. L. (1989) 'Fascism and the French Revolution', *Journal of Contemporary History*, vol. 24, no. 1, pp. 5–26.

Mulgan, G. (1994) *Politics in an Antipolitical Age* (Cambridge: Polity Press).

Müller, W. C. and V. Wright (1994) *The State in Western Europe: retreat or redefinition?*, special issue of *West European Politics*, vol. 17, no. 3.

Nairn, T. (1981) *The Break-up of Britain: crisis and neo-nationalism* (London: Verso).

Norris, C. (1993) *The Truth about Postmodernism* (Oxford and Cambridge, MA: Blackwell).

O'Brien, C. C. (1993) *The Great Melody: a thematic biography and commented anthology of Edmund Burke* (London: Minerva).

Ozouf, M. (1989) *L'homme régénéré: Essais sur la révolution française* (Paris: Gallimard).

Parekh, B. (ed.) (1973) *Bentham's Political Thought* (London: Croom Helm).

Pasquino, P. (1987), 'Emmanuel Sieyès, Benjamin Constant, et le "gouvernement des modernes"', *Revue Française de Science Politique*, vol. 37, pp. 214–29.

Pasquino, P. (1989) 'Le Concept de nation et les fondements du droit public de la révolution: Emmanuel Sieyès', in F. Furet (ed.), *L'héritage de la révolution française* (Paris: Hachette).

Pierson, C. (1995) *Socialism after Communism: the new market socialism* (Cambridge: Polity Press).

Postone, M. (1993) *Time, Labour and Social Domination: a reinterpretation of Marx's critical theory* (Cambridge: Cambridge University Press).

Putnam, R. D. (1994) *Making Democracy Work: civic traditions in modern Italy* (Princeton NJ: Princeton University Press).

Rabinow, P. (ed.) (1986) *The Foucault Reader* (Harmondsworth: Penguin).

Reiss, H. S. (ed.) (1955) *The Political Thought of the German Romantics* (Oxford: Blackwell).

Renan, E. (1992) *Qu'est-ce qu'une nation? Et autres essais politiques*, edited by J. Roman (Paris: Presses Pocket).

Rémond, R. (1992) *Les Droites en France* (Paris: Aubier).

Rosanvallon, P. (1992) *Le sacre du citoyen: Histoire du suffrage universel en France* (Paris: Gallimard).

Ross, A. (ed.) (1989) *Universal Abandon? The politics of postmodernism* (Edinburgh: Edinburgh University Press).

Rousseau, J.-J. (1968) *The Social Contract and Discourses*, translated and introduced by G. D. H. Cole (London and New York: Everyman Library).

Rupnik, J. (1996) 'The Reawakening of European Nationalisms', *Social Reseach* vol. 63, no. 1, pp. 41–75.

Sassoon, D. (1996) *One Hundred Years of Socialism: the West European left in the twentieth century* (London and New York: I. B. Tauris).

Schmidt, J. (ed.) (1996) *What is Enlightenment? Eighteenth-Century Answers and Twentieth-Century Questions* (Berkeley, Los Angeles and Oxford: University of California Press).

Schwarzmantel, J. (1991) *Socialism and the Idea of the Nation* (Hemel Hempstead: Harvester-Wheatsheaf).

Scott, A. (1990) *Ideology and the New Social Movements* (London: Unwin Hyman).

Seton-Watson, H. (1977) *Nations and States: an enquiry into the origins of nations and the politics of nationalism* (London: Methuen).

Sewell, W. H. (1994) *A Rhetoric of Bourgeois Revolution: the abbé Sieyès and what is the third estate?* (Durham and London: Duke University Press).

Silber, L. and A. Little (1995), *The Death of Yugoslavia* (London: Penguin / BBC Books).

Smith, A. D. (1991) *National Identity* (Harmondsworth: Penguin).

Smith, A. D. (1995a) *Nations and Nationalism in a Global Era* (Cambridge: Polity Press).

Smith, A. D. (1995b) 'Gastronomy or geology? The role of nationalism in the reconstruction of nations', *Nations and Nationalism*, vol. 1, part 1, pp. 3–24.

Sternhell, Z. (1978) *La Droite révolutionnaire: Les origines françaises du fascisme* (Paris: Éditions du Seuil).

Sternhell, Z. (1986) *Neither right nor left: fascist ideology in France* (Princeton NJ: Princeton University Press).

Szacki, J. (1994) *Liberalism after Communism* (Budapest, London, New York: Central European University Press).

Taylor, C. (1991) *The Ethics of Authenticity* (Cambridge, MA and London: Harvard University Press).

Taylor, C. *et al.* (1994) *Multiculturalism: examining the politics of recognition* (Princeton, NJ: Princeton University Press).

Tocqueville, A. de (1966) *The Ancien Regime and the French Revolution*, translated by Stuart Gilbert (London: Collins Fontana).

Tocqueville, A. de (1968) *Democracy in America, Vols I and II, edited by J. P. Mayer and Max Lerner (London and Glasgow: Collins, The Fontana Library)*.

Touraine, A. (1995) *Critique of Modernity*, translated by David Macey (Oxford and Cambridge, MA: Blackwell).

Van Kley, D. (ed.) (1994) *The French Idea of Freedom: the Old Regime and the Declaration of Rights of 1789* (Stanford, CA: Stanford University Press).

White, S. K. (1991) *Political Theory and Postmodernism* (Cambridge: Cambridge University Press).

Winock, M. (1990) *Nationalisme, antisémitisme et fascisme en France* (Paris: Éditions du Seuil).

Wood, G. S. (1992) *The Radicalism of the American Revolution* (New York: Alfred A. Knopf).

Wood, G. S. (1993) *The Creation of the American Republic 1776–1789* (New York and London: W. W. Norton).

Index

207